# COOKING WITH JAPANESE FOODS

## A GUIDE TO THE TRADITIONAL NATURAL FOODS OF JAPAN

# JOHN BELLEME

# JAN BELLEME

AVERY PUBLISHING GROUP INC.
Garden City Park, New York

Cover Photo: The Image Bank/ Garry Gay
Cover Design: Ann Vestal and Rudy Shur
Text Design: Louise Sandhaus
Text Illustrations: Emily Soltanoff
Calligraphy: Akinori Takei
Text Photos: John Belleme
Photo of Onozaki family: Kensaku Onozaki

ISBN 0-89529-583-0

Printed in the United States of America

10  9  8  7  6  5  4  3  2

# DEDICATION

*For Takamichi Onozaki,
whose traditional wisdom
and flexible mind are still
a source of inspiration to us.*

*The Onozaki Family Crest*

Growing up in Japan I took for granted the many traditional foods we ate every day. Later I learned from George Ohsawa about food's important role in the health and well-being of all peoples and societies. I found that those delicious traditional Japanese foods I had known from childhood were healthful and nutritious. In combination with whole grains and vegetables they can form the basis for healthy daily eating for everyone.

When my husband, Michio, and I began teaching macrobiotics in the United States in the 1950s we encouraged the importing of traditional-quality Japanese foods and are happy that now most of them are available at natural foods stores around the country. This book, *Cooking with Japanese Foods*, will help many people understand and learn to cook with these foods.

In 1979 Jan and John Belleme expressed their wish to study traditional miso-making. Michio and I introduced them to a friend, who led them to the Onozaki family in the mountains of rural Japan. There the Bellemes not only learned miso production, which they are now doing at the American Miso Company in North Carolina, but they became interested in many of the other foods too. They have used their understanding and enthusiasm to write this book. I hope it will help you discover how easy it is to use Japanese foods, and how delicious and healthful they are.

—Aveline Kushi

We would especially like to thank Takamichi and Itsuko Ono-zaki and family for sharing their home and centuries-old knowledge of Japanese miso craftsmanship with foreigners who could barely speak a word of their language. Their adventurous yet traditional spirit, as well as their example and teaching, has had a profound impact on our lives since our meeting in 1979.

In addition to the Onozakis, we are grateful to all traditional Japanese food manufacturers who are upholding the highest standards of quality in the face of competition from companies using quicker, cheaper, mass production methods. We appreciate the efforts of Japanese exporters, particularly Mitoku Co., Muso Co., and Ohsawa Japan, and American distributors who have made it their business to track down high quality traditional foods and make them available to us here in the United States. Several individuals have contributed tremendously to the awareness of the value of these foods, thereby creating the demand that supports and completes the link from manufacturer to consumer. This list is by no means complete, but certainly the following people have played a major role: George and Lima Ohsawa, Michio and Ave-line Kushi, Herman and Cornellia Aihara, Noboru Muramoto, and William and Akiko Aoyagi Shurtleff. For their extensive efforts in the promotion of soyfoods, we would like to thank Richard Leviton, Stephen Gaskin, and Nahum Stiskin and Bev-erly Stiskin of Autumn Press, the original publishers of *The Book of Tofu*, *The Book of Miso*, and *The Book of Kudzu*.

Our thanks to Akinori Takei, Naoki Kubota, and Naoto Kosugi for help with research and translation of information from Japanese texts.

We also wish to thank all those on the *East West Journal* staff who have helped bring this book together: Leonard Jacobs, Linda Roszak Elliot, Mark Mayell, Louise Sandhaus, Meg Seaker, Pamela Fuller, and Thom Leonard. Special thanks to Leonard Jacobs, our publisher, and to Linda Roszak Elliot, editor, for her support and suggestions, terrific sense of humor, and for providing the exception to the rule that says the relationship between writer and editor is difficult at best.

*A 200-year-old farmhouse in rural Japan is protected by its traditional straw roof.*

In the shade of towering cedar trees in one corner of Takamichi Onozaki's property is a series of primitive tombstones and a small shrine commemorating the ancestors who have lived on this land for over five hundred years. Newcomers in the neighborhood are the families who have been here for less than two centuries. The search for a place to study the traditional art of making miso led John and me to this peaceful corner of rural Japan, where no one spoke more than a few words of English, in the fall of 1979. The Onozakis welcomed us to their farm as family, and we experienced a complete cultural immersion.

We worked hard alongside the Onozakis six-and-a-half days a week. We lived in their 300-year-old grass-roofed house with no heat except that provided by a *kotatsu* (a small table with a heating unit underneath), and ate their traditional foods each day. The meals were usually very simple, but they were delicious and satisfying and were always made and presented with care.

There we saw and experienced the real value of the various aspects of traditional diet, lifestyle, and health that we had been studying in the U.S. for several years in an abstract way. The strength, energy, good humor, and stamina of the rural Japanese people clearly demonstrated to us the health-giving qualities of traditional diet and lifestyle.

Japanese civilization is ancient, yet the traditional diet has continued to survive to the present. The cuisine is still one of the healthiest in the world. Anyone interested in creating simple, nutritious, beautiful meals can benefit tremendously from learning its principles. The most basic principle—selecting and preparing food in harmony with the seasons and locale—is actually the foundation of all traditional diets and can be applied to any style of cooking. Learning to select and use high-quality, nutritious Japanese foods will enable you to create authentic Oriental dishes as well as enhance the flavor and healthfulness of Western cooking.

Reverence for nature and a strong artistic sense underlie the special appeal of traditional Japanese food preparation. Only the freshest ingredients are selected, and each is eaten in its own season. Like most age-old dietary principles, seasonal eating is simply common sense. We are attracted to lighter and cooler foods in summer. And since appetites can disappear altogether when it is very hot, an extra effort is made to present foods that are aesthetically appealing. One unseasonably hot day in May we came out of the Onozaki *koji* (miso "starter") incubation room after working for hours in nearly 100 percent humidity and over 100° F. heat. We were exhausted and totally uninterested in eating. But when we sat down to dinner and were presented with clear, cut-glass bowls of white somen noodles floating in ice water and delicately garnished with fresh red shiso leaves, our spirits revived and our appetites were stimulated.

In winter hearty, warm dishes such as soups, baked beans, casseroles, and stews with large chunks of root vegetables are appealing. In nature there are fewer bright colors and less variety and contrast in winter; this is reflected in our food. Also, the method of preparation is very different from winter to summer. Some of the warmest memories I have of the Onozakis are connected to the simmering one-pot meals cooked right at the table on the coldest nights. Though the temperature inside the house was regularly below freezing on winter nights and early mornings, because of the appropriate selection of foods and cooking methods we rarely felt uncomfortably cold.

Another characteristic of Japan reflected in its cuisine is lack of waste. Besides the expert use of meal leftovers, there are thousands of examples, from the use of rice husks as insulation to the common practice of reserving the dregs that remain after shoyu or tamari is pressed and bottled. "Waste" products such as these are used for animal feed or fertilizer.

We were usually impressed each time we witnessed an example of such frugality, but there were a couple of times when it became more than we could feel comfortable with. The first of these came just after New Year's when we were invited to a friend's home for dinner. He served us each a small fish taken from a local stream. Our host explained that the fish were a rare delicacy which are always eaten whole—head first! Since he was Mr. Onozaki's best friend, I didn't want to offend him by not accepting his special offering, so I closed my eyes, held my breath and, barely chewing at all, managed to get it down. Actually, it wasn't as bad as I expected, but when John surreptitiously maneuvered his fish onto my plate, I knew I couldn't manage a repeat performance.

Another time we sat down for lunch and one of the neighbors who worked with us opened her beautiful lacquer lunchbox. Always curious about what would be inside and how it would be arranged, I looked in. In one of the little compartments was a pile of large, shiny black insects that looked like grasshoppers. The woman told us that these insects can do considerable damage to rice crops, so people pick them off the plants and pickle them. Pickled grasshoppers are not eaten in all regions of Japan and certainly are not a significant part of the diet, but it's a good example of how the Japanese make use of everything they have available to them. My co-worker noticed me staring at the leggy objects and offered me one. I politely declined.

The Japanese affinity with nature is reflected in the simplicity of the dishes and the balance within each meal. Foods are simply prepared by methods that maintain and enhance their natural flavors, bright colors, and nutritional value. Seasonings in dipping sauces and broths are generally light and subtle, allowing the essence of the principal foods to come through, but a meal will often include strong, stimulating flavors, too. The result is a meal that is deeply satisfying, natural, beautiful, and

*Top, Jan Belleme (left) is presented with a handmade wooden cooking utensil known as a* sushioke *by seventy-eight-year-old Sen "Obason" (grandmother) Onozaki. Bottom, rural rice growers perform the tedious work of transplanting young rice plants.*

*Miyo Shinoda, one of Japan's last traveling peddler women* (gyoshoyasan), *passes the Onozaki's miso shop on her journey through the mountains.*

delicious. These qualities would be reason enough to take a long look at Japanese cuisine, but there is more—Japanese foods are healthful, nutritious, and low in calories.

The diet of most traditional societies in temperate climates is centered around grain. Rice is the staple grain in the Japanese diet. It is accompanied by land and sea vegetables, fermented foods, beans and bean products, fish, and fruit. Sea vegetables supply a wealth of minerals. Fish is rich in protein and low in cholesterol. Tofu and other soybean products are excellent sources of protein and are low in fat, calories, and cholesterol.

This style of eating, which relies on whole grains as the staple food, is often referred to in this book as a "grain-based diet" or a "grain-based, mostly vegetarian diet." "Macrobiotics" is a term for the recent revival of grain-centered cuisine based on traditional wisdom.

As recently as the 1960s advocates of a return to a more natural, wholesome diet were often ridiculed. But in 1976 the U.S. Senate Select Committee on Nutrition and Human Needs published a landmark report entitled *Dietary Goals for the United States*, which directly linked several major degenerative diseases, including cancer and heart disease, with the modern American diet. The committee advocated a diet consisting of more whole grains, vegetables, and fruit, and less saturated fat, cholesterol, refined sugar, salt, and artificial additives and preservatives. Recommendations were made to substantially decrease the amount of red meat, to rely more on fish and poultry, and to use vegetable oils (polyunsaturated fats) rather than saturated fats such as butter and shortening.

Since that time similar reports and statements have been issued from government, science, and medicine. Studies carried out by medical researchers at Harvard University have demonstrated specific benefits of the macrobiotic way of eating, including a reduction in cholesterol and high blood pressure. These reports and studies have helped influence many people in the direction of more sensible eating.

The elderly people we met in Japan were the greatest testimony to the benefits of their traditional diet. They were an inspiration, and their health, good humor, and vitality made a deep and lasting impression. Many work hard well into their seventies and even eighties. During our stay, one 74-year-old man came each day for several weeks to repair a portion of the thatched roof. A 79-year-old man plastered the Onozaki's new storage building—in midwinter. Each morning, the plasterer told us, he arose at six o'clock, had breakfast, made himself a light lunch, donned his foxtail scarf and leather jacket, and made the bitter cold six-mile trip on his ten-speed bike! He worked outside all day and never missed a single day's work. We never tired of listening to the stories of our favorite old-timers—the 70-year-old barrel maker who came to repair Mr. Onozaki's huge miso vats, a 72-year-old peddler woman who carried a 65-

pound pack of wares from farm to farm, and the bustling 78-year-old Onozaki grandmother.

After returning to the U.S. and setting up our own miso-making "shop," we began to study the properties, manufacture, and uses of other Japanese staple foods. Our main interest was in traditional fermented products. The most characteristic and indispensable seasonings used in Japanese cooking—shoyu, miso, rice vinegar, sake, mirin, and umeboshi—are all fermented foods. More than just delicious and stimulating, when made by traditional methods these foods have unique health benefits. Soon our curiosity spilled over to other important Japanese foods such as shiitake mushrooms, daikon radish, and sea vegetables. As we learned more about these unique products our excitement grew. Now we would like to share this information with others.

Our goals are to introduce traditional Japanese foods, offer recipes to guide you in their use, and provide the information necessary for you to determine the quality of the products you purchase.

When industrially made by modern techniques, foods can be inferior in flavor and, in some cases, of such poor quality as to be hazardous to your health. Perhaps the most important question you can ask about what you eat is how it was made or grown—an important consideration for all conscientious cooks as well as natural foods manufacturers, wholesalers, and retailers. I hope that you will use this book as a shopping guide, ask questions at the shops where you make your purchases, and read labels carefully.

Though many of these traditional foods may seem exotic at first, they are easy to use. The simple recipes I have provided should help you feel comfortable and I hope they will soon serve as a springboard for your own creativity. You will discover that Japanese foods are extremely versatile and can be incorporated into any style of cooking. For example, umeboshi (pickled Japanese plums) can be used instead of salt in many dishes, and will add tangy flavor and unique health benefits to anything from *o-kayu* (rice porridge) to guacamole. Protein-rich seitan (seasoned wheat gluten) is equally at home in sukiyaki or pot pie.

Please read the introduction to each section before proceeding with the recipes. There you will find cooking hints and information to help you determine a commercially-made product's quality; explanations of how the products are made; cultural and historical information; and in some cases there will be a discussion of medicinal and nutritional qualities. We are very fortunate that most of traditional Japanese foods included here are now available in natural foods stores in the U.S. In some cases vegetables may be easier to find at Oriental markets.

I hope this book will encourage you to include these delicious and healthful foods in your everyday cooking. The quality of our food directly affects the quality of our lives. It is rewarding to prepare simple, wholesome meals and watch your family

*Top, John Belleme (left) assists Itsuko Onozaki and barrel maker Haru Arai with the repair of a large cedar vat used for fermenting miso. Bottom, Itsuko takes a tea break during rice planting.*

blossom and become healthier.

One last word of advice to help ensure success: Have fun! When you are giving your energy and creating with joy, positive energy flows through you and is received by all who eat your food.

Scientists now believe that humanity's most ancient cultivated plants are not grains or vegetables, but rather the microscopic organisms—molds, yeast, and bacteria—that cause foods to ferment. In the distant past humanity learned, probably quite by accident, that adding just the right amount of salt to foods cultivated "friendly" organisms, thereby preventing spoilage and formation of dangerous toxins. Although our ancestors' concern was probably for food storage, fermentation accomplished much more than that. It transformed molecular structure, making foods more flavorful and more digestible while preserving them—sometimes for years! Driven by the basic need to preserve food, we had harnessed the microbial world to do our "fireless cooking." We discovered one of nature's most precious gifts, fermentation.

The evolution of fermented foods has culminated, in twentieth century Japan, in an incredible diversity of colors, tastes, and textures. From the rich, dark saltiness of *tamari* to the clear, amber sweetness of *mirin*, Japanese fermented foods stimulate the creativity of cooks around the world.

As you gain confidence and experience in cooking with these delicious and versatile foods, you will want to incorporate them into almost every meal. From simple everyday cooking to gourmet banquets, Japanese fermented foods can make a real difference both in your eating enjoyment and in your health.

Japan's fermented foods industry is now highly technical, using sophisticated equipment in large modern factories. In traditional shops of the past, however, manufacturing fermented foods was considered a complex craft requiring special training and long experience. Although much of the work once done by skilled craftsmen is now performed by machines, some high-quality fermented foods are still made in Japan—the minimum requirements for which are the use of traditional ingredients and unhurried natural aging. Only by meeting these can a manufacturer achieve the taste and aroma and nutritional characteristics of traditional fermented foods.

# MISO

For centuries Japanese craftsmen, using natural fermentation, have transformed soybeans and grains into many types of *miso,* a rich, thick paste used for flavoring a wide variety of dishes. Each miso, like fine wine, has its own distinct flavor, color, and aroma. Throughout Japan each region has developed its own particular type of miso, and though many Japanese are currently turning to Western cuisine, most still start their day with a hot, stimulating bowl of miso soup.

With the growing interest in natural foods and health, miso is steadily gaining in popularity in the West. Many types of miso are now available in America, most of these imported from Japan and some made right here.

Miso is a source of essential amino acids, vitamin $B_{12}$, and minerals, and is low in calories and fat. The daily use of miso, considered a medicinal food by many Japanese, is credited with numerous health benefits. It is said to break down and discharge cholesterol, aid in neutralizing the effects of smoking and environmental pollution, alkalinize the blood, and prevent radiation sickness. Like yogurt, unpasteurized miso contains lactic acid bacteria and enzymes, which aid digestion and food assimilation. Scientists studying Japanese populations have also discovered that those who regularly drink miso soup suffer significantly less from some forms of cancer and heart disease. Japan's Tohoku University has recently isolated chemicals from miso that cancel out the effects of some carcinogens.

Although methods used in making miso differ depending on the type of miso being made and the level of technology employed, the basic process dates back to pre-industrial Japan. Cooked soybeans are mixed with *koji* (grain inoculated with *Aspergillus* mold), salt, and water. This mixture is placed in a container to ferment. Gradually enzymes supplied by the koji, along with microorganisms from the environment, break down the complex structure of beans and grains into readily digestible amino acids, fatty acids, and simple sugars.

Since it is a manufactured food, miso's quality varies depending on production methods and ingredients. There are three methods of miso production: temperature-controlled; naturally-aged; and traditionally-made. Ingredients may be grown either organically or with chemical fertilizers and insecticides.

Like most modern beer, vinegar, and soy sauce, much Japanese miso is made by the fast, completely automated temperature-controlled process using chemically-grown ingredients. Red miso, for example, which at natural temperatures must ferment for one to two years, can be made in just six weeks by this process. The result is a dark, often dry miso with a flat, sometimes burnt, taste. Fortunately, very little of this type of miso is sold in American natural foods stores. Usually carrying a Japanese label, it is the most common type sold in

*Top, Jan Belleme helps out at the Onozaki Koji-Ten, a miso shop in Yaita, Japan, by tossing cooked soybeans to cool them. Bottom, left to right, Itsuko Onozaki, Jan Belleme, and Toshiko Onozaki pour cooked soybeans into a crushing machine. The soybeans will be mixed with rice koji, salt, and water to make red miso.*

*Top, Jan Belleme and Toki Watanabe scoop amazake koji into wooden boxes to be incubated overnight in the koji room. Bottom, left to right, Toshiko Onozaki, Jan, and Itsuko Onozaki cool rice koji by tossing it after it has been inoculated with* Aspergillus *mold.*

Oriental foods markets. This miso is pasteurized to prevent further active fermentation so that it can be shipped in sealed plastic bags or other sealed containers. Temperature-controlled miso may also contain additives such as alcohol to retard bacterial growth.

With few exceptions miso sold in natural foods stores is naturally aged. A few large old factories that changed to automated production methods after World War II are still setting aside small amounts of miso in seasoned wooden vats for natural aging. (Although it is made using the automated process, the fermentation is not temperature controlled.) It is then pasteurized and packaged for natural foods distributing companies under each distributor's private label.

Quality of ingredients in naturally-aged miso can vary widely, so it is best that you try to use only the traditionally-produced varieties. In homes and small shops both in Japan and America, a limited amount of miso is made by methods dating to 19th century Japan. Produced by craftsmen concerned with flavor, health, and tradition, this miso's high quality derives from handmade koji, organic ingredients, slow cooking and cooling of soybeans, and long aging in wooden vats. The traditional process allows for the introduction of many types of "wild" microorganisms from the environment. Their contribution to fermentation adds to the deep, rich taste and heady aroma of traditionally made miso. Fresh and unpasteurized, it has subtle, balanced flavors that only great care, high quality ingredients, and long natural aging can produce. It should be kept refrigerated, and direct contact with air, which adversely affects taste and color, should be avoided. Look for this fine variety of miso in the refrigerator of natural foods stores in small tubs or the recently introduced plastic bag with a one-way valve that prohibits the entrance of air but allows carbon dioxide, a natural byproduct of active fermentation, to escape. Read labels on tubs and packets—they will let you know what you're getting.

The quality of the miso you use will affect the taste of your food and, particularly if used on a daily basis, may affect your health. Organic, unpasteurized, traditionally-made misos should always be preferred. In the preparation of uncooked foods such as dips and salad dressings, the fresh taste of unpasteurized miso is delicious. The powerful enzymatic action of unpasteurized miso is a natural digestive aid and tenderizing agent. In the digestive system miso enzymes aid the body's own resources in breaking down complex food molecules. The same principle applies when miso is added to marinating sauce. Place shrimp or fish in a miso marinade an hour before cooking and notice the delicious taste and tender texture.

In American dishes such as soups, gravies, casseroles, and salad dressings, a little miso, added like bouillon, gives rich flavor as well as eleven grams of protein per tablespoon. For those people moving toward a more wholesome, natural way of eating,

the meat-like flavor of dark miso and the dairy-like flavor of light, sweet miso can help ease the anxiety of that transition. For the experienced natural foods, Japanese, or gourmet cook, miso's possibilities are truly endless.

Although there are a few exceptions, for food preparation miso can be divided into two groups based on color and taste. Sweet miso is usually light in color (white, yellow, or beige) and high in carbohydrates. It is marketed under such names as "mellow miso," "sweet miso," and "white miso." Because it is high in koji and low in salt, sweet miso ferments naturally in just two to eight weeks, depending on the specific recipe and the temperature of aging. It is important to understand that each miso has its own recipe that determines the proper length of fermentation. For instance, white miso is not red miso aged for less time.

*John Belleme (left) and Takamichi Onozaki scrape finished koji from boxes.*

Miso with a higher salt content, lower koji content, and proportionally more soybeans is darker in color and saltier in taste than sweet light miso. It must be fermented for a longer period of time, usually at least one summer but as long as two or three years. This type of miso is marketed under such names as "red miso," "*kome* miso," "rice miso," "brown rice miso," "*genmai* miso," "barley miso," and "*hacho* (soybean) miso."

The miso found in Oriental and natural foods stores is labeled according to color or koji content. For example, barley miso is made with barley koji, and soybean miso, which contains no grain, is made using soybean koji. Confusion arises when both color and koji content are used to describe the same miso. "Red miso" and "rice miso" are actually two names for the same product. In the following recipes I have specified the name most commonly used for each miso; however, if a recipe calls for sweet miso, any sweet or "mellow" miso will do. The same is true for dark, salty miso.

Each type of miso has its own use in both health maintenance and cooking. In terms of health or food value, light, sweet miso is high in simple sugars and contains about twice the niacin and ten times the lactic acid bacteria of dark, saltier miso. Dark miso is higher in protein and, because of its larger proportion of soybeans, contains more fatty acids, which have been shown effective as anti-carcinogenic agents.

The key to miso cookery is not to overpower dishes with a strong miso taste, but to integrate the more subtle aspects of its color and flavor in a gentle balance with the other ingredients.

The light color, sweet taste, and creamy texture of sweet miso suggests its application in American-style cooking: it is an excellent dairy substitute. For example, try a little sweet miso instead of milk in mashed potatoes or creamed soups, and with tofu and lemon or rice vinegar in place of sour cream for dips and spreads. To realize the full potential of sweet miso, explore its uses in salad dressings and sauces. A combination of mellow white miso and rice vinegar creates a delicious, refreshing

*Top, Jan Belleme places the last few pounds of red miso in a huge cedar vat that holds up to 8,000 pounds of miso. Bottom, she washes a 200-year-old cedar vat in front of the Onozaki's house.*

tartness. Sweet miso and sake or mirin combine well in sauces for baked, broiled, or stir-fried vegetables or fish. Think of sweet miso for festive occasions and light summer cooking. In southern climates mellow barley miso is excellent for year-round cooking.

Foods such as raw tofu, beans, and tomato products may cause digestive discomfort, particularly in young children. Because of its mild character, sweet miso can be used to help balance these foods and aid in their digestion. Occasionally I make a tomato sauce containing up to 10 percent mellow barley miso and no added salt. We have friends who say they are allergic to tomatoes, but miso spaghetti sauce does not cause any reaction. This "buffering" effect of miso has not been investigated by scientists, but I have personally experienced it many times.

A combination of sweet miso and tofu in dips, spreads, and salad dressings is easily digested, delicious, and nutritious. Just one four-ounce serving of Creamy Dill (page 10) or Creamy Garlic Chip Dip (page 176) contains the following percentages of the U.S. Recommended Daily Allowance of protein, vitamins, and minerals:

> *Protein...... 20%*
> *Thiamine.... 4%*
> *Niacin....... 4%*
> *Calcium.... 12%*
> *Iron......... 16%*

The F.D.A., which has strict guidelines for nutritional labeling, considers a single serving of food containing 10 percent of the recommended daily allowance of protein "high" in protein. For vegetarians, tofu-miso dishes can be an important source of protein and amino acids.

The readily digestible amino acids, fatty acids, and simple sugars, and relatively low salt content of sweet miso make it ideal for the delicate constitutions of babies and young children. A very dilute mellow miso broth is fine for children starting at age six to eight months.

Dark, saltier miso is best for basic winter cooking in cold climates. Its hearty quality combines nicely with beans, gravies, baked dishes, and vegetable stews and soups. Try dark miso in thick soups using root vegetables such as burdock, carrots, and daikon radish. A lentil loaf made with red miso warms the body and supplies a large quantity of complete protein. Remember that dark miso is stronger in taste than sweet miso, so use it sparingly.

Any discussion of miso is incomplete without considering its use in miso soup. Miso soup and rice, with pickles and tea, constitute a meal by Japanese standards. In Japan the ingredients, texture, and color of miso soup reflect seasonal changes and geographic location. While in winter more grain products such as mochi, fu, and dumplings are used along with root and sea vegetables and hardy greens, spring brings the addition of fresh shiitake, wild vegetables such as cress and wild onions, and thinnings from the earliest garden crops. In summer, light, cooling tofu and succulent vegetables are emphasized, followed in late summer and fall by Chinese cabbage, daikon, and leeks. In the south sweet barley miso, which gives miso soup a beautiful yellow to beige color, is used. In the north it is hearty red miso, often in combination with carrots, burdock, and *wakame* seaweed, giving the soup an earthy color and flavor. Don't be afraid to experiment with the countless possibilities of miso soup. However, since miso is the dominant taste here, unpasteurized miso should be used, and added only at the very end of cooking to prevent boiling the miso.

According to ancient Japanese mythology, miso was a gift from the gods. It is an integral part of a traditional Japanese diet, and has evolved with other foods in that diet. It is closely associated with such foods as rice vinegar, sake, and mirin, which are often used with miso for the purposes of nutritional balance and flavor.

## KYOTO-STYLE MISO SOUP

Although one mellow miso may generally be substituted for another, this recipe is the exception to the rule. The beautiful color of this savory soup can only be achieved by using fresh mellow white miso. Other vegetables may be added or substituted, but simplicity and a flavorful stock are the keys to this authentic miso soup.

*6-inch piece kombu*
*4 cups cold water*
*¼ cup bonito flakes*
*¼ lb. tofu, cut into ½-inch cubes*
*1 scallion, sliced very thin*
*¼ cup mellow white miso*

Place kombu and water in saucepan and bring to a simmer, uncovered, over medium heat. Remove kombu as soon as the water begins to boil. (It may be reused to make soup stock, or cooked with beans or vegetables.) Stir bonito flakes into simmering stock, then remove pan from heat and let sit for 2 minutes. Strain the broth, pressing liquid from flakes with the back of a spoon. Return broth to pan and reheat, adding tofu and scallion, and simmer for 2 minutes. Turn off heat. Soften the miso in a little broth, add to soup, and allow to rest briefly before serving.

**SERVES 4**

## MELLOW MISO SOUP

*6 cups kombu stock or water*
*3-4 scallions, cut into ½-inch*
  *lengths*
*1 carrot, sliced thin*
*1-1½ cups chopped greens*
  *(such as kale, cabbage, or*
  *bok choy), tightly-packed*
*5-6 level tablespoons mellow*
  *white or mellow barley miso*

To make kombu stock, put a 6-inch piece of kombu into a saucepan with 6 cups cold water. Place over medium heat, uncovered, and remove kombu just as water comes to a boil. (Reserve kombu for another use.) Add scallions to stock, then add carrots, and simmer for 10 minutes. Add greens and simmer, uncovered, for 5-7 minutes. Turn off heat. Dilute miso in a little of the broth, then add to soup and allow to rest briefly before serving. Garnish with minced scallion.

This soup is especially satisfying in the warmest months. For a delicious cool weather soup, use 4 level tablespoons red (rice) or barley miso in place of the mellow miso. Other vegetable combinations, such as potato-leek-wakame, daikon-Chinese cabbage, or shiitake-turnip greens, may be substituted. In Japan, the choice of ingredients in the daily miso soup is varied often but always reflects the seasons.

Diluted 50 percent with water, Mellow Miso Soup is a favorite with young children.

**SERVES 4**

## MISO SOUP WITH SHIITAKE

*6 cups water*
*5 dried shiitake mushrooms*
*1 carrot, sliced, or 1 small*
  *potato, diced (peel if not*
  *organic)*
*1½ cups chopped greens,*
  *(such as kale, cabbage,*
  *Chinese cabbage, or mus-*
  *tard greens), tightly-packed*
*¼ cup barley or red (rice)*
  *miso*

The shiitake stock lends an especially rich flavor to this hearty soup. Other vegetables may be substituted, but if shiitake are omitted it is best to start with vegetable or kombu stock rather than water.

Soak shiitake in the 6 cups water overnight or for at least 2 hours. Remove shiitake, cut off and discard tough stems, thinly slice the caps, and place in a pot with the soaking water. Bring to a simmer, add sliced carrot, and cook for 10 minutes. Add greens and cook for 5-10 minutes more. Turn off heat. Dilute the miso in a little of the broth, then add to soup. Allow to steep briefly before serving.

**SERVES 4**

# NAVY BEAN SOUP

Soak beans for several hours, then drain. Combine beans, water, and kombu in a pressure cooker, bring to a simmer, and boil uncovered for 5-10 minutes. Cover, bring up to pressure, and cook for 50-60 minutes. (If pot-boiling instead of pressure cooking add more water as needed and simmer for 2 hours or until beans are completely tender.) Meanwhile, heat oil in a skillet, sauté onion until translucent, add carrot and celery, and sauté together briefly. Cover and cook over very low heat for 10 minutes. Uncover and set aside.

When beans are cooked, remove from heat and allow pressure to return to normal, or to reduce pressure quickly, place cooker in sink and gently run cold water over the top until pressure is completely released. Add salt, vegetables, and herbs to beans. Simmer for 20 minutes and remove from heat. Dissolve the miso in a little water or broth, add to soup, and let sit a few minutes before serving. Garnish with parsley if desired.

SERVES 6-8

*2 cups navy beans*
*10 cups water*
*3-inch piece kombu*
*1 teaspoon light sesame or other unrefined vegetable oil*
*1 large onion, diced*
*2 carrots, diced*
*1 rib celery, thinly sliced*
*1 ¼ teaspoons sea salt*
*1 bay leaf*
*½ teaspoon summer savory*
*¼ teaspoon thyme*
*4 level tablespoons mellow barley or mellow white miso*

# MELLOW MISO SALAD DRESSING

Place all ingredients in a blender and blend until smooth. For a delicious variation with an entirely different appearance and flavor, add several sprigs of fresh dill before blending.

When cooked, the flavor of this dressing changes and it becomes a wonderful sauce for broiled fish or tofu. Simply broil as usual and brush on sauce for the last minute of cooking. Garnish with paprika and parsley and serve hot.

MAKES 1 CUP

*¼ cup unrefined light sesame or safflower oil*
*¼ cup water*
*¼ cup mellow white miso*
*1 ½ tablespoons brown rice vinegar*
*2 tablespoons rice syrup or 1 scant tablespoon honey*
*1 rounded tablespoon chopped onion*
*¼ teaspoon dried mustard powder (optional)*

⅓ lb. fresh tofu
¼ cup mellow white miso
2½-3 tablespoons rice vinegar
   or apple cider vinegar
2 tablespoons light sesame oil
2 tablespoons tahini
⅓ cup (approximately) water
2 tablespoons chopped onion
¼ cup chopped fresh parsley
   (optional)

## MISO-TOFU SALAD DRESSING

Creamy, nutritious, and low in calories, this dressing is excellent on fresh green salads and sea vegetable salads.

Tahini, usually associated with Middle Eastern cooking, is finely ground sesame seed paste. Its non-dairy richness and nutty flavor blend well with traditional Japanese foods. Look for tahini in natural foods stores, Middle Eastern markets, and supermarkets.

Blend all ingredients well. If time permits, chill dressing before serving.

MAKES 2 CUPS

⅓ cup natural mayonnaise
2 tablespoons natural catsup
1 scant teaspoon stoneground
   mustard
2 teaspoons mellow white miso

## MOCK ''THOUSAND ISLAND'' DRESSING

Combine all ingredients and mix until smooth.

MAKES ½ CUP

8 oz. fresh tofu
¼ cup mellow barley miso
2 tablespoons brown rice vinegar or lemon juice
2 tablespoons light sesame oil
1 or 2 cloves garlic
several sprigs fresh dill

## CREAMY DILL DIP

This dip is high in protein and low in calories. It's great for parties, snacks, or to keep hungry dinner guests happy when you're running a little behind schedule.

Place tofu in boiling water to cover. Turn off heat, cover, let sit a few minutes, then place the tofu in cold water briefly to cool. Remove tofu, wrap in cheesecloth or porous cotton, and gently squeeze out excess water.

Place all ingredients in a blender and blend until smooth. Let rest, refrigerated, for at least two hours to allow flavors to heighten. (It is best not to attempt to adjust seasonings before it has rested.)

If you can't find fresh dill, substitute two tablespoons dried onion or three tablespoons fresh minced onion. Stir in onion after blending all other ingredients.

MAKES 1½ CUPS

# SAVORY MISO-SUNFLOWER SPREAD

Roast the sunflower seeds in a dry skillet over medium heat, stirring constantly until golden brown and fragrant (about five minutes). Place roasted seeds in a blender. Blend briefly on "chop" or "crumb" until it is a fairly fine meal. Add the next five ingredients and blend until well mixed. Add miso and tahini and blend. Crumble the tofu with your hands and add it to the blender, one-third at a time. Blend until smooth.

It may be necessary to stop from time to time, scraping the sides of the blender and pressing the mixture down to eliminate air pockets. If your tofu is very firm, you may have to add a *little* more water, but be careful not to overdo it or you'll end up with a dip instead of a spread.

Serve on crackers, bread, or toast, or use with alfalfa sprouts in a sandwich.

MAKES 3 CUPS

*½ cup sunflower seeds*
*2 tablespoons lemon juice or rice vinegar*
*2 tablespoons rice syrup*
*2 cloves garlic*
*2 tablespoons chopped onion*
*water to blend (⅛ to ¼ cup)*
*3 tablespoons red miso (or any rice miso)*
*1 tablespoon tahini (optional)*
*1 lb. fresh tofu*

# MISO-TAHINI SPREAD/SAUCE

To prepare this quick, versatile sauce, simply mix all ingredients well in a saucepan and bring slowly to a simmer, stirring constantly. Cook for 1-2 minutes while stirring, then remove from heat.

Spread on bread, rice cakes, or crackers. For a sauce, add a little more water before simmering. Serve over grains such as couscous, rice, or bulghur, or with steamed or boiled vegetables (try a carrot-cauliflower-broccoli medley), or on broiled tofu. For an interesting variation, try adding ¼ teaspoon dried basil before simmering.

MAKES ½ CUP

*4 tablespoons tahini*
*4 tablespoons water*
*1 level tablespoon red or barley miso*
*1 rounded tablespoon minced onion, scallion, or chives (optional)*

*½ cup mellow white or mellow barley miso*
*2 tablespoons lemon juice*
*2 tablespoons honey (or 4 tablespoons rice syrup)*
*1 tablespoon mirin (optional)*
*1 tablespoon tahini*
*1 clove garlic, pressed or finely minced*
*1 teaspoon ginger juice (peel and grate fresh ginger and squeeze to extract juice)*

## PIQUANT MISO-GINGER SAUCE

Combine all ingredients and mix well.

This easy and versatile sauce "concentrate," which stores well, is generally used diluted about 1:1 with water. Use full strength as a marinade for fish, shrimp, or chicken. For a sauce to enhance steamed or boiled vegetables, combine ¼ cup sauce with ⅛ to ¼ cup water and simmer for 1 minute. Pour over cooked vegetables such as green beans, turnips, broccoli, rounds of daikon, or cauliflower. Combine equal parts sauce and water and add to your favorite wok or stir-fried dishes during the last two minutes of cooking.

For a delicious, protein-rich entree, broil ½-inch thick slices of tofu or 1½-inch pieces mochi. Place a teaspoonful of sauce (thinned with water to desired strength) on each piece one minute before end of cooking time.

MAKES ¾ CUP

*1½ tablespoons olive oil*
*1 onion, diced*
*1-2 cloves garlic, minced*
*3 tablespoons whole wheat or unbleached white flour*
*3 tablespoons nutritional yeast (optional)*
*1⅔ cups (approximately) water*
*3 level tablespoons mellow barley miso*
*¼ teaspoon dried basil*
*several sprigs fresh parsley, chopped (optional)*
*1 tablespoon white wine or mirin (optional)*

## HEARTY GRAVY

This gravy does as much for potatoes as Grandmother's does, and is delicious over grains, especially bulghur and millet.

Heat oil in a medium-sized skillet, add onion and garlic, and sauté over medium heat for 3 to 5 minutes. (Other vegetables such as sliced mushrooms or diced bell pepper may be added if desired.) Lower heat and add flour and nutritional yeast. Stir constantly for about 1 minute, then slowly add 1½ cups water while stirring briskly to keep the flour from lumping. Stir frequently until gravy begins to simmer and thicken.

Combine the miso with 2 to 3 tablespoons of water, then add to pan along with the basil and, if desired, parsley and wine or mirin. Simmer gently, uncovered, for about 15 minutes, stirring occasionally. Keep warm until serving. If gravy is too thick add a *little* more water; if too thin, cook down to desired consistency or slowly stir in one tablespoon arrowroot flour dissolved in one tablespoon water.

MAKES 2 CUPS

*2 level tablespoons mellow white miso*
*3 tablespoons tahini*
*1 tablespoon lemon juice*
*6 tablespoons water*

## WHITE SAUCE

Mix all ingredients thoroughly in a small saucepan. Bring slowly to a simmer, stirring frequently with a whisk. Simmer for 1 minute. If too thick, add a little more water. Delicious over steamed vegetables, noodles, or grains.

MAKES ⅔ CUP

## MISO MARINADE

Mix all ingredients well. Cut one pound of shrimp, fish, chicken, or tofu into bite-sized pieces. Toss in marinade and let sit for about 1 hour unrefrigerated, tossing occasionally, before broiling or including in a recipe of your choice. The following recipe is one delicious way to use any of these marinated items.

¼ cup mellow miso
¼ cup mirin
1 teaspoon shoyu
1 clove garlic, minced

## JOHNNY'S STIR-FRIED SHRIMP AND VEGETABLES

A wok is ideal for this type of preparation, but a large skillet is fine. Endless variations can be created by using different vegetables or substituting other types of seafood, or tofu or chicken, for the shrimp. Try to use attractive combinations of colors and harmonious flavors. Begin sautéeing with those foods that take longest to cook.

Peel and devein shrimp. To devein, make a ¼-inch-deep slit down the back of each shrimp and remove the blackish vein. Cut each shrimp into 2-3 bite-sized pieces, toss in Miso Marinade and let sit for 30-60 minutes unrefrigerated. Meanwhile, wash and slice all vegetables.

Heat oil in wok or skillet and brown ginger over medium heat. Add onion and sauté for 1-2 minutes, add carrot, and sauté for another minute. Add celery and sauté for 5 minutes, then remove and discard ginger. Add green pepper and sauté for 1 minute. Add mushrooms and salt and sauté for 3 minutes. Add Jerusalem artichoke and toss and sauté for another minute, then add shrimp and marinade and sauté for just 1 minute more. Add stock, cover, and simmer briefly while preparing kuzu.

Crush lumps of kuzu with the back of a spoon before measuring, then thoroughly dissolve the kuzu in a small amount of water. Add kuzu to pot, stirring constantly for 1 minute or just until broth thickens. Add more water or kuzu if necessary to achieve the consistency you prefer.

Serve immediately over freshly cooked white rice. (This is one instance where I prefer to serve white rice instead of brown.)

SERVES 3

⅔ - 1 lb. large shrimp
1 tablespoon sesame oil
2 thin slices fresh ginger
1 medium onion, thinly sliced
1 cup thinly sliced carrots
1 cup thinly sliced celery
½ large green bell pepper, thinly sliced
3 cups sliced mushrooms
⅛ teaspoon sea salt
⅔ cup sliced Jerusalem artichoke (optional)
½ cup vegetable or kombu stock or water
1 tablespoon kuzu

*3 cups green beans, cut on
diagonal into 1½-inch
lengths*
*pinch sea salt*
*3 tablespoons sesame seeds*
*1 teaspoon light sesame oil*
*2 level tablespoons barley
miso or red (rice) miso*
*1 tablespoon mirin (optional)*
*1 teaspoon lemon juice*
*1 tablespoon rice syrup or ½
tablespoon honey*

## GREEN BEANS IN SESAME-MISO

Place green beans and salt in boiling water and cook, uncovered, until just tender. Drain and cool. Toast sesame seeds in a dry skillet, stirring constantly over medium heat for about 2 minutes or just until they are fragrant or begin to pop. (If over-toasted they become bitter.) Grind seeds in a *suribachi* or mortar and pestle, add oil and mix, then add miso and mix. Add mirin, lemon juice, and sweetener. The mixture will be thick and somewhat coarse and dry. Add green beans and toss gently with dressing until evenly coated.

Arrange small portions attractively in individual serving bowls or on small plates.

SERVES 4

*1 large onion*
*1 teaspoon unrefined vegetable
oil*
*3-4 parsnips*
*small pinch of sea salt*
*2 level tablespoons mellow
miso*
*2 tablespoons mirin*
*1-2 tablespoons water*
*chives for garnish*

## "SCALLOPED" PARSNIPS

Cut onion in half, then into thin half-moons. Heat oil in a medium-sized skillet (preferably cast iron) and sauté onion for a few minutes or just until translucent. Cover and cook over very low heat for 15-20 minutes. (This long, slow cooking makes the onions very sweet.) Meanwhile, slice parsnips. If they are small, cut on the diagonal into ⅛-inch thick slices; if large, cut in half lengthwise, then slice.

Add parsnips and a small pinch of salt to onions, sauté together briefly, then add water to just cover the bottom of the pan. Cover and simmer until parsnips are nearly tender. Combine miso, mirin, and water. Pour over vegetables and toss gently. Simmer for a few minutes more. Serve garnished with chopped chives for a splash of color.

SERVES 3

## MACARONI SALAD

Combine water and salt in a large pot and bring to a rapid boil. Add noodles and cook until just tender (about 7-10 minutes, depending on type of noodle). Drain, and cool immediately and thoroughly under running water, then drain again and set aside.

While noodles are cooking, cut vegetables. (Wrap minced onion in porous cloth and knead and wring out under cold running water to eliminate its "bite.") Toast sesame seeds in a dry pan over medium heat for 1-2 minutes, stirring constantly. Remove from pan and allow to cool.

Blend miso, tahini, lemon juice, water, and ginger until smooth. (If you don't have a blender, grate the ginger and mix all dressing ingredients together well.) Combine noodles, seeds, and vegetables except for about half the parsley. Add dressing and mix well. Garnish with remaining parsley.

Serve with cornbread and lightly steamed greens for a cooling and satisfying summer lunch.

SERVES 4-6

*2 quarts water*
*3/4 teaspoon sea salt*
*8 oz. noodles (elbows or shells, or fetuccine or long noodles cut into 1½-2-inch lengths after cooking)*
*1 cup seeded and diced cucumber*
*¾ cup thinly sliced celery*
*⅔ cup thinly sliced red radish*
*½ cup minced onion or scallion*
*¼ cup minced parsley*
*3 tablespoons sesame seeds*
*3 level tablespoons mellow white or mellow barley miso*
*3 tablespoons tahini*
*2 tablespoons lemon juice*
*¼ cup water*
*1-inch piece fresh ginger, peeled and sliced*

## LENTIL LOAF

Wash the lentils and combine with kombu, bay leaf, ¼ teaspoon of the oregano, and 3 cups water in a pot. Bring to a boil, then lower to a slow simmer and cook with lid ajar for 30-40 minutes or until lentils are tender and most of the liquid is absorbed. Check frequently toward end of cooking time, adding a *little* water as necessary to avoid scorching.

Meanwhile, bring ¾ cup water to a boil in a small saucepan, then add bulghur and a small pinch of sea salt. Stir and simmer for 1 minute, then cover, remove from heat, and let sit for at least 15 minutes.

When lentils are cooked, they should still be moist. If dry, add about ¼ cup water or stock. Add rolled oats and mix. Add bulghur, ½ teaspoon oregano, and all remaining ingredients. Mix well. Press mixture into an oiled loaf pan, cover with foil, and bake at 350° F. for 40-45 minutes. Remove foil for the last 10-15 minutes.

Cool on a wire rack for 30 minutes if time permits. (This makes it easier to remove loaf from pan.) To remove, run a knife or spatula around the sides of the loaf and invert over a serving plate. Slice, ladle a little Hearty Gravy or other sauce over the top, garnish with a sprig of parsley, and serve with additional gravy on the side.

*1 cup green lentils*
*4-inch piece kombu (optional)*
*½ bay leaf*
*¾ teaspoon dried oregano*
*½ cup bulghur*
*⅔ cup rolled oats (uncooked)*
*½ cup minced scallion*
*2 cloves garlic, minced*
*½ teaspoon dried basil*
*1 tablespoon light sesame or other unrefined vegetable oil*
*1 teaspoon lemon juice*
*2 level tablespoons barley miso thinned in 2 tablespoons water*
*½ cup minced parsley (optional)*

This loaf is especially attractive surrounded by lightly-steamed broccoli and/or braised cherry tomatoes. A delicious, warming dish, Lentil Loaf is especially satisfying in the cooler months and is at its best served with Hearty Gravy or a miso-based tomato sauce. The combination of beans and grains provides an abundance of high-quality complete protein. Leftovers are good sliced and pan-fried, in sandwiches, or simply reheated.

SERVES 6

## LENTIL-NOODLE CASSEROLE

*1 cup lentils*
*3½ cups water*
*3-inch piece kombu*
*½ bay leaf*
*½ teaspoon dried oregano*
*1-2 teaspoons light sesame or*
*corn oil*
*1 large onion, diced*
*1-2 cloves garlic, finely*
*minced*
*1 carrot, diced*
*1 rib celery, sliced thin*
*1 cup (dry) noodles*
*¼ teaspoon sea salt*
*2 level tablespoons barley or*
*red miso*
*⅓ cup minced parsley*

This hearty and nutritious casserole is best served in the fall or winter.

Wash lentils. Combine first 5 ingredients in a pot, bring to a boil, then simmer with lid ajar for 40-45 minutes or until lentils are tender and most of the liquid is absorbed. Meanwhile, heat oil in a skillet and sauté onion, then add garlic and sauté briefly. Add carrot and celery and sauté for a few minutes more. Lower flame, cover, add a little water if necessary, and cook for 10 minutes more. Turn off heat, remove cover, and set aside. Boil the noodles in lightly salted water for about 5 minutes. (They should be undercooked.)

Preheat oven to 350° F. Combine lentils, vegetables, and noodles in casserole dish with ¼ teaspoon salt and 2 tablespoons miso thinned in 2 tablespoons water. Bake, covered, for 30 minutes. Mix in parsley, reserve a little for garnish, and bake for 10 minutes more. Garnish with remaining parsley and serve.

A few tablespoons of freshly grated parmesan cheese is a delicious addition—combine cheese with other ingredients when adding to casserole dish.

SERVES 4

## QUICK MISO PICKLES

Small amounts of light pickles, fresh and crisp, can be part of every meal. Miso pickles are nutritious, an aid to digestion, and are easily prepared and ready to eat in 1-3 days. Although any type of miso will do, I prefer to use a dark miso rather than a light sweet one. My favorite method, however, is to use a blend of equal parts of barley miso and mellow barley miso, or red miso and mellow white miso (both rice misos). Combine the misos and proceed.

Place a 1-inch layer of miso in the bottom of a non-metal container. Add a layer of selected vegetables (as listed below), then cover with miso. No weight is necessary.

☐ Young whole turnips (1-inch diameter) will pickle in 2-3 days. If using larger ones, quarter or slice. Rinse and slice before serving.
☐ Cabbage leaves can be pickled in 1 day. Submerge whole leaves in miso and cover container. Rinse before eating.
☐ For celery pickles, simply cut stalks into lengths appropriate for your container, submerge, cover, and leave for 2-3 days. To serve, rinse, and slice diagonally.
☐ Whole pickling cucumbers may be washed and dried, rubbed with salt and kneaded briefly, then submerged in miso in a covered container for 2-3 days.
☐ Cut tofu into ¾-inch thick slices, wrap in a towel to absorb excess water, then cover with miso for half a day.

Experiment with other vegetables. For a stronger flavor, pickle longer but serve less. Very strong pickles may be minced and sprinkled over rice or millet as a condiment.

Although the miso will be diluted by liquid from the vegetables, it may be reused at least 2-3 times. After it becomes too weak, a little salt and sake may be added to increase flavor and enable the miso to be used for another batch or two of pickles.

## SHOYU

The world's love affair with Japanese soy sauce, *shoyu*, probably began with Dutch traders in Nagasaki in the 17th century. Those early traders sent barrels of shoyu back to Europe and it found its way into the royal kitchens of Louis XIV of France. Since that time shoyu has gained international recognition as a versatile and delicious seasoning, and its production has become one of Japan's leading industries. Although many people associate soy sauce only with Chinese "chow mein," it is a wonderful seasoning for a wide variety of dishes from soup to salad.

*Top, a worker at the Johsen Shoyu Miso Company in Sendai, Japan, places shoyu* moromi *into cotton cloths. The cloths are then run through a hydraulic press. Bottom, natural shoyu ferments in 1,000-gallon vats.*

The methods used today to manufacture traditional shoyu were pioneered during Japan's 16th century. Although modern machines wash and cook ingredients, the few manufacturers that still make the traditional product use whole rather than defatted soybeans, natural fermentation (at least one to two years) rather than accelerated high temperature fermentation, and they age their shoyu in old, seasoned wooden vats. Although this type of shoyu is usually pasteurized before bottling, no preservatives or additives of any kind are used.

The traditional manufacturing process begins with toasting the cracked wheat and steaming the soybeans. These are mixed together in approximately equal parts and inoculated with spores of an *Aspergillus* mold. After a three-day incubation period the wheat and soybeans are covered with a fragrant, fluffy mold mycelium. Now called *koji*, the mixture is added to a brine solution. The thick solution of brine and koji is called *moromi*. After fermenting for one to two years in large wooden vats, with occasional agitation by long wooden rakes, the moromi is placed in cotton sacks and pressed under great force to extract its dark liquid, a mixture of shoyu and soy oil. The oil, which rises to the surface, is removed and the shoyu is ready for pasteurization and bottling.

High quality traditional shoyu accounts for less than one percent of Japan's shoyu production. Over ninety-nine percent is commercial shoyu, using defatted soybeans, fermented at high temperatures for three to six months and often bottled with additives. Served in Japanese restaurants throughout the world, commercial shoyu has a similar flavor but lacks the richness of traditional shoyu.

Synthetic "soy sauce," usually sold in supermarkets, is a different product. Made from hydrolized vegetable protein, hydrochloric acid, corn syrup, caramel coloring, salt and water, it bears little resemblance to natural shoyu. When shopping for traditional shoyu read labels carefully. Look for natural aging of one to two years using only wheat, soybeans, sea salt, and water. The best place to shop for high-quality shoyu is in natural foods stores. Asian shops usually sell only commercial and synthetic soy sauces.

Like miso, shoyu contains amino acids, minerals, and some B vitamins, but it is used in such small quantities that its nutritional value is greatly overshadowed by its outstanding seasoning properties. However, even in small quantities, the ability of shoyu to buffer acidic foods, such as tomatoes, and aid in the digestion of grains is pronounced. Shoyu is high in glutamic acid, a natural form of monosodium glutamate (MSG), which makes it an excellent flavor enhancer, great for marinating, pickling, and sautéeing.

In any cooking style, shoyu can enhance flavor and keep foods tasting fresh. In general, when using shoyu to season foods it should be added only during the last few minutes of cooking. Brief cooking mellows its flavor and enables it to blend with and heighten rather than dominate other flavors in the dish. In longer cooking, shoyu's complex, delicate flavor and slightly alcoholic qualities are lost. When using shoyu to season soups or sauces, I often get the best results by adding just a little sea salt early in the cooking to deepen the flavors of the ingredients, then adding shoyu to taste shortly before serving.

To preserve the fine qualities of traditionally made shoyu, the cap should be tightly closed after each use and the bottle should be refrigerated. Heat and air can oxidize shoyu, turning it dark and adversely affecting its flavor and aroma. To ensure that your shoyu is always in good condition, buy only about a one-month supply, and observe the above guidelines.

A related product, discussed in the next section of this chapter, is called *tamari*. Except for those in the tamari section and a few others that specifically call for tamari, the recipes in this book are calculated for traditional shoyu, which has a little stronger flavor than tamari.


## ONION SOUP

This is a Japanese variation on a popular theme.

Soak kombu and shiitake in the water for 30-60 minutes in a soup pot, then place over medium heat and allow to simmer uncovered for 5-10 minutes. Remove kombu and shiitake and reserve for another use.

Slice onions thinly into half moons. Heat the oil in a medium-sized skillet, add onions and a pinch of salt, and sauté over medium-low heat until the onions are translucent. Lower heat, cover, add a *little* water only if necessary to prevent scorching, and cook for 15-20 minutes. Add salt, bay leaf, and sautéed onions to stock and simmer for 15 minutes. Add shoyu and celery seed and simmer for 5 minutes more. Garnish with minced parsley and croutons and serve hot.

For croutons, cut whole grain bread into ½-inch cubes and deep fry until golden-brown and crisp in vegetable oil heated to 325° F.

**SERVES 3-4**

*6-inch piece kombu*
*3-4 dried shiitake mushrooms*
*4 cups water*
*1-2 teaspoons unrefined vegetable oil*
*5 medium onions*
*½ teaspoon sea salt*
*½ small bay leaf*
*1 tablespoon plus 1 teaspoon shoyu*
*small pinch celery seed (optional)*
*parsley for garnish*
*croutons (optional)*

6 cups kombu-shiitake stock
1 teaspoon vegetable oil
1 onion, thinly sliced
1 pound mushrooms, sliced
pinch white pepper (optional)
1 teaspoon sea salt
1 tablespoon sake or mirin
    (optional)
¼ cup chopped celery leaves
    or parsley
⅔-1 tablespoon shoyu (to
    taste)

## MUSHROOM SOUP

Prepare stock as for Onion Soup. Heat oil in a skillet and sauté onion until translucent, then add mushrooms, a pinch of sea salt, and, if desired, a pinch of white pepper. Sauté over medium heat for about 5 minutes. Add contents of skillet to the simmering stock along with one teaspoon sea salt and, if desired, sake or mirin. Simmer for 15-20 minutes then add celery or parsley and shoyu and simmer for 2 minutes more. Serve hot.

**SERVES 4**

1 lb. (1 large block) fresh tofu
2 tablespoons mirin
1 tablespoon sake or dry white
    wine
2½ tablespoons shoyu
2-3 teaspoons toasted or light
    sesame oil
1 teaspoon grated fresh ginger
    (optional)
2 tablespoons finely minced
    scallion

## TERIYAKI TOFU

This flavorful and attractive tofu dish is quick and simple to prepare. It's perfect when you have unexpected guests.

Cut tofu crosswise into five equal slices. Wrap the slices in a clean, dry kitchen towel to absorb excess water, then lay them flat on a baking pan or platter. Combine the mirin, sake or wine, and shoyu and pour the mixture over the tofu. Turn tofu to coat all sides and set aside to marinate for 15-20 minutes. Turn the tofu once or twice while marinating.

Heat the oil in a large skillet (cast iron if possible) over medium-low heat. Remove tofu from marinade, setting marinade aside. Drain excess liquid from tofu and fry on one side until lightly browned. (Browning will enhance flavor and appearance, but be careful—tofu burns easily.) Carefully turn and cook for 2-3 minutes more. Blot the pan between tofu slices with a paper towel to remove any excess oil, then add marinade and cook for another two minutes.

Place 1 slice tofu on each serving dish. Spread a half teaspoon or so of liquid left in the pan over each slice and, if desired, sprinkle with a few drops of juice squeezed from the grated ginger. Garnish with minced scallion and serve hot.

**SERVES 5**

## THREE-MINUTE TAHINI-SHOYU SAUCE

The exact amount of water needed for this quick sauce will vary depending on the consistency of your tahini and how thick you want the sauce. It thickens as it cooks, so start with the mixture fairly thin.

Add the water to the tahini a little at a time, mixing until smooth after each addition. Add shoyu and, if desired, lemon juice and bring slowly to a simmer while stirring constantly. Cook for one minute. If too thick, add a little more water; if too thin, simmer a little longer to thicken.

This sauce is particularly delicious mixed with an attractive combination of steamed vegetables such as cauliflower, broccoli, and carrots. Cut each vegetable into bite-sized pieces. Carrots take the longest to cook, so steam them for 10 minutes before adding cauliflower. Steam 5 minutes more, then add broccoli and steam for another 5-7 minutes (just until broccoli is tender but still bright green).

Remove cover immediately to prevent greens from overcooking, place vegetables in a serving bowl, and gently toss with sauce.

Simmered until thick, this simple sauce is a good topping for broiled tofu; made thin enough to pour easily, it is excellent over couscous, bulghur, or noodles.

MAKES ⅔ CUP

*¼ cup tahini*
*⅓-½ cup water*
*2 teaspoons shoyu*
*1 teaspoon lemon juice (optional, but recommended)*

## PARBOILED GREENS SALAD

Wash greens and remove tough stems from leaves. Fill a large pot halfway with water, bring to a boil, add a pinch of sea salt, and add as many whole leaves as will comfortably fit (you may have to cook them in batches). Boil greens just until tender (about 7 minutes for collards and kale, a little less for chard and bok choy). When tender, remove greens immediately and plunge them into cold water to stop the cooking and hold the color. Drain, gently squeeze out excess water, and slice thinly. (If leaves are very large, cut in half lengthwise first.) Boil carrots for 2-3 minutes, remove, and cool under running water.

Combine shoyu, lemon juice, ½ tablespoon water, and ginger juice. Toss with greens and carrots in a mixing bowl, then place in a serving bowl and garnish with the sesame seeds.

SERVES 4

*1 large bunch collards or other leafy greens such as kale, chard, bok choy, and so on.*
*½ carrot, cut julienne (into ''matchsticks'')*
*1 tablespoon toasted sesame seeds*
*1 tablespoon shoyu*
*1 tablespoon lemon juice*
*½ tablespoon water*
*1 teaspoon juice from grated fresh ginger*

# TAMARI

Even before the development of shoyu, Japanese miso makers were using *tamari*, the rich, dark liquid that pooled on the surface of fermenting miso, to season foods and pickle vegetables. By the thirteenth century a purposely wet soybean miso was being prepared, and after fermentation its liquid was pressed out and decanted. This was the birth of Japan's small but productive tamari industry, which today survives in Aichi, Mie, and Gifu prefectures and accounts for about three percent of Japan's soy sauce production.

When Western natural foods distributors first began importing soy sauce from Japan, by accident they labelled it "tamari," though what they were getting was actually high quality shoyu. Thus began one of the most confusing controversies of the modern natural foods movement.

In the broader use of the term, shoyu and tamari both are types of soy sauce—fermented seasonings derived from soybeans. Reduced to its simplest terms, the main difference between tamari and shoyu is the type of starter, or koji, used. For shoyu koji, equal parts of cracked wheat and soybeans are inoculated with *Aspergillus* mold spores and incubated for three days. Tamari koji is made with only soybeans. Although ancient tamari makers used a thick miso-like paste to produce tamari, modern manufacturers use a wet mush made by adding soybean koji to a brine solution. After the koji is made, therefore, tamari production is similar to that of shoyu. The subtle yet significant difference between these two delicious seasonings is in the absence of wheat in true tamari. However, if a recipe calls for shoyu, an equal amount of tamari can usually be substituted with good results. If you want to fine-tune your cooking skills, though, learn the qualities of each and take advantage of their unique characteristics.

The subtle sweetness of shoyu and its alcoholic bouquet are both the result of wheat fermentation. Much of the rich taste and aroma of shoyu is lost during cooking because of evaporation of alcohol, so tamari is the choice when longer cooking is called for.

Since real tamari contains no wheat, its cooking qualities are different. Made solely from soybeans, tamari has a significantly higher amino acid content, which is responsible for its thick texture and rich taste. Unlike alcohol, amino acids are not volatile, so they remain to impart flavor to foods even after lengthy cooking. Tamari also contains more glutamic acid than shoyu. I like to use tamari whenever it is better to add seasoning other than sea salt early in the cooking. For example, when cooking certain foods such as shiitake, or bland or oily foods such as fresh, dried, or deep-fried tofu, all of which are enhanced by long simmering in a seasoned liquid, tamari is the better choice. Its thicker consistency and slightly deeper taste also make it good for dipping sauces and pickling.

When shopping for real tamari, read labels carefully. Look for long natural aging (one to two years), and only soybeans, water, and sea salt as ingredients. Most natural foods stores now stock excellent tamari. A few are organic, and one has mirin added, making it good for marinades and dipping sauces as well as for general purpose seasoning.

## TEMPEH HORS D'OEUVRES WITH TOFU-MUSTARD TOPPING

For those of us who don't entertain often, hors d'oeuvres can be a stumbling block. Elegant yet easy to prepare, this one fills the bill.

Tempeh is an Indonesian fermented soyfood that is rapidly becoming popular in the U.S. Versatile and delicious, it is an excellent vegetable source of protein and vitamin $B_{12}$.

If your tofu is not fresh, cover it with water and bring it to a boil in a small saucepan. Turn off heat and let pan sit, covered, for a few minutes. Drop the tofu into cold water and let rest until cool enough to handle, then proceed.

To measure tofu, press it into a measuring cup. Wrap tofu in a clean towel and gently squeeze to remove excess water. Grind or mash in a suribachi or bowl until smooth. Add mustard, tamari, and salt and mix well.

Heat ⅓ inch of unrefined vegetable oil (safflower works well) in a small skillet over medium heat to about 325° F. (hot enough to sizzle as soon as the tempeh is added, but not so hot that it smokes). Put in about seven or eight pieces of tempeh, fry until golden on one side (about 1 minute), turn, and fry for about 30 seconds more. Remove and drain on a wire rack placed over absorbent paper, or directly on the paper. Continue with the rest of the tempeh. Always remove all pieces from one batch before adding more tempeh to the oil.

Neatly place a small mound (about a rounded half teaspoon) of tofu-mustard on top of each square of tempeh. Pierce each with a toothpick down through the top and arrange on a serving plate. Mix tamari and water and place one or more small shallow dishes of dip beside the plate.

**MAKES 25-30 PIECES**

⅔ cup fresh tofu
2 tablespoons (or to taste)
  prepared natural mustard
½ teaspoon tamari
pinch sea salt
oil for frying tempeh
8 ounces tempeh, cut into ¾-
  inch squares
toothpicks

DIP:
1 tablespoon tamari
1½-2 tablespoons water

*1¼-1½ cups slivered carrots*
*1 cup green beans, cut on the*
*diagonal in very thin strips*
*1 pound mung bean sprouts*

DRESSING:
*1 tablespoon unrefined light or*
*toasted sesame oil*
*2 tablespoons tamari*
*1½ tablespoons brown rice*
*vinegar*

## PARBOILED SALAD WITH JAPANESE DRESSING

Though traditionally the Japanese did not eat raw salads, lightly parboiled vegetables with a Japanese version of vinaigrette dressing has long been a favorite summer side dish. Other parboiled vegetables such as shredded cabbage or Chinese cabbage, thinly sliced red onions, and green pepper can be substituted for the ones here, or add raw cucumber, radish, or lettuce.

Bring three inches of water with ⅛ teaspoon sea salt to a boil in a large saucepan. Meanwhile, rinse and drain bean sprouts, and cut carrots and green beans into fine slivers 1-1¼ inches long. When water reaches a full boil, add carrots and green beans and simmer for just 2 minutes, then add bean sprouts. As soon as water returns to a simmer, drain vegetables into a colander or bamboo basket and gently toss or vigorously fan to cool quickly. Gently squeeze out excess water.

Combine dressing ingredients and mix well. Put vegetables in a bowl and toss with dressing just before serving in salad bowls or on small plates.

SERVES 5

## QUICK TAMARI PICKLES

These simple pickles take but a few minutes to prepare and are ready to eat in 2-4 days. We find them most appealing in fall and winter.

Fill a wide-mouthed jar with either carrot or rutabaga cut into thin, inch-long "matchsticks." (Other vegetables may be substituted, but these two are particularly good.) Cover with a mixture of half tamari and half water, screw on the jar cover, and let sit for at least 2 days before beginning to eat them. When the vegetables are pickled enough to have lost their raw taste they should be refrigerated. These pickles keep well, though they get a little stronger with age.

When the pickles are gone, the leftover tamari mixture can be used for at least one or two more batches of pickles. However, it will have become diluted by juice drawn out from the vegetables so fresh tamari should be added until the brine's strength approximates that of the original mixture. If you have forgotten the taste, mix ½ teaspoon tamari with ½ teaspoon water for a comparison.

# BROWN RICE VINEGAR

Refreshing and delicious, naturally brewed brown rice vinegar is a wonderful seasoning. Characterized by a light sweetness, it is full bodied yet mild, without the sharpness or "bite" often associated with other vinegars. In cooking, brown rice vinegar adds interest by providing a stimulating contrast of flavors. It helps balance salt and reduces the craving for strong sweets.

Since ancient times vinegar has been used throughout the world, both as a seasoning agent and as a home medicinal remedy. Rice vinegar was brought to Japan from China in the fourth century A.D., at about the same time that the closely related technique for brewing rice wine (sake) was introduced. Natural rice vinegar maintained its popularity in Japan until the early 1900s, when the quicker and cheaper alcohol vinegar brewing method was developed.

Top-quality natural rice vinegar is made only from cooked rice, rice koji, pure water, and seed vinegar. (The "seed" is some of the mash reserved from a batch of mature vinegar.) These four ingredients are mixed together and placed in earthenware crocks to ferment. First the enzymes in the koji break down the complex starches in the rice, converting them to simple sugars. Yeast from the koji and seed vinegar converts the sugars to alcohol. Bacteria present in the seed vinegar then convert the alcohol to acetic acid (vinegar). This process takes about a year, as compared to synthetic vinegars, which are quickly and inexpensively produced.

There are several brands of brown rice vinegar, all of which are of high quality. However, that a vinegar is labeled "rice vinegar" does not assure its quality. Any vinegar made in Japan that contains 40 grams of rice or rice wine dregs per liter can be called rice vinegar, even if it is mixed with synthetic vinegar. Therefore, be sure to check the label on any rice vinegar. It should contain only rice, rice koji, and water, and should be naturally fermented for about one year.

Naturally brewed brown rice vinegar should not be confused with inexpensive, low-quality vinegars found in supermarkets. Some are synthetic products made from glacial acetic acid, a petroleum product. Others are made from alcohol produced for industrial use. Avoid any vinegar labeled "distilled," which is the most highly refined and least healthful. Distilled vinegar is sometimes referred to as "white vinegar" or "grain vinegar." There are other types of naturally-brewed vinegars, such as some apple cider and wine and malt vinegars. However, besides its superior, mild flavor, and whole rice in the fermenting mixture, high-quality brown rice vinegar has a significantly higher amino acid content. The presence of amino acids is partly responsible for vinegar's ability to counteract the effects of lactic acid buildup caused by strenuous physical exertion.

Excess lactic acid in the blood causes fatigue, stiff, sore muscles, and irritability, and contributes to atherosclerosis.

Naturally-brewed vinegar neutralizes lactic acid, cleaning the blood and helping to restore a balanced condition. A major cause of sickness is an acid blood condition. Natural vinegar has an alkalinizing effect on the blood, which helps maintain health.

Generally, vinegar is more appealing in the warmer seasons. According to Kuroiwa Togo, author of *Rice Vinegar: An Oriental Home Remedy*, this is because of the large amount of lactic acid naturally occurring in the body then. You can enjoy brown rice vinegar in all the ways you use other vinegars. Combined with a little *ume su* (umeboshi "vinegar," see page 50) and/or olive oil, it is delicious on fresh salads.

Traditionally-brewed, unfiltered rice vinegars often contain a rice sediment, which, if disturbed, causes them to look muddy. Rather than being a cause of concern, this sediment is a sign of high quality.

## ITALIAN DRESSING

Combine equal amounts of Italian olive oil, brown rice vinegar, and ume su in a jar. Cover and shake vigorously before using. When serving this dressing, I like to sprinkle some dried herbs over the salad. The Seelect company markets a perfect blend of sweet basil, tarragon, and savory under the name "Natural Salad Herbs." The herbs can also be added to the dressing, or try substituting oregano, basil, and a little finely minced garlic.

## TOFU AVOCADO SALAD DRESSING

Blend all ingredients except parsley until smooth. Add parsley and mix it in with a spoon. This is a mild dressing, and goes best on tossed green salads.

**MAKES 3 CUPS**

*⅓ block tofu (approximately ⅓ pound)*
*1 ripe avocado, peeled and pitted*
*1-2 cloves garlic*
*2 tablespoons chopped onion*
*3 tablespoons brown rice vinegar*
*⅓ to ½ cup water*
*¼ cup safflower or light sesame oil*
*¼ cup mellow white miso*
*¼ cup minced parsley*

## MARINATED VEGETABLE/BEAN SALAD

Other vegetables may be substituted, but use a variety of colors. Hard vegetables, such as carrots and broccoli, should be *briefly* steamed or parboiled in lightly salted water, then immediately cooled under running water and drained.

To prepare marinade, bring first 7 ingredients to a simmer, then turn off heat, cover, and let steep. Separately parboil or steam green beans and cauliflower as described above (for 1-2 minutes). Drain and cool.

Combine marinade, vegetables, beans, and scallion and/or parsley. Refrigerate for at least several hours (preferably overnight) to allow flavors to blend and heighten. Toss occasionally. Serve over lettuce in small bowls.

**SERVES 6**

*½ cup unrefined Italian olive or light sesame oil*
*⅓ cup brown rice vinegar*
*1½ teaspoons sea salt*
*1 bay leaf, broken into 2-3 pieces*
*1 clove garlic, minced*
*pinch white pepper or cayenne (optional)*
*1 teaspoon dill seed or caraway seeds*
*10 green beans, cut into 1½ to 2-inch lengths*
*several bite-sized pieces cauliflower*
*1 red onion, thinly sliced*
*1 small green pepper, thinly sliced*
*8 mushrooms, sliced or quartered*
*2/3 cup kidney beans or chick peas, cooked but not mushy*
*3 tablespoons minced scallion and/or chopped parsley*

*1 bunch mustard or turnip
   greens (about 6 cups
   chopped and tightly-packed)
1-2 teaspoons unrefined vegetable oil (light sesame, safflower, or corn)
2 cloves garlic, finely minced
1 to 1½ teaspoons shoyu
approximately 2 teaspoons
   brown rice vinegar*

## VINEGARED GREENS

Vinegar complements the flavor of greens. Properly prepared, this simple vegetable dish is colorful, refreshing, and stimulating.

Wash greens carefully, chop, and set aside. Heat oil in a large skillet and sauté garlic briefly. Add greens and sauté for 2-3 minutes. Add enough water to just cover the bottom of the pan, cover, and let steam for 5-10 minutes (until greens are nearly tender but still colorful). Sprinkle with shoyu, add vinegar to taste, toss, cover, and let steam for 1-2 minutes more.

If not serving immediately, remove from heat and uncover to prevent greens from losing their bright color.

SERVES 3-4

*1½ lbs. (3½ cups) daikon or
   pickling cucumbers, sliced
   ⅛ -inch thick
2 teaspoons sea salt
½ cup brown rice vinegar
½ cup water
1 tablespoon mirin
1 tablespoon honey or 2 tablespoons rice syrup
2-3 pinches sea salt*

## QUICK BREAD 'N BUTTER PICKLES

Toss sliced vegetables with 2 teaspoons salt. Let daikon stand for 5 hours or just overnight (no longer, or they will be too soggy). Cucumbers need to stand for only one hour. *Gently* squeeze to drain off excess water, but do not rinse. Mix last 5 ingredients together, boil for just 1 minute (no longer), then cool to room temperature. Combine vegetables and liquid in a jar or other covered container and put in a cool place or refrigerate.

These are ready to eat after 2-3 days. Refrigerated, cucumber pickles will keep up to one month before losing their crispness, daikon up to one year.

## SAKE (JAPANESE RICE WINE)

My interest in Japan might have actually begun with a sip of hot sake at a party in Boston. Hot sake seems to hit all the senses at once; you taste it, smell it, and feel it simultaneously. The sensation left me wondering what other uncommon pleasures this distant culture had to offer.

Sake is one of Japan's oldest beverages; its origins are buried deep in ancient legend and myth. Even today drinking sake has special meaning, especially for older people, and Shinto rituals dating back centuries are still celebrated with sake. The crystal clear fragrant liquid served today in tiny delicate cups and used as a seasoning in cooking is very different from the primitive fermented rice gruel from which it probably originated. That thick, *amazake*-like alcoholic drink is still made today in rural homes in some parts of Japan. Gradually over many years sake gained popularity among the nobility and clergy. By the tenth century privileged classes were enjoying a more liquid, milky drink with a much higher alcohol content than the thicker gruel of rural peasants. In the last 200 years advances in technology have made possible the large-scale production of crystal-clear sake that has an alcohol content of from 15 to 17 percent.

Good quality sake is available at many wine stores in the U.S. Although most sake sold in Japan contains additives such as glucose and ethanol, sake made for export is of higher quality. The finest quality sake, however, is made in the U.S. The Kimoto Brewing Company in Berthoud, Colorado is making a completely natural sake using brown rice and traditional methods. Almost all other sake in Japan and the U.S. is made with white rice. If you are interested in a regular supply of good quality sake, ask your local wine store to order this brand.

Sake, called "rice wine" in this country, is related more to other koji-fermented foods such as amazake, miso, and rice vinegar than to wine or beer. Natural sake contains only rice, water, koji, and yeast. Manufacturing begins with the steaming of rice to make koji. The koji is added to water and cooked rice along with a special strain of yeast. Koji enzymes turn complex rice carbohydrates into simple sugars, which the yeast then ferments to alcohol. After about sixty days most of the sugar has been converted to alcohol and the white mash, called moromi, is ready for pressing, filtering, and bottling. (This is a simplified explanation of modern sake production.) Although most sake is now made in automated factories, we were surprised to find a few sake shops in Japan still making koji by hand and using old wooden vats for fermentation.

Before considering the use of sake in cooking, we should distinguish between the two types of sake. The process described above results in a sake that is not particularly sweet because almost all the simple sugars supplied by the rice are converted to alcohol. This type, called *karaguchi* (dry mouth sake), is preferred by serious sake drinkers. If more cooked rice is added to finished sake, koji enzymes convert rice carbohydrates to sugars. The result is *amaguchi* (sweet mouth) sake, which is preferred as a seasoning in cooking. Although this distinction is not critical, if you have a choice, consider what your purpose is, then choose accordingly.

Although sake is sometimes drunk cold, particularly in summer, it is more often served warm. To serve, fill a small serving container, called a *takkuri*, with sake and place it in 2-3 inches of water in a small saucepan over a medium-low flame. Since alcohol boils at a lower temperature than water, do not let the temperature of the sake go above 140°F. or the alcohol will evaporate. Sake is served in small cups called *saka-zuki*. A little simple etiquette should be observed, particularly when serving Japanese friends. It is considered impolite to fill one's own cup, or to have a guest fill his or her own cup. Even in your home it is customary for your guest to fill your cup and vice versa. When your friend pours for you, raise your empty cup a few inches to acknowledge the gift. When you have had enough

*Top, on special occasions sake is drunk at room temperature directly from its traditional container, the* sakadaru. *Bottom, a giant, wood-filled cauldron is readied for steaming rice at a traditional sake shop in Tochigi Prefecture, Japan.*

sake, leave your last cupful standing. Finally, when serving sake with a meal, rice is traditionally not offered until your guests have had their fill of sake, so serve rice last, just before tea. All this ceremony may seem a little complicated at first, but with all the pouring and raising of cups, a simple dinner can turn into a party, with everyone relaxed and having fun.

Although overconsumption of alcohol was not considered good temple etiquette, Zen monks responsible for cooking found sake indispensable as a seasoning. Sake enhances the flavor of other foods. Along with shoyu, miso, mirin, and dashi, it is one of the most important seasonings in Japanese cuisine. Much as the French use wine in sauces, marinades, and stocks for soups and simmered dishes, the Japanese use sake. Sake is unsurpassed for reducing strong odors of foods such as fish, is an excellent tenderizer, and helps to de-emphasize saltiness.

If you want to add a truly authentic Japanese taste and spirit to your meal, use sake both as a beverage and a seasoning.

## SAKE-SEASONED CLEAR SOUP

BROTH:
*7 cups water*
*6-inch piece kombu*
*3 dried shiitake*
*1 teaspoon sea salt*
*2 tablespoons sake*
*2 tablespoons tamari or shoyu*

To prepare the broth, soak the kombu and shiitake in the water for 15 minutes. (You will need to use a saucer or other object as a weight to keep the shiitake submerged.) Place soaking water, kombu, and shiitake in a pot and bring to a boil over medium heat. Remove kombu as soon as the water begins to simmer. Cook shiitake for 5 minutes, then remove. Reserve the kombu and shiitake for another use. Add salt, sake, and tamari or shoyu to the broth, and simmer for 2 minutes.

VARIATION I:
Ingredients in clear soups should be kept simple, attractive, and generally sparse. Properly prepared and served, their simple beauty calms the spirit. The following are two examples, but you can improvise endlessly.

For **each** bowl of soup you
   will need:
*3 pieces zeni fu (see page 91)*
*2 tablespoons chopped par-*
   *boiled spinach, turnip*
   *greens, or other bright,*
   *leafy green*

Soak fu in lukewarm water for 10 minutes, then gently squeeze out excess water between the palms of your hands. Add to the broth and simmer for 10 minutes. Meanwhile, parboil carrot flowers in lightly salted water until *just* tender.

Parboil spinach for just 30-60 seconds, remove, drain immediately and chop. If substituting other greens, they may require longer cooking, but be careful not to overcook until they lose their color.

Arrange the fu in soup bowls along with the greens and carrots, ladle the broth into the bowls, and serve hot.

VARIATION II:
If tofu is not absolutely fresh, I suggest using the dumplings. Cook dumplings in a pot of lightly salted water, then remove and drain. If using carrot flowers, parboil as described in option I. Tofu, scallions, and watercress need not be precooked. Arrange ingredients in soup bowls, cover with piping hot broth, and serve.

SERVES 6

*3 carrot flowers (slice carrot into ⅛ -inch thick rounds and scallop edges to make flower shapes)*

For **each** bowl of soup you will need:
*several ½-inch cubes fresh tofu or 3-5 dumplings as in Vegetable Soup with Dumplings (see page 127)*
*3-5 parboiled carrot flowers, or a sprinkle of minced scallion*
*a few sprigs of watercress, cut into 2-3 pieces*

# BRAISED CARROTS AND SNOW PEAS

Braising is a simple technique that involves sautéeing briefly in a small amount of oil, then adding a little liquid to the pan, covering, and steaming until tender. The result is more flavorful than just steaming. The use of sake makes this quick and colorful braised dish especially good.

Cut the carrot on the diagonal into ⅛ -inch thick slices, then cut each slice lengthwise into 2-3 pieces. Heat the oil in a medium-sized skillet and add the ginger, carrot, and a small pinch of salt. Sauté briefly, then add 3-4 tablespoons water, cover, and cook until nearly tender. Check occasionally and add a *little* more water if necessary to prevent scorching. When carrots are almost tender, remove and discard ginger. The pan should be nearly dry. If not, uncover, and cook off excess liquid by stirring constantly over medium-high heat for a minute or two. Add the peas, sake, and shoyu, toss with the carrots, cover, and steam for just 1-2 minutes.

If it is not possible to serve immediately, uncover the pan and remove it from the heat to prevent the vegetables from overcooking.

SERVES 2-3

*1 large or 2 medium-sized carrots*
*1 teaspoon light sesame oil*
*1 slice fresh ginger, ⅛ -inch thick (optional)*
*pinch sea salt*
*¼ lb. snow peas or other edible-pod peas*
*2 tablespoons sake*
*1 teaspoon shoyu*

*1 pound grouper or other thick
  white fish fillet such as
  snapper, cod, or tile fish*
*⅔-1 lb. tofu*
*12 ⅛ -inch thick carrot slices*
*12 snow peas*
*sea salt*
*4 tablespoons sake*

DIPPING SAUCE:
*¼ cup shoyu or tamari*
*¼ cup lemon juice*
*¼ cup water*

GARNISHES:
*⅓ cup grated daikon*
*2-3 tablespoons finely minced
  scallion*

# BAKED FISH, TOFU, AND
# VEGETABLE MEDLEY

This simple, nutritious, and low-calorie preparation is cooked and served in individual ovenproof containers. If you don't have small gratin dishes or appropriately-sized Pyrex or Corningware containers, cook all together in a small baking pan or a loaf pan and serve in individual bowls.

As always, fish and tofu should be very fresh. Preheat oven to 425 °F. Rinse fish in cold water, then pat dry, sprinkle lightly with salt, and cut into bite-sized pieces. Cut tofu into one-inch cubes. Slice carrots and, if desired, cut into flower or other decorative shapes. Parboil carrots in lightly salted water for just two minutes, then remove and drain. Parboil snow peas for 30 seconds, drain, and set aside.

Arrange fish, tofu, and carrots in individual ovenproof serving containers. Sprinkle a pinch of salt and a tablespoon of sake over the ingredients in each container, cover with foil and bake for 20-30 minutes. Cooking time will vary according to thickness of fish and type of container. Check often to avoid overcooking. When done, the fish will be white throughout, not translucent. Add snow peas for the last minute or two of cooking. Remove from oven, remove covers, and serve hot.

Combine ingredients for dipping sauce and divide among four custard cups or other small containers. Place grated daikon and minced scallion on the table and allow each diner to add them to their dip.

SERVES 4

For **each** person being served
  you will need the following:
*⅓-½ lb. large-flake fish fillet
  (grouper, snapper, salmon,
  cod, flounder or tile fish)*
*pinch sea salt*
*2 teaspoons sake*
*small pinch ground red
  pepper (optional)*
*1 teaspoon Italian olive oil or
  light sesame oil*
*squeeze of lemon juice plus
  lemon wedge*
*piece of aluminum foil for
  wrapping fish*

# FRESH FISH BAKED IN FOIL

This is a variation of a delicious trout recipe I learned from a Japanese friend. The foil keeps the juices sealed in so that, assuming the fish is fresh, the result will be moist and flavorful.

Preheat oven to 325 °F. Sprinkle the fish with the salt and sake and, if desired, a little red pepper. Set the fish aside for 10 minutes, then spread the oil evenly over the surface and sprinkle the fish with lemon juice. Moisten the center of the foil with oil to keep it from sticking to the fish. To be sure the juices are kept in, wrap the fish by bringing the two ends of the foil together over the fish and fold at least twice in ½-inch folds. Next fold each side in toward the center at least twice. Place the fish on a cookie sheet and bake for 20-30 minutes. Cooking time will vary depending on the variety and thickness of the fish, so check occasionally. When done, the flesh will be solid white throughout, not translucent at the center. Unwrap and serve hot with a wedge of lemon and, if desired, a sprig of parsley or watercress for color.

# BROILED MARINATED HADDOCK

Here's an easy and tasty fish recipe. The actual preparation time is only about five minutes.

Rinse fish under cold running water, then pat dry. Combine the liquid marinade ingredients in a pie plate or 8-inch square baking pan. Lay the fish in the marinade, then turn it over. (The marinade is not meant to cover the fish, so this coats the top while the other side is marinating.) Tuck several slices of ginger under the fish. If desired, lightly sprinkle with cayenne pepper or Japanese 7-spice. Marinate for 15 minutes then turn, again placing the fish on top of the ginger. Sprinkle with a little more cayenne, if using, and marinate for 15 minutes more. Spoon a little of the marinade over the top of the fish once or twice while marinating.

Preheat the broiler and oil a baking sheet. Remove the fish from the marinade and place it on the baking sheet, reserving marinade. Broil fish on one side for about 5 minutes. Turn, spoon a little marinade over, and broil for about 3 minutes more. (Broiling time will vary according to the thickness of the fish. The fish is done as soon as the flesh is solid white throughout. If still translucent at the center, cook for a couple of minutes more and check again.)

Serve hot on individual dishes or standard dinner plates. If desired, sprinkle a teaspoon or two of the marinade over each serving and garnish with a wedge of lemon and a sprig of parsley or watercress.

Japanese 7-spice, or *shichimi*, is a blend of red pepper, sesame seeds, orange peel, nori, and other ingredients. It adds flavor, but is very hot. Look for 7-spice in Japanese markets, but don't buy the variety that contains monosodium glutamate.

SERVES 3-4

*1½ pounds fresh haddock steaks or fillets (or substitute cod or sole)*

MARINADE:
*3 tablespoons shoyu or tamari*
*2 tablespoons sake*
*2 tablespoons mirin*
*1¼-1½-inch knob fresh ginger, peeled and sliced thinly*
*red pepper powder (cayenne) or Japanese 7-spice (optional)*
*several lemon wedges*
*parsley or watercress for garnish (optional)*

*4 level tablespoons barley, red
(rice), or mellow white miso*
*1 tablespoon water*
*1½ tablespoons sake*
*2½ tablespoons rice syrup
(reduce to 1½ tablespoons if
using mellow white miso)*
*2 teaspoons lightly grated
lemon rind*

## SWEETENED MISO SAUCE

This sauce goes well with steamed or boiled vegetables such as
daikon, cauliflower, broccoli, green beans, or turnips. It is also
good on broiled tofu, mochi, or white fish. When made with
barley or red miso, its dark color provides an attractive contrast
to white foods such as whole baby turnips peeled and cooked
until tender.

Thoroughly mix all ingredients in a small saucepan and bring to
a simmer over low heat while stirring constantly. Continue to
cook and stir until sauce thickens (about 2 minutes), then remove
from heat. To serve, place cooked vegetables, tofu, mochi, or
fish in individual serving bowls or on small plates and spoon a
little sauce over the top.

MAKES ½ CUP

## MIRIN

My discovery of *mirin* (Japanese sweet rice cooking wine) filled
a gap in my understanding of cooking. My early study of
macrobiotics taught me to rely heavily on salt, shoyu, miso, and
umeboshi as seasonings. I have now found that the use of mirin
and other seasonings, especially rice vinegar and herbs, balances
salt and reduces the craving for strong sweets. You will find
many recipes that incorporate mirin throughout this book.

Mirin is related to sake (rice wine). Like sake, traditional
mirin manufacture begins with a mixture of rice koji (see Koji,
page 37), cooked white rice, and water. However, after a one-
month fermentation, the resulting white, slightly alcoholic mash
undergoes a distillation process that is not part of traditional
sake-making. The clear distillate, called *shochu*, is mixed with
cooked sweet rice—the variety of rice highest in natural
sugars—and more rice koji. After three months of additional fermentation, the *shochu* is pressed, and the resulting clear liquid is
aged for six months to two years in ceramic containers. The
thick, sweet, golden liquid removed from the containers is mirin,
Japan's answer to fine brandy. Prized by wealthy women in feudal Japan as a beverage, mirin slowly evolved into one of Japan's
most valued cooking seasonings. Today, mirin is virtually
always used for cooking, while sake is usually served hot as an
alcoholic beverage. Cooking quickly evaporates mirin's 13-14
percent alcohol content, leaving only its sweet essence.

Authentic natural mirin is as scarce and costly as it is delicious. Many brands of mirin, especially those sold in Oriental
markets, are not naturally brewed and are sweetened with sugar
or corn syrup. However, in most cases the mirin available in
natural foods stores is a high-quality, naturally fermented product

made with slight modifications of the traditional process described above. Unlike those brands containing added refined sweeteners, the sweetness of naturally made mirin derives only from sweet rice and rice koji. Mikawa mirin is the brand I am familiar with, though there are others. Even when shopping in natural foods stores it is necessary to read the label carefully to see whether it was naturally fermented, and to check for purity of ingredients (sweet rice, rice koji, and water are the only ingredients in authentic mirin).

A related product, known as *aji no haha* in Japan, is often marketed under the name "mirin" in this country. In terms of its manufacture, this mirin-like seasoning is actually more like sake, except that additional cooked rice, koji, and water are added to the sake and fermented for two more weeks to produce sweet sake. Unlike mirin, it contains no sweet rice or distilled alcohol. After pressing, 2 percent salt is added and the liquid is allowed to age for three to four months. Its alcohol content is only about ten percent. To determine which product you are buying, simply read the list of ingredients. High quality aji no haha "mirin" contains only rice, rice koji, water, and sea salt. The rice koji may or may not be listed. This type of seasoning is sweet, like authentic mirin, but also has some of the qualities of sake. Though the result will not be exactly the same, it can be used in place of sake and mirin in any of the recipes in this book.

Sometimes mirin and its related products are sold in Oriental or gourmet shops under names such as "Chinese cooking wine" or "sweet cooking wine." Read the ingredients list before purchasing these products.

Mirin is indispensable in Oriental cooking. The traditional sweetening agent long before the arrival of white sugar, mirin is still commonly used in Japan to provide a balance for salty seasonings and to enhance the flavor of vinegared dishes. With a little experience you can use mirin in a variety of ways to enhance Western-style cooking as well. It is excellent in marinades, vinaigrettes, sauces, noodle broths, simmered vegetable or fish dishes, with sautéed vegetables, fried noodles, and in dips for tempura or sushi. Mirin's mild sweetness rounds out the flavor of many dishes, providing a satisfying, balanced taste.

*1 pound tofu*
*3 level tablespoons mellow*
*white or mellow barley miso*
*2 tablespoons mirin*
*1 tablespoon rice syrup or ½*
*tablespoon honey*
*1 tablespoon lemon juice*
*(optional)*
*2 tablespoons tahini*
*1 teaspoon juice squeezed from*
*grated fresh ginger*
*2 tablespoons water or stock*

## BROILED TOFU WITH SAUCE

This delicious protein-rich entree is quick and easy to prepare.

Cut the block of tofu into six ½-inch thick slices and drain on absorbent paper or kitchen towel. Place on lightly oiled cookie sheet or baking pan and broil until golden. Turn and broil other side. Meanwhile, combine all remaining ingredients and mix well. Spread a thin layer of sauce on each piece of tofu and broil for about 1 minute more. If desired, garnish with parsley or chives to serve.

SERVES 3

*3 tablespoons mirin*
*2 tablespoons shoyu*
*2 tablespoons water or stock*
*1 finely minced clove garlic*
*(or 1 teaspoon grated fresh*
*ginger)*
*2 teaspoons lemon juice*
*(optional)*

## MIRIN MARINADE

Combine all ingredients and mix well. Place bite-sized pieces of 1 pound of any of the following: any firm-fleshed white fish, shrimp, scallops, or chicken in a bowl and pour marinade over. Let marinate for 30-60 minutes, turning occasionally. The addition of any of these turns a simple sautéed or stir-fried dish into a gourmet delight.

To marinate fresh tofu, cut a 1-pound block of tofu into ½-inch thick slices and drain on paper towel. Cut into 1"x1½" pieces and place in a bowl. Pour marinade over and set aside for 30-60 minutes, turning occasionally. Use in simple sautés and stir-fries such as Mushroom-Tofu Sauté.

MAKES ½ CUP

# MUSHROOM-TOFU SAUTÉ

Marinate tofu as in Mirin Marinade. Heat oil in a skillet, add mushrooms and salt and sauté over medium heat for 3 minutes. Add broccoli and tofu, toss gently, and add marinade. Cover, and simmer for 5 minutes. Turn off heat, remove cover immediately to prevent broccoli from losing its color, and serve hot.

SERVES 4

*1 lb. marinated tofu*
*2 teaspoons light sesame oil*
*½ lb. fresh mushrooms, sliced*
*pinch sea salt*
*2 tablespoons Mirin Marinade*
*4 cups small florets broccoli*

# GLAZED BEETS

Mirin and kuzu sauce add a sheen that brightens the beautiful magenta of the beets in this simple vegetable dish.

Heat oil in a skillet, add sliced beets and salt, and sauté briefly. Add water to cover bottom of skillet, lower heat, cover, and cook for 20-30 minutes or until beets are nearly tender. (Check occasionally and add more water if needed to prevent scorching.) Add mirin and cook for about 5 minutes more, then add shoyu and cook for another minute. Add water to a depth of ¼ inch.

Crush lumps of kuzu into a coarse powder before measuring. Thoroughly dissolve kuzu in 1 tablespoon water and add to beets while stirring. Stir constantly until liquid returns to a simmer. Cook for 1-2 minutes more, adding a little more water if too thick.

Dill goes well with beets. For variety, add 2-3 tablespoons chopped dill weed when adding the shoyu. You can also add (or substitute) ¼ to ⅓ cup minced parsley if desired.

SERVES 6-8

*1-2 teaspoons unrefined vege-*
*table oil (light sesame, saf-*
*flower, or corn)*
*4 medium-large beets, quar-*
*tered and sliced thin (about*
*3½ cups)*
*small pinch sea salt*
*1 tablespoon mirin*
*1 teaspoon shoyu*
*1 tablespoon kuzu*

# KOJI

The sweet, fragrant aroma of incubating *koji* fills the air of fermented foods shops throughout Japan. Koji is the catalyst and most important ingredient in the traditional manufacture of such diverse Japanese fermented foods as miso, amazake, vinegar, shoyu, and sake. Simply stated, koji is either a grain or bean that has been cooked, cooled, and inoculated with the spores of a particular *Aspergillus* mold, and then incubated in a warm, humid place for about fifty hours. At the end of this time, the grain or bean is covered with a soft, fluffy, pure-white mold, and is loaded with enzymes.

Koji actually begins the work of the digestive system. When a particular koji (such as rice, barley, wheat, or bean koji) is mixed with other ingredients such as cooked beans as in miso, or cooked rice as in sake, its enzymes begin to change proteins, carbohydrates, and fats into simpler molecules through fermentation. Yeast and bacteria, naturally present in the mixture, then reduce these partially-digested molecules into simple amino acids, fatty acids, and sugars. Koji-fermented foods, therefore, are an excellent source of "predigested" nourishment, especially for people with a weakened condition.

The distinctive taste, aroma, color, and texture of each fermented food is determined by this complex sequence of biochemical reactions, started by a particular koji, aided by natural organisms and fueled by other ingredients in the recipe. Many traditional brewmasters feel that the key to high-quality fermented foods is strong, active koji. Although most koji today is made by a completely automated process, a few small shops still make koji by hand—a labor-intensive process requiring years of experience.

Using white rice koji, brown rice koji, and barley koji sold dry in natural foods stores, many people are now fermenting amazake, sake, pickles, and even miso in their homes. We have heard of people using koji as a leavening agent in baking, and we have used it to aid beer fermentation.

According to the directions in *The Book of Miso* (William Shurtleff and Akiko Aoyagi, Ballantine Books, 1976), small amounts of koji itself can be made at home. Koji spores (*Aspergillus*) are now available from natural foods distributors and can be special-ordered through your local natural foods shop.

## FOUR-HOUR WINTER PICKLES

Pickles are an important part of a whole grain-based diet. They aid digestion as well as provide stimulating flavor and color to your meals. These fail-proof pickles can be made quickly and keep well in the refrigerator.

Soak kombu until it completely opens up (5-10 minutes). Cut in half lengthwise and slice crosswise into slivers. Slice carrot on the diagonal, then sliver. Combine the next 4 ingredients in a saucepan and boil for just one minute. Immediately pour over slivered vegetables in a bowl. Mix well and cover bowl with a cotton towel to keep heat in but allow steam to escape. Allow to cool slightly (for about 15 minutes), add koji, and stir. Mix occasionally, then set in a cool place or refrigerate. These pickles are ready to eat in about 4 hours. (For more koji pickle recipes, see Rice Bran section, page 102.)

In general, serve small pieces and small amounts of any pickle, since they are often quite salty and are meant to be a condiment and an aid to digestion.

*3-inch x 12-inch piece kombu*
*1 large carrot, slivered*
*¼ cup shoyu*
*¼ cup brown rice vinegar*
*¼ cup mirin*
*2 tablespoons sake (optional)*
*2-3 tablespoons koji*

## AMAZAKE

Amazake is a creamy, rich "pudding" traditionally used in Japan as a sweetener or as the base for a warming drink during the colder months. A fermented product made by incubating a mixture of cooked sweet rice and rice koji for 6-10 hours, amazake is abundant in natural sugars as well as enzymes that aid digestion and elimination. As a sweetener, amazake is a natural in puddings and custards. It adds a rich, moist quality to breads, pancakes, waffles, cakes, and cookies.

Amazake is gradually becoming more well known in this country, and more and more natural foods stores are carrying homemade or commercially-made amazake pudding and beverage. The amazake available in Oriental markets almost always contains sugar, so for the recipes here, use either homemade amazake or amazake from your natural foods store. Also, the recipes have been devised with thick amazake rather than the beverage, which is too thin and dilute to use as a sweetening ingredient.

If you have never tasted amazake, you will be surprised at its sweetness. When making homemade amazake, you can determine how sweet it will be by the amount of koji you use. If you plan to use it mainly as a sweetener in desserts and as the base for amazake beverage, use more koji. If you intend to eat the pudding as is, use less.

*Jan Belleme prepares a batch of amazake at the Onozaki miso shop. The large vat in the background is for miso.*

*4 cups sweet brown rice*
*8 cups water*
*1-4 cups rice koji, depending*
*on sweetness desired*
*pinch sea salt*

## AMAZAKE ''PUDDING''

Wash sweet rice and combine with water in pressure cooker. (If pot-boiling, use 10 cups of water.) It is recommended, but not necessary, to soak the rice for several hours or overnight. Pressure cook for 40 minutes (or boil for one hour). Allow pressure to come down, then remove rice to a large ceramic bowl and beat vigorously with a rice paddle or large wooden spoon for 5-10 minutes. This helps cool it quickly and, if you crush the grains against the side of the bowl while beating, the koji will be able to penetrate and do its work faster. After this time, you should be able to insert your finger into the center of the rice and hold it there without burning, although it will still be hot.

Add koji and mix well. Cover with a dish towel and place in a warm oven (not over 140°F.—if this is not possible, periodically turn oven on for a few minutes, then turn off, or place the bowl on a radiator or in another warm spot). Let the mixture incubate for 8-10 hours, stirring once every hour or so. Add a small pinch of salt during the first or second stirring. When finished, it will have a rich, sweet aroma and taste. Blend or put through a food mill for a smooth consistency if desired, and refrigerate in a covered container. This rich pudding may be enjoyed as is, or used in any of the following ways.

MAKES 3 QUARTS

## AMAZAKE BEVERAGE

We find nothing more satisfying than a creamy, hot cup of amazake drink on a cold day. To make this invigorating beverage, combine one part amazake with 1-1½ parts water in a saucepan and bring just to a simmer, stirring occasionally. For a smooth, milky consistency, puree in a blender. Amazake's ambrosial flavor can be enhanced by adding a pinch of grated fresh ginger just before serving.

Cooled to room temperature, or slightly chilled, amazake beverage also makes a delicious summer drink. Experiment by blending seasonal fruits or a little carob powder into the amazake and water before heating, or add a few drops of vanilla extract or fruit concentrate before serving.

# VANILLA AMAZAKE PUDDING

To make almond milk, drop ¾ cup almonds into enough boiling water to cover for 10 seconds, turn off heat, and let sit for 2-3 minutes. Drain, and remove skins. Combine almonds with 3 cups cold water, ⅛ teaspoon sea salt, 2 teaspoons light sesame oil, and 2 tablespoons rice or barley malt syrup (or 1 tablespoon honey) in blender and blend for 1-2 minutes. Strain through cheesecloth, squeeze out all liquid, and store in a covered container in the refrigerator. Use strained almond meal in Almond Cookies (see page 97) or in Amazake Macaroons (page 43). Almond milk will stay fresh for about 6 days and can be used in many of the same ways as dairy milk.

Blend amazake and ¾ cup almond milk for 2 minutes on high speed in blender. Combine with salt and maple syrup in a small saucepan. Sprinkle kanten flakes over and bring to a simmer over medium heat without stirring. Let simmer for 1-2 minutes, stirring occasionally. Thoroughly dissolve the arrowroot in the remaining ¼ cup almond milk and add to pan while stirring briskly. Return to a simmer and cook for 1-2 minutes. Remove from heat and stir in vanilla. Pour into dessert dishes and chill. The pudding will set as it cools.

For variation, fold in berries, sliced bananas, or other fruits before chilling.

SERVES 4

*1 cup almond milk*
*1 cup amazake*
*small pinch sea salt*
*1 tablespoon maple syrup*
*1 slightly rounded tablespoon*
 *kanten flakes*
*4 teaspoons arrowroot powder*
*1 teaspoon vanilla*

# AMAZAKE CREME PUFFS

Deliciously rich yet delightfully light, this is a real gourmet treat. Follow directions for Vanilla Amazake Pudding, adding 2 teaspoons lightly grated lemon rind with the vanilla. Allow to cool and set. Meanwhile, prepare puff shells. (They are much easier to make than their reputation would have you believe.)

Preheat oven to 400° F. Sift flours and salt together twice. Combine water and oil in a heavy saucepan, bring to a simmer, and add flour all at once, stirring quickly. Continue to stir briskly just until the mixture forms a ball and no longer sticks to the sides of the pan or to the spoon (about 30 seconds). Immediately remove from heat. (Overcooking will prevent the dough from rising.) Let rest a minute or two, then add eggs one at a time, beating well after each until batter loses its shiny appearance. Mixture will be stiff.

*¼ cup whole wheat pastry*
 *flour*
*¼ cup unbleached white flour*
*pinch sea salt*
*½ cup water*
*3 tablespoons corn oil (or use*
 *a combination of corn oil*
 *and melted butter)*
*2 eggs (they must be at room*
 *temperature)*

Drop by rounded tablespoonfuls onto a lightly oiled cookie sheet. If you have a plant or laundry mister, give them a light spray of water. Bake at 400° F. for 10 minutes, then at 325° for 25-30 minutes more. They should be firm. Remove and cool. Slice off tops and remove any wet dough that may be inside. Beat amazake creme with a spoon to fluff, and fill shells just before serving. Replace tops lightly.

MAKES 12

## NEOPOLITAN PARFAIT

3½ cups amazake
1 cup almond milk
2 tablespoons carob powder
pinch sea salt
3 level tablespoons kanten
    flakes
3 level tablespoons arrowroot
    powder
vanilla
½ cup fresh strawberries,
    raspberries, or pitted cher-
    ries

This dessert is fun to serve to guests.

1. Blend amazake and almond milk for 1-2 minutes on high speed in blender.
2. Strain amazake mixture to remove any rice grits.
3. Return ⅓ of amazake mixture to blender and blend with the carob powder.
4. Combine carob-amazake mixture with a small pinch of sea salt in a saucepan, sprinkle 1 tablespoon kanten flakes over, and bring to a simmer without stirring. Simmer for 1-2 minutes, stirring occasionally, then dissolve 1 tablespoon arrowroot in 1 tablespoon water and add to pan while stirring briskly. Simmer for 2 minutes.
5. Remove pan from heat and add ¼ teaspoon vanilla.
6. Pour into parfait glasses, tilt, and let chill for an hour or so or until firm.
7. Repeat steps 3-6, adding the fruit instead of carob in step 3. (Carob portion should be firm before adding the next layer to parfaits.)
8. The last third is plain (vanilla only). Omit step 3. Repeat steps 4-6, increasing vanilla to ½ teaspoon in step 5. Also, don't tilt the glasses while this last layer is setting.

MAKES 4 PARFAITS

## CAROB AMAZAKE BROWNIES

These moist, delectable brownies are sweetened only with amazake. Though my family finds them satisfying, if you are accustomed to a stronger sweet taste, you may wish to add ¼ cup concentrated sweetener such as honey or maple syrup when combining the liquid ingredients.

Preheat oven to 350° F. and oil a 9″ x 9″ baking pan. Combine
corn oil, amazake, and vanilla in a medium-sized bowl. Add egg
and mix well. Sift next four ingredients together in another
bowl. Combine dry and wet ingredients and mix just until batter
is evenly moist. Fold in the nuts. Spread batter evenly in the
pan and bake for 30 minutes. Brownies are done when they pull
away from the sides of the pan and spring back when lightly
pressed. Cool in pan on a wire rack.

*¼ cup corn oil*
*⅔ cup amazake*
*½ teaspoon vanilla*
*1 egg, lightly beaten*
*¼ teaspoon sea salt*
*½ teaspoon baking powder*
*⅓ cup carob powder*
*½ cup whole wheat pastry
  flour*
*⅔ cup chopped walnuts*

## BOB'S COCONUT-AMAZAKE MACAROONS

Preheat oven to 350° F. Combine all ingredients and mix well.
Drop by slightly rounded teaspoonfuls onto a lightly oiled cookie
sheet. Batter will be wet, but should hold its shape. Bake for
10-15 minutes or until bottoms are brown and tops golden. If
necessary, flip cookies for the last 5 minutes of baking.

**MAKES 24 SMALL COOKIES**

*1 cup unsweetened coconut
  flakes*
*1 cup amazake*
*1 teaspoon tahini or sesame
  butter*
*3 tablespoons almond meal*
*1 teaspoon sesame seeds*
*2 tablespoons rice or corn-
  barley malt syrup, or 1
  tablespoon honey or date
  sugar*
*1 tablespoon any flour*
*½ teaspoon vanilla*
*¼ teaspoon almond extract*
*⅛ teaspoon sea salt*

*1½ teaspoons dry yeast*
*3½ cups whole wheat flour*
*1 cup corn meal, wheat germ,*
*    or wheat bran*
*½ teaspoon sea salt*
*2 tablespoons corn or light*
*    sesame oil*
*1 cup amazake*
*1⅓ cups (approximately)*
*    water*

## AMAZAKE BREAD

Sweet and flavorful, this bread is a favorite of ours.

Add yeast to ⅓ cup tepid water and let sit for about 10 minutes or until frothy. Meanwhile, combine flour, corn meal, and salt. Add oil and mix by rubbing between your hands. Add amazake and mix well. Add yeast mixture, then gradually add enough water (about 1 cup) to form a workable, not too sticky, dough. Knead about 300 times, adding a little flour if the dough becomes sticky. Oil a bowl lightly and place the dough in, turning it once to coat with oil. Cover the bowl with a damp cloth. Let rise in a warm place for about 90 minutes.

Punch down, knead a few times, and roll into a loaf, sealing the edges by pinching along the seam. Press the loaf into a lightly oiled bread pan. (Or form 2 small round loaves and place on a lightly oiled cookie sheet.) Allow to rise for 30-40 minutes. Bake at 350° F. for about 1 hour for a large loaf, or 45 minutes for small ones. Bread should be golden brown and should sound hollow when tapped on the bottom. Cool on a wire rack for 5-10 minutes before removing loaf from pan.

For variation, add 1 teaspoon cinnamon to the dry ingredients and work ⅔ cup raisins into the dough after the first rising.

MAKES 1 LARGE OR 2 SMALL LOAVES

## UNYEASTED AMAZAKE BREAD

*6 cups whole wheat flour*
*½ teaspoon sea salt*
*2-3 tablespoons light sesame*
*    or corn oil*
*3 cups amazake (at room tem-*
*    perature)*
*water to make workable dough*
*    (approximately 1¼ cups)*
*approximately 1 cup extra*
*    flour (whole wheat or*
*    unbleached white)*

This moist, chewy bread is simple to make and very satisfying. It is especially good thinly sliced and toasted.

Combine flour and salt, add oil, and mix by rubbing between the palms of your hands. Add amazake and mix well, then add enough water to form a workable dough. (It should form a ball, not too sticky.) Knead at least 300-350 times, adding a little more flour as dough becomes sticky. You will probably have to add flour several times throughout the kneading. Be sure dough is not sticky when you finish kneading. Divide dough in half, shape into loaves, and press into oiled bread pans. Make a 1-inch deep slit down the center of each loaf, cover pans with a damp towel, and put them in a warm place for 8-12 hours.

Preheat oven to 300° F. Slit the loaves again. Bake at 300° F. for 20 minutes, then raise temperature to 350° and bake for another hour and 15 minutes. When done, bread should be golden brown and sound hollow when tapped on the bottom. Allow bread to cool in the pans for just 10-15 minutes, then carefully remove. You may need to run a knife around the sides of the pan to loosen. Now comes the hardest part: allow to cool thoroughly before slicing!

MAKES 2 LOAVES

## PICKLES

The ability to preserve food and its nutritional value has always been of prime importance. It is not surprising, then, that various imaginative and effective ways of food storage have evolved. Japan has developed one form—pickling—to its fullest. Using many methods such as pickling with bran, salt, vinegar, miso, shoyu, and sake lees (the solid residue left after pressing sake), the Japanese pickle almost everything: roots, shoots, flowers, seeds, fruit, fish, and meat. A visit to the pickle section of a modern Tokyo supermarket is a sensual extravaganza of diverse colors, textures, and exotic smells. Over the centuries pickles have become an indispensible part of traditional Japanese cuisine, and in many respects they symbolize the conservative yet creative nature of this ancient culture.

While living in Japan we were told (by the man of the house, of course) that until recently a main criterion by which a wife's worth was judged was her ability to make a variety of delicious and interesting pickles. Apparently this was such a commonly-held and respected standard that if two couples were dining together and one man complimented the other's wife for her pickles, it was both an affront to his own wife and, by showing too much overt interest, a cause for jealousy by the other man.

In the several months we spent with the Onozakis, not a single meal was ever served without pickles. Like the use of fresh and wild vegetables in Japanese cooking, the type of vegetable pickled and the method of pickling is always appropriate, first to the season and second to the other foods being served. It is not simply a matter of serving long-aged, salty pickles in winter and quick, light, pickles in summer. For example, out-of-season vegetables are never purchased and pickled in a seasonally appropriate way, and the pickle served in winter with a meal including fish is usually not the same variety as would be chosen to complement a meal consisting of grains and vegetables. Properly selected, pickles never fail to stimulate the appetite and refresh the palate.

*Customers buying directly from the Onozaki miso shop are afforded the bonus of a few traditional pickles on the top of each bucket of miso.*

The traditional pickling process used by the Japanese is technically known as "lactic acid fermentation," one of nature's oldest and safest ways of preserving food. The key to good pickling is the early establishment of lactic acid-forming bacteria before other bacteria have a chance to multiply. The latter, which can spoil pickling vegetables, cannot tolerate the high acidity produced by lactic acid bacteria or the high salt concentration used in most pickling methods. To help establish beneficial bacteria, traditional makers use enough salt and mix it well, and store developing pickles in a cool place (40-65 °F. is ideal).

The importance of pickles in the mostly vegetarian, grain-based diet of traditional Japan cannot be overemphasized. Pickles contain large amounts of *lactobacilli* bacteria, which are important to the digestion of grains and vegetables. Scientific research has shown that these "friendly" bacteria survive the trip through the acidic juices of the stomach to the small intestine. In the small intestine they aid pancreatic enzymes in the transformation of dextrin (a carbohydrate found in grains) into simple sugars that can be readily used by the body.

*Lactobacilli* have other functions in the digestive system. In the large intestine they help synthesize B and K vitamins and they inhibit the growth of putrefying bacteria. The role of intestinal bacteria in human metabolism is extremely complex. Dr. Phillip Evans, a Colorado physician and the author of *The Biochemical Basis for Disease and Disorders*, feels that an overall sense of well-being cannot be experienced without a healthy population of appropriate intestinal flora.

Other benefits of pickles relate to specific types, such as the alkalinizing properties of umeboshi and the high niacin content of bran pickles. One property common to all pickles is high fiber, so important to proper intestinal cleansing and functioning.

Having stressed the importance of pickles, I must now add that most pickles served in Japanese restaurants and sold in Asian food stores are probably the most adulterated of all foods. They are dyed, sweetened with refined sugar, and pickled with commercial salt, synthetic vinegar or soy sauce, and preserved with various chemicals. The good news, however, is that some truly delicious and natural Japanese pickles are now available in well-stocked natural foods stores. Some are long-aged and heavily salted, such as miso pickles, excellent for helping the body adjust to cold weather. Others, such as "sushi pickles," are lightly salted and use vinegar and herbs, making them refreshing in hot weather.

*Miso-Tamari Pickles*: The rich, dark, salty liquid that accumulates in miso during fermentation is called "miso tamari," one of Japan's most prized pickling agents. In summer and early fall, when vegetables are plentiful, traditional pickle makers place cucumbers, carrots, daikon, burdock, and ginger in vats with miso tamari. Under the pressure created by large stones on a wooden pressing lid, vegetable juice is slowly extracted and replaced by the tamari. Throughout the winter and following summer the pickling process continues, and in the fall a delicious, dark, salty pickle is ready to eat.

Look for miso-tamari pickles in small vacuum-packed plastic bags, marketed under the name "Miso Pickles." To serve, cut miso pickles very thin or mince them finely and sprinkle a small amount over grains and vegetables. They are also delicious served before dinner with hot sake on cold winter nights.

*Shoyu and Tamari Pickles*: The thick, rich, fermented mash (moromi) from which shoyu and tamari are extracted has a long history of use as a pickling medium. By a process similar to that used in making miso-tamari pickles, vegetables are placed in the moromi and pressed for from two months to over a year. The result is a flavorful, salty pickle. Though generally a little milder than miso-tamari pickles, they should be thinly sliced or minced and served in small quantities. They go well with whole grains, especially brown rice.

Shoyu and tamari pickles usually come in vacuum-packed pouches. Delicious, excellent quality pickles made from organically-grown vegetables and organic shoyu or tamari are available in some natural foods stores. Read labels to determine the quality.

*Takuan Pickles*: Takuan, or daikon pickled in rice bran, is one of the most important and traditional of all Japanese pickles. Rich in B-vitamins and *lactobacilli*, they are still commonly made in rural Japanese homes every fall and eaten throughout the winter. For more information on their unique qualities, the availability of commercial takuan, and a recipe for making your own, see page 115.

*Sushi Ginger Pickles*: This is one of our favorites. Young, tender ginger roots are thinly sliced, briefly salt-pressed, then pickled in a vinegar mixture. They are so named because they are almost always served with sushi or sashimi (raw fish). If you have ever been to a sushi bar, you have no doubt seen mounds of these paper-thin, pink or beige pickles. Sushi ginger pickles can be served year-round as a digestive aid and taste complement with meals, especially those including fish, but they are particularly refreshing in summer.

Although the sushi ginger pickles available in Oriental food stores and sushi bars nearly always contain sugar and dyes, and are almost certainly pickled in low-quality vinegar, there are some excellent quality ginger pickles available in natural foods stores. They are unsweetened, or sweetened only with mirin, and their color is naturally derived from red *shiso* (perilla herb) leaves.

Japanese natural foods importers have recently introduced cucumber and daikon pickled in shoyu, rice vinegar, and various herbs and seasonings under the name "Sushi Pickles." Though they differ considerably from sushi ginger, sushi cucumber and sushi daikon are light and refreshing, tasty, and of good quality.

*Umeboshi*: I feel certain there are even today few house-holds in Japan that do not keep these venerable and medicinal salt-pickled plums on hand. You will find information on how they are made as well as some of their uses both as a seasoning and a home remedy on pages 48-50. Excellent quality umeboshi are available in many natural foods stores. Most brands found in Oriental markets, on the other hand, are not naturally made and contain red dye.

*Shiso Senmai*: Shiso senmai are whole red shiso leaves pickled in umeboshi vinegar, the salty-tart liquid extracted from umeboshi kegs. They are delicious substituted for nori in making wrapped or rolled foods such as Rice Balls or Nori-Maki. Unless you plan to steam the stuffed leaves to warm them before serving, briefly rinse shiso senmai to remove excess salt before stuffing. Pickled shiso leaves are also good chopped and used as a seasoning inside nori rolls or briefly rinsed, then chopped and tossed with steamed cauliflower or greens such as cabbage, Chinese cabbage, or bok choy. They can also be sliced and steamed or sautéed along with these or other vegetables. In this case, rinsing isn't necessary. Shiso senmai are available in some natural foods stores.

Several pickle recipes are included in this book—consult the index for a complete listing. It is best to keep a variety of homemade or good quality commercial pickles on hand so you will have some for any type of meal or occasion. Besides aiding digestion, enhancing the appetite, and providing other health benefits, pickles can add stimulating flavor and interesting color and texture to meals. Remember that pickles, especially very salty ones, should be taken in very small amounts.


# UMEBOSHI

*Umeboshi* (salt-pickled Japanese plum) is a lively and versatile seasoning that adds a pleasant tartness to salad dressings, cooked vegetables, and sauces. It is also commonly served in Japan as a condiment with rice, or tucked inside a rice ball wrapped with nori. In summer we enjoy thick cucumber rounds spread thinly with umeboshi paste. Sparingly spread on cooked sweet corn it is more healthful and just as delicious as butter and salt.

The healthful qualities of Japanese plums (*ume*) have been recognized for virtually hundreds of years. People began to salt-pickle them over 1000 years ago as a means of preserving this important food-medicine and ensuring a year-round supply. Although particularly effective for all sorts of stomach disorders from hyperacidity and indigestion to ulcers, umeboshi also coun-teracts fatigue, increases endurance, and stimulates the liver's and kidneys' function of dissolving and expelling toxins, thus purifying the blood. Its powerful antibacterial properties make umeboshi effective in preventing rice from spoiling. Ancient medical texts also credit umeboshi with preventing food poisoning. Umeboshi's alkalinizing effect makes it a wonderful general tonic. Added to "soft rice" (rice cooked 7-10:1 with water until very soft), umeboshi is the Japanese cure-all for sick children.

While we were living with the Onozaki family in Japan, umeboshi were frequently served at breakfast, to be eaten with the rice, and were also used medicinally on several occasions. Though no one really got sick during those seven months (which I believe was largely a result of the natural lifestyle, hard work, and strong, balanced meals), some credit must certainly be given to Mrs. Onozaki's quick and judicious use of umeboshi as a preventive. She had an uncanny ability to tell when someone was on the verge of becoming sick. Often before the person was aware of their impending illness she had prepared a tea with shredded umeboshi, or soft-cooked rice with umeboshi, as her female ancestors had done for generations.

Umeboshi are made by alternately soaking unripe Japanese *ume* (commonly called plums, but actually a variety of apricot) in brine, then sun-drying and returning them to the brine. The pink color of umeboshi is derived from red *shiso* leaves, which are pickled together with the ume. Red shiso (perilla) is a mineral-rich herb, particularly high in iron. In addition to lending its beautiful color, shiso adds its abundance of minerals to the high concentration of vitamin C and other virtues of the ume. Umeboshi is available in two forms: whole plums pickled with or without shiso leaves, and as umeboshi "paste," a convenient puree made from red umeboshi.

As someone who suffered from chronic digestive discomfort before changing to a grain-based vegetarian diet, I can certainly attest to umeboshi's effectiveness as an antacid and digestive aid. More than once, eating one whole umeboshi relieved me of severe abdominal cramps in a matter of minutes. For more information on other products made from Japanese plums see Ume Su (page 50) and Ume Extract (page 53).

## ORANGE-UME DRESSING

This is a refreshing summer dressing for tossed salads and noodle salads.

Toast sesame seeds in a dry skillet over medium heat for 2-3 minutes, stirring constantly. Remove from pan. Blend first 5 ingredients in a blender until smooth. As an alternative, grind the seeds in a suribachi, mix in next 3 ingredients, then add orange juice and mix well. Mix in scallions or chives if desired, and chill for 30 minutes before using.

MAKES 1 CUP

*3 level tablespoons toasted sesame seeds or 3 tablespoons tahini*
*2 teaspoons umeboshi paste or minced umeboshi*
*2 tablespoons light sesame or Italian olive oil*
*1 tablespoon lemon juice*
*juice of 1-1½ oranges*
*1 teaspoon minced scallion or chives (optional)*

*1 cup water*
*1 bunch broccoli (or equal*
  *amount of other vegetable),*
  *cut into florets*
*1½ tablespoons umeboshi*
  *paste or minced umeboshi*
*1½ tablespoons kuzu*
*1-1½ cups water*

## UME-KUZU BROCCOLI

Ume-kuzu sauce, which combines the medicinal qualities of ume-boshi and kuzu, is excellent for restoring and maintaining health and strengthening digestion. It works well with steamed vege-tables such as broccoli, cauliflower, green beans, and daikon (Japanese white radish).

Bring 1 cup water to boil in a large skillet or pot. Add broccoli and simmer, covered, until *just* tender and still bright green. Remove cover and allow broccoli to cool slightly. Dissolve kuzu in ¼ cup cold water, add umeboshi and remaining ¾ cup water, and mix well. Add mixture to broccoli, toss lightly, and bring slowly to a simmer, gently stirring constantly to avoid lumping. Simmer for 1-2 minutes. If too thick, add a little more water.

SERVES 3-4

*½ head cabbage*
*2 teaspoons light sesame oil*
*1½ tablespoons umeboshi*
  *paste or minced whole ume-*
  *boshi*

## CABBAGE WITH UMEBOSHI

Cut cabbage half into halves. Remove core and slice it thin. Slice cabbage quarters ⅛ - to ¼-inch thick. Heat oil in a skillet, add umeboshi, and sauté briefly, then add cabbage. At first the umeboshi will not disperse evenly, but as you continue tossing and sautéeing, it will evenly coat the cabbage. If no juice has come out of the cabbage, add a *little* water, cover, and simmer over low heat until tender (15-20 minutes).

SERVES 3

## UME SU

Though *ume su* translates as ''plum vinegar,'' it is actually the brine drawn from kegs of mature umeboshi. Ume su contains all the healing qualities and nutrients associated with umeboshi, and it is easy and convenient to use. Both pleasantly tart and salty, it is a versatile seasoning that's especially refreshing on a hot after-noon. Use ume su to liven up salad dressings, cooked vegetables (especially members of the cabbage family), homemade quick pickles, and tofu spreads. When substituting ume su for vinegar, reduce substantially or eliminate the salt in the recipe. By fol-lowing the recipes below, you will begin to become familiar with ume su and will soon be discovering new ways to use this deli-cious and healthful seasoning.

## UME-TOFU DRESSING

Crumble tofu, and chop garlic and scallion. Combine all ingredients in a blender and blend until smooth. If time permits, it is best to chill the dressing before serving. Serve over tossed or pressed salads.

MAKES 1⅔ CUPS

¼ to ⅓ pound fresh tofu
1 clove garlic
1 scallion
¼ cup unrefined safflower oil or light sesame oil
¼ cup water
2 tablespoons ume su
1 tablespoon lemon juice or rice vinegar
1 tablespoon tahini
1 tablespoon mirin (optional)
½ cup parsley
2 tablespoons rice syrup or 1 tablespoon honey
¼ teaspoon dried mustard (optional)

## TANGY GREENS

Ume su adds a pleasantly pungent flavor to cooked leafy greens, especially cabbage and Chinese cabbage, and also goes well with cauliflower, broccoli, or green beans. Steam or sauté vegetables until tender but still colorful. Drain if necessary, place in a serving bowl, and toss with ume su to taste (about 1 tablespoon ume su for one small head of cabbage).

## GUACAMOLE

*1 large or 2 small ripe avoca-*
*does, peeled and pitted*
*(about 1¾ cups mashed)*
*1 level tablespoon grated*
*onion*
*1½ tablespoons ume su*
*1 teaspoon lemon juice*
*(optional)*

This quick and easy recipe makes a delicious spread for toast, crackers, or flatbread, or a stuffing for celery or cucumber "boats."

A highly nutritious fruit, avocado contains significant amounts of several essential vitamins, and is particularly abundant in vitamin C. Since the vitamin C content begins to decrease once exposed to air, this spread should be made just before serving.

Use mature avocadoes. When ripe, an avocado will give slightly to gentle thumb pressure, but should not be so soft that there are rotten spots or a gray color under the skin. The skin should peel easily and the flesh should be easy to mash.

To prepare, remove pit and mash avocado with a fork or potato masher. Add the remaining ingredients, mix well, garnish with a sprig of parsley, and serve immediately.

## SIMPLE SWEET 'N SOUR PICKLES

*4 cups thinly sliced turnip,*
*daikon, red radish, carrot,*
*or cucumber*
*1½ teaspoons sea salt*
*¼ cup ume su*
*¼ cup rice vinegar or cider*
*vinegar*
*¼ cup mirin*
*¼ cup water*

Combine vegetables and salt. If using turnips or daikon, let sit 5 hours or overnight (no longer). Leave carrots 24 hours or press overnight. Red radish requires 2-3 hours, and cucumbers only 1 hour.

Press vegetables gently with the back of your hand and drain off salt water. Mix the ume su, vinegar, mirin, and water in a saucepan and boil for 1 minute only. Allow to cool. Place vegetables in a quart jar, pour the liquid over them, cover, and put in a cool place or refrigerate. Pickles will be ready to eat in 24 hours (if refrigerated it may take 2 days). Once pickled, store in refrigerator.

## MEDICINAL TEAS

*Ume-Shoyu-Ginger-Kukicha* tea, taken warm, helps combat fatigue, improve circulation, and aid digestion. Bring 1 cup of kukicha tea (see page 192) to a boil. Remove from heat, add ½ to 1 whole umeboshi, a few drops of shoyu, and a few drops of juice squeezed from grated fresh ginger, and let steep for 1-2 minutes.

*Ume-Shoyu-Kuzu* is excellent for diarrhea, stomach pain, hyperacidity, and indigestion. Dissolve a heaping teaspoonful of kuzu in 1-2 tablespoons water and add, along with 1 whole umeboshi, to a cup of cold water or cool kukicha tea. Bring to a boil while stirring constantly. Reduce heat and simmer for 1-2 minutes. Add ½-1 teaspoon shoyu. (A few drops of fresh ginger juice may be added if you like.)  Drink hot.

## UME EXTRACT (BAINIKU EKISU)

The virtues of Japanese plums (*ume*) and the various products made from them cannot be overstated.  *Umeboshi* (salt pickled whole plum) and *ume su* (umeboshi "vinegar") are both used in cooking.  Ume extract (*bainiku ekisu*) is not; it is a time-tested, traditional Japanese folk remedy that is effective for relief of a variety of minor ailments.  As far as I'm concerned, ume extract is one of the greatest products ever invented—I don't know what I'd do without it!

For over 2000 years first the Chinese, then the Japanese, sought to develop ideal ways to preserve and concentrate the active medicinal components of ume.  The Japanese first developed the technique of salt pickling, resulting in umeboshi and its byproduct, ume su, before the year 1000. These products have an indefinite shelflife and various uses as both food and medicine, but some who understood the exceptional qualities of the plum continued to try to find a way to capture its medicinal essence without the use of salt, since the high salt content of pickled plums makes them inappropriate as a remedy for certain conditions and for young children.

Finally, in the late 1700s or so, it was discovered that slow cooking of the immature fruits to reduce them to about 1/50 of their original weight results in a thick, dark syrup that retains ume's medicinal qualities in a highly concentrated, salt-free form.

Ume extract is used primarily as an antacid, and it can be useful for Westerners.  Our modern diet and lifestyle are conducive to an acid blood condition, which makes us less able to expel toxins and resist disease, and more easily fatigued.  A pea-sized amount of ume extract, "the king of alkaline foods," dissolved in ⅓-½ cup hot water, kukicha tea, or barley tea can neutralize excess acid and relieve in a matter of minutes the acute stomach pains that often accompany the condition.

According to Mr. Kosai Matsumoto II, author of *The Mysterious Japanese Plum: Its Uses for Healing, Vigor and Long Life* (Woodbridge Press, 1978), ume extract's high concentration of citric acid provides other health benefits.  Citric acid aids the body in the absorption of calcium, making it an especially good tonic for pregnant and nursing women.  Some signs of a lack of sufficient calcium include irritability, tiredness, and sleeping disorders.  Citric acid helps overcome fatigue by neutralizing excess lactic and pyruvic acid and by metabolizing excess sugar and converting it to energy.

Ume stimulates the liver and increases the liver's and kidneys' ability to dissolve and expel toxins and thereby purify the blood. Mr. Matsumoto's studies have shown that this is because of the picric acid in the plum.

The strong antibacterial qualities of Japanese plum concentrate led to its use by the Japanese army to guard against bacterial diseases such as dysentery. It has a purifying effect on the intestines.

Another benefit of ume that is important for everyone is its effect of regulating the bowels. It also helps prevent morning sickness and motion sickness, both common in the early months of pregnancy.

Ume extract has a sour taste that some people object to. Recently a convenient, granular form of ume was developed that does not have such a strong taste. There are so far at least three varieties of ume "tablets."

One, known as *meitan* in Japan and often called "plum balls" in this country, is a combination of 70% ume extract and 30% rice flour. Like the others, these hard, round, pea-sized balls are now available in handy compact dispenser packs. They are usually taken as is, three or four at a time, and dissolved in the mouth. Another type combines 50% ume extract and 50% dried and powdered jinenjo (wild yam). Jinenjo is a highly regarded digestive aid that is also said to be beneficial to the kidneys and liver. (For more information on this traditional food-medicine, see page 130.) "Umeboshi tablets" are somewhat smaller round balls that are a mixture of umeboshi purée and rice flour. The extract seems to me more effective, but the tablets are convenient.

I have the highest regard for ume extract and the other ume products and recommend that you keep one or more forms on hand and carry some with you when you travel.

## BONITO FLAKES

The bonito, a member of the mackerel family of fish, has been a mainstay in the Japanese diet for centuries. Once bonito's ability to preserve well was discovered in the fifteenth century, it became highly treasured by samurai warriors as a field ration.

To make dried bonito (*katsuobushi*), the fish are filleted and cut lengthwise into quarters. After being steamed, sun-dried, and wood-smoked several times until they are thoroughly dried, the fillets are placed outdoors on racks for about three months to ferment. This ancient method, which uses natural fermentation to increase bonito's nutritional values and "vegetalize" its composition, is still used today.

Once fully mature, the dried fillets will maintain their quality almost indefinitely if kept cool and dry. The bonito fillets are shaved into flakes on a *katsuo kezuri-ki* (bonito shaver) just before use. Bonito flakes also come prepackaged in small, convenient cellophane envelopes that preserve their freshness well. These "single serving" packets of shaved bonito are much preferred over large bags or boxes, in which the flakes rapidly lose their flavor and quality.

Bonito is valuable whenever a mild fish flavor is appropriate. It is most commonly used along with kombu sea vegetable in making a flavorful stock for various types of soups and noodle broths and for simmered root vegetable dishes.

## FISH OR OYSTER CHOWDER

To make soup stock, combine water and kombu in a pot and bring to a simmer, uncovered, over medium heat. Remove kombu and reserve for another use. Add bonito flakes, remove from heat, and let rest for 1-2 minutes. Strain soup to remove flakes. Press all liquid from flakes into stock and discard flakes.

Rinse fish or oysters, pat dry, rub fish with a small pinch of salt, and set aside. Heat oil in a medium-sized skillet and sauté onion or leek over medium-low heat until translucent. Add celery, carrot, potato, and a small pinch of sea salt, and sauté for 5 minutes. Add arrowroot or flour and toss briefly to evenly coat vegetables. Add half the stock to the skillet and stir until it begins to simmer. Add contents of skillet to remainder of stock in soup pot along with ¾ teaspoon salt. Bring to a boil, lower heat, and simmer for 20 minutes. Cut fish into 1-inch squares. Add fish, shoyu, and white pepper to soup and simmer for 5 minutes more. You may also add a small pinch of garlic powder and/or thyme or tarragon. Serve hot with a sprinkle of minced parsley as garnish.

SERVES 4-5

*6 cups water*
*6-inch piece kombu*
*1 packet (¼ cup) bonito flakes*
*¼ pound white fish fillet or oysters*
*1 teaspoon light sesame oil*
*1 onion or leek, sliced thin*
*1 rib celery, sliced thin*
*1 carrot, sliced thin*
*1 potato, diced*
*4 tablespoons arrowroot powder or unbleached white flour*
*¾ teaspoon sea salt*
*pinch white pepper (optional)*
*2 teaspoons shoyu (or to taste)*
*parsley for garnish*

*6 cups water*
*6-inch piece kombu*
*1 package (¼ cup) bonito*
*flakes*
*1 teaspoon light sesame oil*
*1 leek*
*1 large carrot*
*½ teaspoon sea salt*
*½ cup elbow noodles*
*2 cups chopped kale (loosely*
*packed)*
*2 tablespoons shoyu*

## HEARTY VEGETABLE-NOODLE SOUP

Prepare kombu-bonito stock as in Fish or Oyster Chowder.

Cut leek into ¼-inch thick diagonal slices. Cut carrot in half lengthwise, then into ¼-inch thick diagonal slices. Heat oil and sauté leek briefly. Add carrots and a small pinch of sea salt. Toss, lower heat, cover, and cook for 5-10 minutes. Check occasionally and add a little water only if necessary to prevent scorching.

Add vegetables to stock along with ½ teaspoon salt. Simmer for 5 minutes, then add noodles. Return soup to a simmer and stir to prevent noodles from sticking to the bottom of the pot. Add greens and simmer, uncovered, for 7-10 minutes more or until noodles are tender. Add shoyu 1-2 minutes before end of cooking time. Serve hot.

SERVES 4

*4 cups kombu-bonito stock*
*¼ teaspoon sea salt*
*½ lb. fresh tofu, cut into ½-*
*inch cubes*
*1½ tablespoons shoyu or 3*
*level tablespoons mellow*
*white miso*
*2 cups watercres., chopped*
*into 1½-inch pieces*
*minced scallion*

## TOFU-WATERCRESS SOUP

This is a simple soup, but nonetheless attractive, flavorful, and nutritious.

Prepare kombu-bonito stock as in Fish or Oyster Chowder. Add salt to stock, bring to a boil, add tofu, and simmer gently for 5 minutes. Add shoyu and simmer for two minutes more. Add watercress for last minute of cooking. If using miso rather than shoyu, dilute the miso in a little broth and add to soup just before serving. Garnish with scallion and serve immediately.

For a decorative touch, cut carrot slices into flower shapes, parboil until just tender and place 3 in each bowl as a garnish.

SERVES 3

## NATTO

Japanese folklore has it that a certain farmer wrapped his cooked soybeans in straw and unwrapped them a day or two later to discover *natto*, a fermented soyfood with a slippery texture and an aroma reminiscent of strong cheese.

Early makers of natto relied on microorganisms naturally occurring in rice straw to start fermentation. Today natto is made by soaking soybeans overnight, then draining and boiling or pressure cooking until the beans are nearly tender. The beans are then drained again, cooled somewhat, and inoculated with *Bacillus natto*. Next the warm beans are placed in small Styrofoam containers with holes that allow for the necessary circulation of air or in perforated plastic bags wrapped in straw.

During the 14-18 hour incubation period the temperature of the natto must be kept between 104° and 113° F. Since it produces its own heat while fermenting, natto can easily overheat if not carefully regulated. Temperatures over 120° F. will quickly ruin the batch.

As you would expect with soybeans, natto is high in protein (17 percent) and low in calories. It is also an excellent source of iron (16.8 mg per 100g) and a good source of B vitamins, including $B_{12}$, and calcium. Like some other fermented foods, such as miso and lactic acid fermented pickles, natto is more than the sum of its parts. The level of several nutrients increases as a result of the process of fermentation. In Japan natto is commonly understood to be beneficial to the digestive system.

So why is this nutritious fermented soyfood, which is easy to produce, not gaining in recognition and popularity in this country as quickly as others such as shoyu, miso, and tempeh? Perhaps because natto is one of those foods that people often decide they don't like even before tasting it. Many, perhaps most, Americans see it as an unattractive, gooey substance with an offensive odor. Though I liked natto the first time I tried it and have been enjoying it since, my husband's reaction is probably more typical—he doesn't even like to be in the same room with it! I do think that if more people would try it, they would agree that it is delicious. If eaten when fresh, the aroma is mild, though it still has the slippery quality akin to melted mozzarella cheese that some people object to.

Since I have been unable to arouse any enthusiasm for this exotic food in my home, I have not experimented much with its culinary possibilities. I usually eat it in the traditional way— mixed with a dab of mustard, a dash of shoyu, and sometimes some minced scallion, on rice or in nori-maki. Natto's cheesy taste and stretchy quality could lead an adventurous cook to experiment with natto pizza, natto-rice burritos or burgers, natto-topped tacos, or deep-fried natto nuggets. In Japan natto is also used on pan-fried or grilled mochi, sautéed with scallions or leeks, as a topping for udon noodles, and even in soup.

When purchasing natto, be sure it is fresh or buy it frozen. Good quality natto forms slippery threads that stretch a good distance before breaking when you pick up a spoonful. Fresh, its shelflife is only about a week, and the odor gets stronger with age. By the time it has "gone by," the taste and smell will be so strong that even real natto lovers will be put off. Most of the time natto is packaged in its natural state, without the addition of chemicals or preservatives. However, some brands have added monosodium glutamate, so read the label to be sure the one you are buying doesn't.

Natto is still a rare commodity in natural foods stores. Asian markets, though, especially Japanese-oriented ones, almost always carry natto. It is usually sold frozen and is best kept frozen and thawed only just before use.

*At the Onozaki's house, neighbor Sachiko Watanabe readies homemade udon to be cooked.*

The Japanese are experts when it comes to noodles. It's quite certain that noodles originated in China and passed to Japan where they have been a favorite food for centuries. More noodles are probably eaten in Japan today than any other food except rice. Light and easy to digest, quick and simple to prepare, yet delicious and satisfying, Japanese eggless noodles are a versatile food. They make a filling lunch, convenient snack, or, served with one or two side dishes, a complete dinner. Noodles can be served in piping hot broth to warm us in winter, and in salads or floating in a bowl of ice water accompanied by a chilled dipping sauce to cool and refresh us in summer. Whether in soups and salads, sautéed with vegetables, deep-fried, baked, or topped with sauce, noodles are delicious. Quick to prepare, they provide the perfect solution when you have unexpected guests or find yourself at mealtime with nothing "in the works." In the time it takes for the noodle water to boil and the noodles to cook, you can prepare a broth or sauce and a vegetable and voila! in twenty minutes you have a delicious and satisfying meal.

Although many commercially available noodles are made from wheat that has first been stripped of its nutritious outer layers then ground into flour and "enriched" with synthetically-produced vitamins and minerals, there are also many varieties of nourishing whole grain noodles. They come in a variety of thicknesses and are made from different grains or combinations of grains, sometimes with the addition of vegetables or herbs.

Extra time and energy spent in processing high quality Japanese noodles, as well as the blend of flours used, results in a superior product. The Japanese add a specific proportion of salt to the water used for making the noodle dough. This affects flavor and texture by regulating the rate at which the gluten in the flour is activated. After thorough mixing and kneading, the dough is allowed to rest for several hours to develop the gluten. It is then rolled into sheets of the appropriate thickness and run across a set of knives that slice it lengthwise into strips. Another cutter cuts the noodles into the desired length. Not willing to compromise quality, many Japanese manufacturers still hang the noodles over bamboo rods to dry at natural temperatures. Fans are used in the drying rooms to keep air circulating, but artificial heat is not used to speed drying since it adversely affects quality. From start to finish, this method is based on the way noodles were traditionally made at home.

Most American noodles are made on an extruder, a machine that squeezes the dough through a dye and then cuts it into various sizes and shapes. The extruding method is quick and easy, but taste and texture suffer. Though a few traditional manufacturers in this country cut the sheets of dough by running them over knives, the kneaded dough is not allowed to rest before processing and artificial heat is used to hasten drying. On the other hand, quality-conscious American noodle manufacturers use a variety of wheat significantly higher in protein than that used by Japanese makers.

Though there are many varieties within each group, there are two main types of Japanese noodles, those made from buckwheat (*soba*) and those made from wheat (*udon*). Since buckwheat requires cooler, drier growing conditions, the thin brownish-gray soba is popular in northern Japan while udon, a thick, chewy, beige wheat noodle, is favored in Kyoto and southern Japan. In winter both types are most often enjoyed in hot broth, either plain or with other accoutrements, such as tempura or simmered vegetables, attractively arranged on top. Soba is eaten cold in summer with a chilled dipping sauce, but southerners prefer either *hiyamugi* or *somen*—thin, vermicelli-type wheat noodles—in summer. Udon is not traditionally served cold.

The Japanese feel that their traditional "fast food" must be eaten immediately, before the piping hot broth has made the noodles limp. This means you must take in a cooling breath with each bite. The resultant slurping sound can be strange to Western ears, but it is a sign of enjoyment in Japan. In fact, eating noodles slowly and quietly is offensive to the cook. The day we arrived in Japan we were taken to a "noodle bar" for lunch. The sound of fifty or more businessmen all slurping noodles at once is something I'll never forget!

Noodle bars abound in Japanese cities, and many of them still offer *teuchi* (hand made) soba and udon. At the window of a steamy little noodle shop you are enticed by the sight of a Japanese chef kneading and slicing fresh pasta dough, noodles rolling in a cauldron of boiling water, and a variety of tempting noodle dishes being served up for eager customers. This is a rare instance when, unless you make your own noodles—a task that is not difficult but of course does require time and experience—you can actually get something better in a restaurant than at home. You simply can't beat the fresh taste and texture of professionally-made *teuchi* noodles.

A single serving is 3½ to 4 ounces of dry noodles. Although Japanese noodles can be used in a variety of ethnic dishes, the Japanese almost always eat their noodles in broth or with a somewhat stronger-flavored dipping sauce. Both are a savory blend of kombu-bonito stock, shoyu, and mirin, the three most important Japanese seasoning agents.

*Top, udon cooks in a cauldron (*kamado*) that sets into a chamber of a traditional Japanese wood-fired stove (*irori*). Bottom, Watanabe places rinsed and cooled noodles in a bamboo basket to drain.*

## COOKING NOODLES

Since most Japanese noodles are made with salt, it isn't necessary or advisable to add salt to the cooking water. Bring water to a full rolling boil in a large pot (about 10 cups of water for every 8 ounces of noodles) and add noodles a few at a time so as not to completely stop the boiling. Stir gently until the water is boiling rapidly again to prevent the noodles from sticking to the bottom of the pan. If too many noodles are added at once the water will not quickly return to a boil and the noodles will be overcooked on the outside and undercooked inside. Also, using too little water results in sticky noodles and uneven cooking.

There are two methods for cooking noodles, both of which are acceptable. The "shock" method involves adding the noodles as described above then, after all the noodles are in the pot, adding one cup of cold water when the water returns to a rolling boil. Repeat 3-4 times, until the noodles are cooked but still firm to the bite ("al dente"). A properly cooked noodle should still be slightly chewy and, when broken in half, it should be the same color throughout. Test often to avoid overcooking. The second method is simply to bring the water back to a rapid boil after adding all the noodles, then cook over medium heat until done.

When cooked, immediately drain and rinse noodles in two or three cold water baths or under cold running water to prevent further cooking and to keep them from sticking together. When they have cooled enough to handle, and while still in the cold bath or under running water, gently rub the noodles between your hands to remove surface starch. Drain and set aside until ready to assemble your dish. If it is necessary to reheat them, place individual servings in a strainer or colander and submerge in a pot of boiling water until just heated. Drain well and serve.

The noodle cooking water can be reserved, allowed to sour slightly, and used as a natural leavening agent in breads, muffins, or pancakes.

# UDON

A thick, cream-colored wheat noodle, udon resembles spaghetti. High-quality udon noodles are made from 100 percent whole wheat flour or whole wheat combined with unbleached white flour. One-hundred percent whole wheat udon is a sturdy noodle with a full whole wheat flavor. *Tsuru* udon (60 percent whole wheat) is a lighter, smoother variety that readily absorbs the flavors of broths, sauces, and seasonings.

Though usually served in broth or with a stronger-flavored dipping sauce, udon is also good pan-fried, as a substitute for spaghetti with tomato or white clam sauce, in noodle salads, or it can be parboiled, then deep-fried, and used to top chow mein. Easy to prepare, udon is ideal when on the road or camping.

## UDON WITH WHITE MISO SAUCE

Cook noodles as described on page 62. Combine remaining ingredients for sauce and bring just to a simmer. If too thick, add a little more water; if too thin, simmer briefly to thicken. Ladle sauce over the noodles in individual serving bowls. Garnish with minced scallion and slivered nori.

If time permits you may wish to top noodles and sauce with a colorful assortment of foods such as carrots cut into $^1/_8$ -inch diagonal slices; butternut squash peeled and sliced; broccoli florets; and tofu cut into cubes. While noodles are cooking, steam or boil the vegetables until just tender. Drain and cool green vegetables immediately to retain color. If using shiitake mushrooms or fresh, dried, or deep-fried tofu, first simmer in 1 cup water with 1 tablespoon shoyu and, if desired, 2 teaspoons mirin for about 15 minutes.

Arrange vegetables and tofu attractively over noodles and sauce. Try to use locally-grown seasonal vegetables and keep in mind an appealing combination of colors and textures.

**SERVES 2-3**

*1 package (8 oz. or 8.8 oz.)
  udon
4 level tablespoons mellow
  white or mellow barley
  miso
2 tablespoons tahini
$^1/_3$ cup water
2 tablespoons lemon juice or
  brown rice vinegar
1 tablespoon mirin
$1^1/_2$-2 teaspoons juice of
  grated fresh ginger
pinch garlic powder, or 1
  clove fresh, minced
pinch (approximately $^1/_8$ teaspoon) dry tarragon
  (optional)*

*1 package (8 oz. or 8.8 oz.)
    udon*
*3 cups water*
*6-inch piece kombu*
*1 packet, or ¼ cup, bonito
    flakes (optional)*
*¼ teaspoon sea salt*
*3-4 dried shiitake mushrooms
    and/or 3 scallions cut into
    ¾-inch slices*
*1 carrot, sliced thin*
*3 tablespoons shoyu*
*2 tablespoons mirin*
*finely minced scallion for gar-
    nish*
*grated fresh ginger, or a pinch
    of cayenne or Japanese 7-
    spice*

## UDON IN BROTH

This is one of the simplest noodle dishes, and we never tire of it.

Cook noodles as described on page 62. Combine water and kombu in saucepan, bring just to a boil, and remove kombu. (Reserve kombu for another use.) Add bonito flakes to stock and remove from heat. Let sit for 1-2 minutes, then strain soup to remove flakes. Squeeze all liquid from flakes back into stock and discard flakes. (If omitting bonito flakes, for flavor I recommend using shiitake that have been soaked for at least 2 hours and sliced. The soaking water should be used as part of the 3 cups of water.) Add salt. Add any vegetables you may be using and simmer for 10-15 minutes or until they are tender. Add shoyu and mirin and cook for a minute more. Turn off heat. If necessary, reheat just before serving.

To serve, place noodles in deep individual serving bowls, ladle hot broth over them to almost cover, and garnish with minced scallion and a little grated ginger or a *small* pinch of Japanese 7-spice or cayenne. A variation appealing in summer is a colorful combination of vegetables or other ingredients arranged over noodles and broth. For example, blanched watercress, steamed or boiled carrots and green beans, and simmered or deep-fried tofu are all lovely and delicious.

The broth in this dish is meant for flavoring the noodles. Although it's delicious, it's quite salty, so I don't recommend drinking the liquid left in the bottom of the bowl.

SERVES 2

## TEMPURA UDON

This variation on the preceding recipe is popular on both sides of the Pacific.

Shrimp and/or vegetables such as mushrooms, sliced winter squash, broccoli, green pepper, carrots, cauliflower, and onion are dipped in batter, deep-fried, and placed on top of noodles and broth. The tempura is dipped into the noodle broth for flavor. Tempura is equally delicious with soba noodles. (For preparation, see *About Tempura* on page 128.)

## UDON WITH SHRIMP FLOWERS

A beautiful dish to serve to guests, this variation takes a little more time to prepare but the result is extra special. You can double or triple the recipe, according to your needs.

Follow the recipe for Udon in Broth, omitting any vegetables. Shell and devein shrimp, being careful to leave tails attached. (To devein, make a slit along the back of each shrimp and remove the dark vein.) Slice backs of shrimp almost halfway through, then press flat. Cut a slit about one inch long down the middle of the back. Push the tail through the slit to form a "flower," but do not pull tight.

Combine the next four ingredients in a saucepan and bring to a simmer. Add shrimp and simmer for about 3-5 minutes or until they are just pink. Place cooked udon in individual serving bowls and add piping hot broth almost to the level of the noodles. Arrange five shrimp "flowers" on each bowl of noodles and garnish each bowl with a sprig of watercress.

SERVES 2

*1 package (8 oz. or 8.8 oz.)*
  *udon*
*10 medium or large shrimp (5*
  *per person)*
*2 cups kombu stock*
*3 tablespoons shoyu*
*¼ cup mirin*
*2 tablespoons sake (optional)*
*2 sprigs watercress*

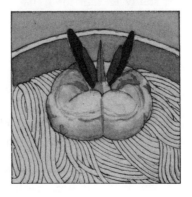

*8 ounces udon*

*2 cups broccoli or green beans, cut into small bite-sized pieces*

*1 cucumber*

*1 scallion, finely minced*

*⅓ cup mellow white miso*

*3 tablespoons brown rice vinegar*

*4 tablespoons water*

## UDON SALAD

This is a simple, tasty noodle salad. It is satisfying on hot summer days.

Cook the noodles as described on page 62. Drain, and set aside. While noodles are cooking, lightly steam the broccoli or green beans until just tender and still bright green. Peel the cucumber, quarter it lengthwise, then thinly slice. Combine the miso, vinegar, and water. Chop the noodles into 2-inch lengths and toss them with the vegetables. Add dressing, mix well, and serve.

SERVES 4-6

## SOBA

Several varieties of soba are available at natural foods stores and Oriental markets. One-hundred percent buckwheat soba is a hearty, delicious, wheat-free noodle. It must be cooked more gently to prevent breaking, so it is not recommended for fried noodles. Most soba noodles are made from 40-60 percent buckwheat flour with the remainder being unbleached white flour. Forty percent *ito* soba is a thin, delicate noodle, which cooks quickly and easily absorbs the flavor of broth, sauces, or seasonings. Like *cha* soba (made with the addition of green tea powder), ito soba, because it is so light, is especially good served cold in summer. *Yomogi* (mugwort) soba, another special variety, contains mineral-rich dried mugwort leaves. Mugwort soba, cha soba and ito soba are not recommended for frying. Jinenjo soba is a popular noodle in Japan. A strengthening food rich in digestive enzymes, jinenjo helps bind the buckwheat flour, resulting in a smooth, soft noodle that is excellent in broth yet sturdy enough for frying. Eighty percent soba, 50 percent soba, and 40 percent *sakurai* soba all have a rich flavor and substantial texture. They may be used in any of the recipes given below.

*1 package (8 oz. or 8.8 oz.) soba*

*1-1½ tablespoons light sesame oil*

*1 carrot, cut julienne*

*1 rib celery, sliced thin*

*cabbage (2 cups sliced thin)*

*4-5 scallions, sliced*

## FRIED SOBA

Parboil noodles until almost tender. Cool, drain, and set aside. Heat oil in a large skillet and sauté vegetables, adding one by one beginning with those that take the longest to cook: first carrot, then celery, cabbage, and finally, scallion. Add a small pinch of sea salt and sauté over medium heat, stirring constantly, until somewhat tender. (The vegetables should still be crunchy, but not raw tasting.) Add ginger and sauté for another minute. Add noodles and toss. Add shoyu and mirin and toss until noodles are hot and evenly mixed with vegetables and seasonings. Serve immediately, garnished with minced scallion if desired.

SERVES 2-3

*small pinch sea salt*
*1½-2 tablespoons fresh*
  *ginger, peeled and finely*
  *minced*
*2½ tablespoons shoyu*
*2 tablespoons mirin (optional)*

## SOBA IN BROTH

The only difference between this recipe and Udon in Broth is that soba broth is generally a little stronger and is traditionally garnished with slivered nori and minced scallion. Soba is seasoned with wasabi whereas udon is usually seasoned with Japanese 7-spice.

Cook soba as on page 62. Prepare broth by following directions for Udon in Broth but increase shoyu to 4 tablespoons. To serve, place noodles in bowls, ladle broth over them to almost cover, and garnish with minced scallion, slivered nori, and a small dab of wasabi paste or a little grated ginger. (Place small bowlfuls of wasabi paste and/or grated ginger on the table so more can be added to suit individual tastes.)

As in Udon in Broth, the salty liquid is meant for flavoring the noodles, and I don't recommend that you drink it.

SERVES 2

## SUMMER SOBA

Cooling and refreshing when nothing else appeals, this traditional noodle dish is a favorite Japanese lunch on hot summer days.

Prepare noodles, broth, and garnishes as for above recipe. Chill broth. Divide cooked noodles and put them into small noodle baskets, plates, or soup bowls. Pour chilled dipping broth into separate small individual bowls. Set out wasabi, chopped scallion, toasted slivered nori, and grated ginger on the table so everyone can add them to the broth to their own taste. (Add about 1 tablespoon scallion and ¼ teaspoon wasabi *or* ginger to ½ to ⅔ cup of broth.) A little grated daikon is a flavorful addition to the dip.

Dip each bite of noodles in broth. If dip becomes weak, replace it with fresh broth.

For **each** person being
served you will need:
*approximately 1¼ cups noodle
broth*
*3½ ounces dry noodles (soba
or udon)*
*3 shrimp, or ½ hard-boiled
egg*
*1 dried shiitake*
*5 slices carrot*
*3 florets broccoli*
*1 square baked or broiled
mochi, about 1¾" x 2½"*

## SOBA SUKIYAKI

This is our favorite winter dish, and a perfect choice for guests.
Besides being beautiful, delicious, and warming, it creates a
lively social atmosphere. However you choose to prepare and
serve it, sukiyaki always sparks conversation and creates good
cheer. Although it may seem complicated at first glance, this is
really a simple one-dish meal that should take under an hour to
complete.

There are three ways to assemble sukiyaki, depending on the
number of people being served and the type of cookware you
have available. The only difference in the first two methods is in
the type of cooking and serving dish. It can be served in small
individual flameproof casseroles, called *donabe*, or, if you are
not serving more than three or four people, you can use a large
skillet (cast iron is best). Using donabe or the third method
described below is preferred when having guests. The skillet
method is more family-style.

The ingredients can be varied, but use an attractive combination
of colors, shapes, and textures. (Other ingredients such as
chunks of steamed or simmered winter squash or daikon rounds,
seitan, deep-fried or broiled tofu, or greens such as watercress or
spinach may be substituted for those here.)

Prepare noodle broth as for Udon in Broth. However, since
more is absorbed by the noodles in this recipe, the broth should
be somewhat weaker. Either omit salt, decrease shoyu by one
tablespoon, or add ½ cup stock from boiling carrots to each 3
cups noodle broth. A little grated fresh ginger adds extra flavor.

Parboil noodles for only 4 to 5 minutes. (If cooked too long
they will become limp and mushy when reheated with the other
ingredients.) Peel and devein shrimp and boil until just pink
(about 3 minutes) in lightly salted water.

Soak shiitake for at least two hours to reconstitute, then remove
and discard stems, score caps with an "X," and simmer whole
mushrooms in 1 cup water or stock with 1½ tablespoons shoyu
and 1 tablespoon mirin for 20 minutes.

Slice carrots ¼-inch thick on the diagonal and parboil until just
tender. Steam broccoli until just tender and still bright green.
Immediately drain and cool to retain color. Bake (at 350° F. for
about 15 minutes) or broil mochi until crisp, golden-brown, and
slightly puffed.

Place noodles in the bottom of each donabe or the skillet and
attractively arrange other ingredients over so colors are balanced
(separate similarly-colored foods, such as broccoli and greens,
with other contrasting ingredients). Add broth to almost cover
noodles, cover, bring to a boil, and simmer for just 2-3 minutes.

Serve immediately. If using a skillet, place it in the center of the table and let the diners fill their bowls from the pan and ladle a little broth over the top.

If you are serving sukiyaki to more than four, the following variation works well and is an interesting way to share a meal with friends. Prepare ingredients as described above, precooking only the shiitake and omitting the egg. You will need more broth—two cups per person. Provide condiments such as freshly grated ginger, minced scallion, lemon wedges, and Japanese 7-spice or cayenne.

Place parboiled noodles on a large platter and arrange other foods over. Pour broth into a large pot or flameproof casserole (large donabe) on a hotplate in the center of the table, or use an electric skillet. Add ingredients to simmering broth, starting with some of the shrimp and the vegetables that take longest to cook. Don't add all the ingredients at once, since the foods should be removed and eaten as soon as they are cooked. Diners ladle broth from the pot into their bowls for dipping and add their choice of condiments. Precooked ingredients are done when heated through, others when tender. When all other foods have been cooked, add noodles. If necessary, add more broth. You may want to have extra parboiled noodles or baked mochi on hand if your guests are particularly hungry.

# SOMEN

Somen is a thin, light summer noodle. The highest quality somen is made from gluten-rich unbleached white flour with a little salt added. Of the many types of Japanese noodles, somen is the only variety used in traditional *shojin* (temple) cooking.

Somen cooks quickly and absorbs the flavor of sauces, dressings, and seasonings well, so it is both convenient and versatile. Try tossing somen with a variety of raw or parboiled vegetables and your favorite salad dressing (miso or umeboshi-based dressings go particularly well). These delicate noodles are also delicious served with a hot miso broth or a hot or chilled shoyu-flavored dipping sauce, garnished with minced scallions, slivered nori, and grated ginger. A sweet and sour vegetable or tofu sauce is excellent served over somen (see Sweet and Sour Noodles, page 72). For an elegant entrée, try somen in Noodle Rolls (page 147).

To prepare, boil 10 cups unsalted water, add 8 oz. somen, and cook for approximately 5 minutes. When still firm, (''al dente'') but not hard or raw tasting, drain, rinse under cold water until thoroughly cool, then drain again.

Although actually a separate variety of noodle, *hiyamugi* is a thin, light, somen-like noodle made from whole wheat.

Traditionally, hiyamugi is almost always served cold. It can be substituted for somen in the following recipes, though some of the visual appeal of Somen on Ice (see page 71) is lost if somen is not used. Hiyamugi requires slightly longer cooking than somen.

## SOMEN IN MISO BROTH

*1 package (8 or 8.8 oz.) somen*
*3 cups water*
*6-inch piece kombu*
*1 packet or ¼ cup bonito flakes (optional)*
*1 small carrot*
*½ cup chopped scallion*
*5 oz. tofu, cut into ½-inch cubes*
*5 level tablespoons mellow white miso*

Prepare somen as described above. Combine water and kombu in a saucepan, bring just to a simmer, uncovered, over medium heat. Remove kombu (save for another use). If using, add bonito flakes, remove pot from heat, and let sit for 1-2 minutes. Strain out bonito flakes, pressing out all liquid from flakes before discarding them. Return stock to heat.

Cut carrot into "matchsticks" and add to stock. Slice scallions into ½-inch lengths and add, reserving a little for garnish. Simmer for 5-7 minutes, add tofu, and simmer for 5 minutes more. Remove from heat. Dissolve the miso in a little of the broth and add to soup.

Fill soup bowls to two-thirds and garnish with minced scallion. Serve noodles in separate individual bowls. If desired, reheat noodles by dipping in boiling water and draining.

Dip individual bites of noodles into soup. (If eaten alone, this broth will taste a little strong, but after dipping the somen, it should be just right for drinking.)

SERVES 2-3

## SOMEN SALAD

Prepare noodles as described on page 62. Cut broccoli into small bite-sized pieces. Bring ½ inch of water and a small pinch of salt to a boil in a saucepan. Add broccoli, cover, and steam over medium-low heat for 5-7 minutes. (Do not overcook. It should be bright green and slightly crunchy.) Remove from heat and drain immediately. Sprinkle on a few grains of salt, toss gently, and allow to cool.

For dressing, combine oil, vinegar, shoyu, and ginger. Chop noodles into 1½- to 2-inch lengths and place them in a bowl along with broccoli and scallion. Add dressing and toss. If possible, allow to sit for 20-30 minutes before serving. Toss again and garnish with 1 tablespoon toasted sesame seeds.

SERVES 3

*5.3 oz. package somen*
*3 cups chopped broccoli*
*pinch sea salt*
*2 teaspoons toasted sesame oil*
*2 teaspoons rice vinegar*
*1 tablespoon shoyu*
*1 tablespoon finely minced*
  *fresh ginger*
*1-2 scallions, minced*
*1 tablespoon sesame seeds*

## SOMEN ON ICE

This cooling dish is most appealing on the hottest summer days.

Bring the water and kombu to a simmer, uncovered, over medium heat. Remove kombu as soon as the water begins to boil. Add shoyu, mirin, and salt and simmer for 2-3 minutes. Remove from heat and refrigerate until cool.

Meanwhile, prepare somen as on page 62. After rinsing cooked noodles in cold water and draining, place somen into small serving bowls (for this dish, glass bowls are lovely). Gently pour into each bowl about 1 cup cold water and, if desired, arrange a few ice cubes around the noodles. Garnish with a single parsley or watercress sprig, a fresh strawberry, or anything simple, cooling, and colorful.

Serve ½ cup chilled dipping broth each in small individual bowls, adding ½ tablespoon scallion and ¼ teaspoon wasabi paste or grated ginger to each. Dip each bite of noodles into broth. When dipping broth becomes weak, replace with fresh broth.

SERVES 2

*2 cups water*
*6-inch piece kombu*
*2 tablespoons shoyu*
*2 tablespoons mirin*
*½ teaspoon sea salt*
*1 package (8 oz.) somen*
*2 tablespoons slivered scallion*
*1 teaspoon wasabi paste or*
  *grated fresh ginger*

## CLEAR NOODLES

*Bifun* is a light, transparent noodle made from rice flour with the addition of 10 percent potato starch. *Saifun* is a similar noodle made from mung bean starch. Wheat-free and salt-free, these noodles take only a few minutes to prepare and are versatile enough for salads, clear soups, sukiyaki, Chinese-style specialties, and fried noodle dishes.

To cook, add bifun or saifun to plenty of rapidly boiling water and boil for 5-6 minutes (be careful not to overcook or it will become mushy). When done, remove noodles and immediately rinse under cold running water until thoroughly cool, then drain.

Sweet potato starch and kuzu powder combine to make *kuzu kiri*, a light-colored noodle traditionally used in sukiyaki and salads. More substantial than bifun, and requiring 20 minutes' cooking, kuzu kiri is sometimes served in a shoyu-flavored broth like udon or soba. A few strands added to clear soups is attractive.

## SWEET AND SOUR NOODLES

*1 package clear noodles (or somen or udon)*
*2 teaspoons light sesame oil*
*2 slices fresh ginger, peeled*
*1 medium onion, sliced thin*
*1 rib celery, sliced thin*
*1 medium carrot, sliced thin*
*1 small red or green bell pepper, seeded and sliced*
*1 cup bite-sized pieces broccoli florets and stalks*
*1 pound tofu, cut into ½-inch cubes*
*½-⅔ cup vegetable or kombu stock or water*
*¼ teaspoon sea salt*
*¼ cup rice vinegar*
*2½ tablespoons honey*
*1 tablespoon shoyu*
*2 tablespoons mirin (optional)*
*1-1½ tablespoons kuzu*

For most sweetened dishes I prefer to use a mild sweetener such as rice syrup or barley malt, but honey works best in this recipe.

Feel free to substitute other vegetables or ingredients such as seitan or deep-fried tofu for those suggested here.

Cook noodles as described above, then rinse under cold running water, drain, and set aside. Heat oil in skillet, add ginger and brown slightly, then add onion and sauté briefly. Add celery, carrot, bell pepper, and a small pinch of salt. Sauté for 1-2 minutes more, then add a little water to prevent scorching, cover, and cook 5 minutes. Add broccoli, tofu, and a little more water if necessary, cover and cook about 5 minutes more (until broccoli is just tender but still bright green). Uncover pan, remove from heat, and remove and discard the ginger.

In a small saucepan combine the stock or water, salt, vinegar, honey, shoyu and mirin. Using the smaller amount of stock will give a more intense sweet and sour flavor; if you prefer a milder taste, use the larger amount. Bring the mixture to a gentle simmer, then remove from heat. Crush the lumps of kuzu with the back of a spoon before measuring, then thoroughly dissolve the kuzu in an equal amount of water and slowly add it to the sauce while stirring briskly. Return pan to heat and simmer for 1-2 minutes, stirring constantly. Mix the sauce with the vegetables and serve over the noodles.

SERVES 2

## FESTIVE NOODLE SALAD

The idea for this recipe, and the artful way of putting the ingredients together, was learned from a friend in Miami. You will be proud to serve it to guests.

Cook noodles as on page 62, then rinse under cold running water, drain, and set aside. Remove large stems from watercress and remove tips and strings from snow peas. Parboil vegetables individually in lightly salted water, then remove, cool under running water, drain, and set aside. (Cook lighter flavored vegetables first. For example, boil carrots for 1 minute, then snow peas for 30 seconds, broccoli for 3 minutes and, finally, watercress for 20-30 seconds.) Chop noodles into 1½- to 2-inch lengths and place in bowl. Chop watercress and add to noodles along with carrots.

For dressing, combine miso, tahini, orange juice, and lemon juice in a blender or suribachi. Just before serving, mix dressing with noodles, carrots, and watercress and place on a platter in a mound. Arrange snow peas around edge of mixture. Place a few broccoli florets on the center of the mound and the rest around the edge.

**SERVES 4**

*1 package clear noodles*
*1 carrot, cut julienne*
*about 20 snow peas*
*several broccoli florets*
*1 bunch watercress*

DRESSING:
*2 tablespoons white miso*
*2 tablespoons tahini*
*juice of 1-1½ oranges (⅓ cup)*
*1 tablespoon lemon juice*
*1 heaping tablespoon chopped scallion*

The diets of traditional agrarian cultures have always been centered around an indigenous grain. Usually one grain provides the focal point, with other grains sometimes playing secondary roles. Rice is by far the most important grain in the Japanese diet. Besides being eaten at almost every meal, rice is used to make other important traditional foods such as miso, koji, vinegar, amazake, sake, and mirin. The more glutinous variety, sweet rice, is mainly used to make mochi, a specialty food served on important holidays.

Wheat, buckwheat, and barley are sometimes served in Japan in place of rice. Wheat and buckwheat are most commonly eaten in the form of noodles. Wheat is also used to make fu and seitan, both forms of protein-rich wheat gluten, and in the manufacture of shoyu. Buckwheat flour is sometimes made into porridge. Barley is used to make barley miso and is also used in stews or cooked with rice.

## RICE

*"Gohan desu!"* With these words the Japanese family is summoned to the dinner table. So basic is rice to the traditional Japanese that *gohan*, "cooked rice," also means "meal." Rice, miso soup, and pickles are the most basic dishes in the traditional Japanese diet, constituting a complete and satisfying meal. Many Asians eat over three hundred pounds of rice per year.

While living with the Onozaki family we ate rice at least twice a day. In two or three meals per week noodles took the place of rice. Though the rice was most often served plain with a side dish of pickles, we never tired of it. The surprise was that, though this was a rural area of Japan and most people, including our hosts, ate rice from their own paddies, no one we met ate whole brown rice. In fact, not even the elderly people had ever tasted it. White rice has been the popular choice ever since milling was industrialized.

Brown rice consists of the whole kernel, with just the tough outer husk removed. Several layers of bran surround the central starchy portion, called the endosperm, and the embryo or germ. Brown rice is a good source of vitamins, minerals, carbohydrates, protein, and fiber. When eaten in a meal with cooked beans or fermented bean products such as miso, or whole sesame seeds, brown rice provides high quality protein with all essential amino acids.

White or "polished" rice, on the other hand, is left after the nutritious bran layers and germ have been milled away. The milling process significantly decreases fiber and fat as well as the B vitamins thiamine, niacin, and riboflavin, and several minerals

*Terraced rice paddies with young rice plants surround a small farming village high in the mountains of Tochigi Prefecture, Japan.*

including iron, potassium, phosphorus and calcium.

Rice was already being polished in Asia long before the Industrial Revolution. In the cities of pre-industrial Japan the local rice miller made his living by placing a customer's brown rice in his hollowed stone and pounding it with a thick stick until the bran was partially removed. Since rice was in short supply, and it took considerable time and energy to polish a sack of rice by this method, white rice was expensive and for a time it remained a luxury of the upper classes. Later, pedal machines that made the process considerably quicker and easier were introduced. In the nineteenth century sophisticated machines that rapidly remove the bran from rice were invented. Today the nutritious bran is mainly fed to farm animals. In the past it was used to make pickles and other foods.

Rice is a versatile and delicious staple. Though organic whole brown rice is recommended for daily use in Western natural foods cooking, white rice can be just the thing for festive occasions and light summer fare. I like to use white rice when making Sushi Rice or Nori-Maki. It is also particularly good in Rice Burgers, Ginger Fried Rice, and topped with Chinese-Style Vegetables.

A well-stocked natural foods shop will carry short, medium, and long grain rice. In general, short grain varieties are adapted for growth in more northern, temperate climates, and medium and long grain varieties are usually suited to cultivation in the southernmost portion of the temperate zone and in subtropical or tropical areas. Choose the type that is most suited to growing in your geographical area, and try to select an organic variety without many scratched or broken grains.

When cooked, short grain types tend to be stickier than long grain rice. Long grain cooks up drier and more fluffy.

Here are basic recipes for brown and white rice as well as a few of our favorite variations.

## PRESSURE-COOKED BROWN RICE

The exact amount of water needed varies a little with the variety of rice used and its freshness, the type of pressure cooker you have, and whether you want a drier or more sticky result. Also, if you are cooking more than two cups of rice, the amount of water needed per cup of rice decreases slightly. Experience is the best teacher of these elements.

Wash the rice by rinsing and draining several times until rinse water is clear. Drain well after the last rinse, then combine rice with measured water and salt in the pot. Cover and bring up to pressure over high heat. When pressure is up, reduce heat to low, place a heat diffuser under the pot to prevent scorching, and cook for 45-50 minutes. Remove from heat and allow pressure to

*2 cups short or medium-grain brown rice*
*2½-2⅔ cups water*
*⅛ teaspoon sea salt*

return to normal. Open cooker and fluff rice, then re-cover loosely and let rest for a few minutes before removing to a serving container such as an unfinished wide wooden bowl. Cover with a bamboo sushi mat (*maki-su*), which will keep in heat yet prevent condensation.

SERVES 4

## POT-BOILED BROWN RICE

*2 cups short or medium grain brown rice*
*4 cups water*
*¼ teaspoon sea salt*

Wash the rice by rinsing and draining several times until rinse water is clear. Drain well, then combine with measured water and salt in a heavy pot with a tight-fitting lid. Bring to a rapid boil over medium-high heat, then reduce heat to low and cook for 50-60 minutes. Do not remove cover while the rice is cooking. Remove from heat and let rest, covered, for 10 minutes before fluffing and serving.

SERVES 4

## SESAME RICE

Cook rice by either of the methods above, then mix with ¼ cup freshly toasted, ground sesame seeds or lightly-salted gomashio (page 188). Cover, and let stand for 5 minutes before serving.

## PARSLEY RICE

Wash and mince a small bunch of parsley. Toss gently with freshly cooked rice, cover, and let stand for 5 minutes before serving.

## RICE WITH SHRIMP

Cook rice. Mince 1 small onion and sauté in a little sesame oil. Shell, devein, and chop 4-6 medium or large shrimp, add to the onion along with a small pinch of sea salt, and sauté together for 2-3 minutes. Sprinkle with a few drops of shoyu. Gently mix the shrimp and onions into the cooked rice, cover, and let stand for 5 minutes before serving.

## RICE WITH BEANS

See Azuki Rice, page 162. If you wish to substitute another type of bean such as pinto beans, soak them for 4-8 hours. Drain beans, parboil for 10-15 minutes, and proceed as for Azuki Rice.

# ROASTED, BOILED RICE

See Fluffy Brown Rice with Hato Mugi, page 94. This produces a lighter, fluffier texture than boiling or pressure cooking.

# FRIED RICE

See Ginger Fried Rice, page 186. Variations on this theme are endless. Use your imagination and whatever vegetables you have on hand to create your own favorites.

# WHITE RICE

Rinse and drain rice several times until rinse water is almost clear, then drain in a strainer for at least 30 minutes. Combine rice and measured water in a heavy pot with a tight-fitting lid. The exact amount of water needed varies slightly with the variety of rice used, its freshness, and the type of pot you use.

Bring rice to a boil over medium heat and cook for 1 minute. Reduce heat to low and cook for 8-10 minutes, then reduce heat to very low for 10 minutes more. (Do not remove cover while cooking.) Remove from heat and let rice stand, covered, for 10 minutes more before fluffing and serving.

Use in any favorite recipe. If desired, sprinkle rice with gomashio or your favorite condiment, or let each person wrap bite-sized portions of rice in strips of toasted nori with a dab of umeboshi paste.

SERVES 4

*2 cups white rice*
*2⅓-2½ cups water*

# SUSHI RICE

This is the lightly sweetened, vinegared white rice used in Japanese sushi. It goes well in Nori-Maki.

Wash rice and drain in sieve or strainer for 30-60 minutes. Cook rice as above. While rice is cooking, combine vinegar, sweetener, and salt in a small saucepan. Warm over low heat to dissolve sweetener and salt, then cool to room temperature by setting container in cold water.

Spread rice in a wide, shallow wooden, glass, stoneware, or plastic (not metal) bowl or tub. Have a friend vigorously fan the rice with a newspaper while you gently toss it with horizontal cutting strokes of a wooden paddle or spoon. While tossing, sprinkle the vinegar mixture over the rice. Continue fanning and tossing until rice is room temperature, then, if not using right away, cover container with a damp, clean cloth.

MAKES 5 CUPS

*2 cups white rice*
*2-2¼ cups water*
*2 tablespoons rice vinegar*
*2 tablespoons rice syrup, or 1 tablespoon plus 1 teaspoon honey*
*¾ teaspoon sea salt*

*In rural Japan, mochi is still often made the traditional way, by pounding sweet rice with a wooden mallet (kin) in a hollowed log (usu).*

## MOCHI

*Mochi* is a delicious whole grain food made from sweet brown rice, a glutinous, high protein rice variety. The sweet rice is soaked, steamed, and pounded, then allowed to dry until it is firm enough to slice. Symbolizing longevity and wealth, mochi is part of the traditional celebration of several important Japanese holidays such as *o-shogatsu* (New Year's). Even today the celebration of o-shogatsu is steeped in tradition and symbolism. Business comes to a standstill and families prepare for this most important holiday for days, even weeks, in advance. The home is thoroughly cleaned from top to bottom and preparations, including making mochi, for the special and elaborate New Year's meal are begun.

In rural Japan one can still see the traditional preparation of handmade mochi. The heavy wooden mallet and large log carved generations before to form a smooth bowl are set in place as the family begins the ritual of mochi pounding. Usually the grandmother steams the rice, places it in the hollowed log, and turns it for her husband after each resonant stroke of the mallet. They work quickly and rhythmically, Grandmother bobbing in then leaning aside as the mallet crashes down and releases a billow of steam from the hot rice. After being pounded until the crushed grains form a homogenous mass, the mochi is formed into small, flat, round cakes, or rolled out to an even thickness and cut into 2″ x 2″ squares on a floured board and allowed to dry. It is then stored in a cold place or refrigerated until it is time to cook it.

Mochi is said to increase stamina. It is especially favored by Japanese laborers and farmers during the colder months. Naturally sweet and filling, mochi is an ideal between-meal snack for growing children.

The process of pounding or mashing the grain makes mochi very easy to digest, so it is excellent for people in a weakened condition. Traditionally, mochi is recommended for such health problems as anemia, blood sugar imbalance, and weak intestines. It is also an excellent food for pregnant women and nursing mothers because it strengthens both mother and child and encourages a plentiful supply of milk. I found it to be so effective that when nursing our son I had to be careful not to eat too much mochi. It's helpful when milk production is low due to exhaustion, stress, or other factors, but can actually cause breasts to become painfully engorged if too much is consumed at a time when you are already producing enough milk. Mugwort mochi is especially recommended since mugwort (a dried green herb) is rich in iron and calcium.

Whole grain mochi is available in many natural foods stores. It can usually be found in the refrigerator or freezer packaged in rectangular blocks weighing about one pound. One brand imported from Japan is sold in vacuum packages containing nine 2″ x 2½″ cakes. Look for this type on the shelf with dry foods.

Many Oriental markets carry mochi made from white sweet rice. Often four or more small, round, flat cakes of white mochi are packaged together on a plastic foam tray and wrapped in plastic. This type is likely to contain additives, preservatives, or sugar, so be sure to check the label before purchasing.

Mochi is versatile and easy to cook. The Japanese often broil or bake it on an oiled sheet until golden and slightly puffed and eat it with a sweet miso topping (see Mochi Dengaku, page 84). Baked mochi can also be cut into bite-sized pieces and added to soups for the last minute or two of cooking. Other favorite ways of cooking mochi include pan-frying and deep-frying. Prepared in those ways, it is usually seasoned with shoyu or dipped in a shoyu and ginger-based sauce (see Pan-Fried Mochi, page 82).

When grilled, broiled, or deep-fried, mochi nearly doubles in size and forms a crisp skin. If cooked too long, the surface will crack and the soft inside part will begin to ooze out, so watch mochi carefully when you are cooking it by any of those methods. Uncooked mochi that has become dry and cracked may be made into a delightful snack: Break it into bite-sized pieces, deep-fry, and lightly salt it. You may soften excessively dry mochi by soaking it for several hours in cold water before preparing it in any of your favorite ways.

*1 teaspoon light or toasted
    sesame oil*
*6 pieces mochi (each approxi-
    mately 2" x 2½")*
*1 sheet nori, toasted*
*2 tablespoons shoyu*
*2 tablespoons water*

## PAN-FRIED MOCHI

Heat the oil in a large skillet, add mochi, and cook, covered, over low heat for 5 minutes or until bottoms are slightly browned. Flip, add 1 tablespoon water to create steam and soften the mochi, cover again, and cook for a few minutes more or just until it is tender. (Watch carefully, and uncover the pan as soon as the mochi is cooked to prevent it from melting.)

Toast nori by passing unfolded sheet over medium heat until its color turns from black to dark green. Cut the toasted nori in half lengthwise, then cut each half into 3 equal pieces. Combine the shoyu and water in a small bowl or dish. Roll the cooked mochi in the shoyu mixture, then wrap each piece in nori. (The nori pieces will not be large enough to completely surround the mochi, which will create a decorative effect.) Serve immediately.

For variation, serve Pan-Fried Mochi with a shoyu-ginger dip: Combine ⅔ cup kombu stock or water with 1 tablespoon shoyu and 2 teaspoons mirin in a small saucepan. Simmer for 1 minute, then allow to cool to lukewarm. Add 1 teaspoon finely grated peeled fresh ginger and, if desired, 3-4 tablespoons finely grated daikon. Serve the dip sauce in small individual bowls.

Deep-Fried Mochi (see page 83) can also be served in either of these two ways. When serving it with shoyu-ginger dip, the grated daikon should be added since it will help digestion of the oil.

SERVES 2

# OZONI (MOCHI SOUP)

This delicious, warming soup is traditionally served as part of the first meal of the New Year.

Soak shiitake in the water for at least 2 hours. Remove, squeeze out excess water, discard stems, and slice caps. Combine shiitake soaking water and kombu in a saucepan and bring to a boil. Remove kombu and save for another use. Add bonito to broth, turn off heat, and let sit for 1-2 minutes. Strain bonito, pressing liquid back into broth, and discard flakes.

Scrub burdock, cut into 2-inch long thin julienne strips, and immediately place in cold water to prevent discoloration. Cut carrot the same as burdock, but a little thicker. Cut scallions into 1-inch lengths. Drain burdock, add to stock along with shiitake and salt, and simmer for 10 minutes. Add carrot and scallion and simmer for 15 minutes. Add shoyu and mirin and continue to cook for 5-10 minutes more.

While soup is cooking, cut each piece of mochi into 4 pieces and place them on a lightly oiled cookie sheet. Bake at 350° F. until slightly browned. (Be careful not to overcook till they burst.) Add mochi to soup for the last minute of cooking only. Serve with a *small* pinch of Japanese 7-spice or cayenne, if desired (place on the table and let each diner season to taste).

SERVES 4

*3-4 dried shiitake mushrooms*
*6 cups water*
*6-inch piece kombu*
*2-3 tablespoons bonito flakes (optional)*
*1 burdock root*
*1 large carrot*
*3 scallions*
*½ teaspoon sea salt*
*1½ tablespoons shoyu*
*½ tablespoon mirin*
*6 pieces mochi (each approximately 2" x 2½")*
*small pinch cayenne or Japanese 7-spice (optional)*

# DEEP-FRIED MOCHI IN BROTH

This simple, tasty, and attractive dish is best during the cooler months.

To prepare broth, bring water and kombu to a boil then remove kombu and reserve it for another use. Add bonito, turn off heat, and let rest for 1-2 minutes, then strain. Press to extract all liquid, then discard flakes. Add shoyu and mirin to stock and simmer briefly. Keep hot (not boiling), or reheat to serve.

Heat oil to 325° F. (until a drop of flour and water batter sinks to the bottom of the pot and immediately rises to the surface). Gently place mochi, 2 pieces at a time, into oil and fry until golden, turning occasionally. Drain on absorbent paper.

In individual serving bowls, place 2 pieces of mochi on the bottom and 1 on top. Pour about ½ cup hot broth over mochi and top with 2 tablespoons grated daikon and a sprinkle of scallion.

SERVES 3

*2 cups water*
*3-inch piece kombu*
*2 tablespoons bonito flakes (optional)*
*2½-3 tablespoons shoyu*
*2 tablespoons mirin*
*oil for deep-frying*
*9 pieces mochi (each approximately 2" x 2½")*
*⅓ cup grated daikon*
*minced scallion for garnish*

## MOCHI DENGAKU (BROILED MOCHI WITH SWEET MISO TOPPING)

¼ cup mellow white or mellow
  barley miso
1 tablespoon lemon juice
1 tablespoon honey (or 2
  tablespoons rice syrup)
1 tablespoon mirin
1 full tablespoon tahini
1 small clove garlic, pressed
  or finely minced
1 teaspoon juice squeezed from
  grated fresh ginger
2 tablespoons water
6 pieces mochi (each 2" x
  2½")

To prepare sweet miso topping, combine and mix first 8 ingredients in a suribachi or small bowl.

Place mochi pieces on an oiled cookie sheet or broiling pan. Broil on both sides until golden and slightly puffed. (Watch carefully to prevent overcooking till they burst.) Spread a thin layer of sweet miso topping on each cake and broil for 1 minute more. Topping should be slightly browned, but not burned. Serve immediately.

SERVES 2

## SWEET MOCHI

For a delicious mochi dessert, cook pieces of mochi as in Pan-Fried Mochi. When tender, dip each piece in warmed rice syrup or corn-barley syrup to coat, then roll in a generous amount of roasted soy flour (kinako).

## SEITAN

Seitan (seasoned wheat gluten, or "wheatmeat") is one of my family's favorite staples, especially in the cool seasons. It is a highly nutritious, protein-rich food, which can be quickly and easily prepared in a variety of interesting ways. Because it resembles meat in taste and appearance, seitan can be used in place of beef or poultry in many recipes. Wheat gluten has long played a significant role in the traditionally meatless diet of Eastern cultures, and it is a favorite among Westerners making the transition to a vegetarian way of eating. Very easy to digest, seitan is also an excellent source of protein for children and sick people.

To make seitan, whole wheat flour is made into dough, kneaded, and then washed to remove the starch (carbohydrate) and bran, thus concentrating the gluten (protein) of the wheat. The gluten is then slowly simmered with vegetables in a shoyu-seasoned broth. The result is a delicious source of high-quality protein. (One 4-ounce serving of seitan contains 15 grams of protein, or 20 percent of the U.S.RDA.)

Just a few years ago seitan was almost unheard of in the U.S., even in natural foods stores, but as it becomes more well-known and popular it is gradually becoming more readily available. Many natural foods stores now offer locally-made seitan sold in bulk or small tubs and/or commercially-made seitan in packages or jars. There are two types made in Japan and sold in jars. One of these, called "Seitan Concentrate," is very salty and is not recommended for use in the following recipes. It is good as a condiment or added to bean soups or stews. The other, called "Seitan Wheatmeat," is fine for general use. However, making seitan at home is not difficult and is much more economical than buying it.

Seitan may be used in stews, soups, spaghetti sauce, chili, deep-fried with or without batter, in deep-dish "meat" pies, sautéed with vegetables, in sukiyaki, sandwiches, stuffings, shishkabob...the possibilities are truly endless. If desired, season the dish you are making with appropriate herbs for a specific flavor. For example, rosemary and/or thyme lend a more meaty taste and, of course, oregano or marjoram, basil, and garlic are indispensable in Italian cooking.

## HOMEMADE SEITAN

Combine 18 cups whole wheat flour and about 11 cups water in a large (8 quart) bowl or a round plastic dishpan. (This makes a lot. This amount works well for my family of two adults and one small boy—we love seitan, and this amount makes a week's worth for us to eat in a variety of dishes. You can halve this recipe or increase it. If you do change the amount, remember to adjust the quantity of cooking broth accordingly.)

Knead the dough, which should be quite sticky, for 5-10 minutes. The easiest way to do this is to set the bowl on a dining table (a counter top is too high) so you can use your weight effectively rather than just using your arm muscles. When flour and water are mixed, vigorously punch the dough with one closed fist, then the other, 300-350 times. Cover dough with cold water and let sit for at least ¾ hour. Knead the dough slowly and carefully in the water until the water becomes thick and white with starch. Pour off the creamy liquid. (This milky, somewhat thick "starch water" from the first few rinses can be saved—it is excellent in bread recipes and as a thickener for stews, sauces, etc.) Gently cover dough with water and knead again. Alternate between warm and cold water rinses, kneading each time to extract the cream-colored starch. A large colander will help in draining off the water from the first several kneadings. At first the dough will seem to be falling apart, and the colander will catch all the little pieces so you don't lose them down the drain. Sometimes a batch of flour disintegrates in the washing, instead of separating into starch, bran, and gluten. In this case you will have to try again with a different type of whole wheat flour.

After about six rinses, the dough should become rubbery gluten. Remaining specks of bran or starch can be rinsed away directly under the tap by pulling the gluten apart and exposing the inside.

Pull off balls, or form gluten into patties, and drop them into boiling water. When they rise, like dumplings, remove and drop them into cold water.

Prepare seitan seasoning stock: In a large pot combine 14 cups cold water, two 6-inch strips of kombu, 1¼ cups shoyu or tamari, ¼ cup grated fresh ginger and, if desired, herbs. For example, try 1 tablespoon each rosemary and sweet basil and 2 teaspoons thyme, or use a combination of bay leaf, garlic, and celery seed. Drop gluten balls into stock, bring to a boil, and cook for 2-3 hours over medium heat with lid ajar. (This may seem like a lot of stock at first, but the gluten absorbs most of it. Also, the length of cooking time depends on the size of your pieces of gluten. I divide the gluten into only four equal pieces and cook them for 3 hours. Smaller pieces take less time.) The seitan is now ready to be used in any of the following recipes.

Seitan will keep for at least one week refrigerated in its cooking broth. For longer storage, add more shoyu or tamari to the broth.

## DELICATESSEN SEITAN SANDWICH

Slice seitan very thin. Spread Quick "Thousand Island" Dressing (see page 10), catsup, or mayonnaise on whole grain bun or sandwich bread and pile several slices of seitan on top. Add a little mustard, if desired, and/or vegetables such as lettuce, tomatoes, sliced red onions, or sprouts. For a real "down home" treat that's sure to please, serve with homemade French fries and beer.

## SEITAN STEW

Bay leaf and rosemary lend a meaty flavor to this delicious and satisfying cold weather dish. It is filling enough to be a meal in itself, or serve a smaller amount at the beginning of the meal in place of soup. Other vegetables such as potatoes or parsnips may be substituted, and ingredients such as elbow noodles or cooked beans may be added.

Bring water and kombu to a boil. Remove kombu and reserve. (It may be re-used to make a stock, or cooked later with beans or vegetables.) Parboil carrots, rutabaga, and green vegetable individually until almost tender. Remove immediately and allow to cool in strainer or colander. Heat oil in a skillet and sauté onion for 3-5 minutes, then add mushrooms and a small pinch of salt, sautéeing for a few minutes more. Add seitan, then vegetables, and sauté all together briefly. Add ½ bay leaf and pinch of rosemary to the 2 cups of stock, then vegetables, and ¼ teaspoon sea salt. Simmer for 5 minutes, add shoyu to taste (about 1 tablespoon), and cook for 2 minutes more. Remove from heat. Dissolve the kuzu in 2 tablespoons water, add to stew, and slowly bring back to a low boil, stirring constantly but gently. Simmer for 2-3 minutes and serve.

For variation, add a little grated fresh ginger along with the kuzu.

SERVES 3

*2 cups water*
*4-inch piece kombu*
*1-2 carrots, cut into bite-sized chunks*
*½ rutabaga (yellow turnip), peeled and cut into chunks (optional)*
*10-12 green beans or Brussels sprouts (or broccoli florets)*
*1 teaspoon unrefined vegetable oil (sesame, safflower, or corn)*
*1 onion, cut into eighths*
*6-8 mushrooms, quartered*
*1½ cups bite-sized chunks seitan*
*½ bay leaf*
*pinch rosemary (optional)*
*¼ teaspoon sea salt*
*1 tablespoon shoyu*
*2 tablespoons kuzu*

## SEITAN POT PIE

This recipe takes a little extra effort, but the result is extra special. You will need some small, deep ovenproof containers. I use 10-ounce heat-resistant glass bowls 4½ inches in diameter and 2 inches deep.

Prepare Seitan Stew as above but reduce the water by ½ cup. Vegetables can be varied according to season and availability. Bite-sized chunks of potato are a favorite addition.

While stew is cooking, prepare double pie crust (see below). Preheat oven to 375° F. Roll out bottom crusts and line the containers. Fill with hot stew to ¼ inch from top. Cover with top crust. Fold edge of top crust under bottom crust and crimp edges well to prevent leaking. Prick a few holes in the top crust with a knife or fork to allow steam to escape. Bake for 45-50 minutes.

MAKES 5-6 4½-INCH PIES

*2 cups whole wheat pastry
    flour
1 cup unbleached white flour
½ teaspoon sea salt
¼ cup light sesame or saf-
    flower oil
¼ cup corn oil
½ cup ice cold water*

## PIE CRUST

For a single crust pie, simply halve the recipe.

Measure all ingredients as accurately as possible. Combine the flours and salt well in a mixing bowl. Add the oils all at once, and quickly and lightly work it into the flour with a fork until the mixture looks like small pebbles. (Do not use your hands to mix pie dough since this results in a less flaky crust.) Add all the water, and with the fork quickly mix the dough until it forms a ball in the center of the bowl. If not using immediately, wrap dough in waxed paper and refrigerate.

Roll out half the dough on an unfloured board or counter, between sheets of waxed paper if you prefer. Start by rolling out from the center in all directions using light, short strokes. As the dough becomes thinner use longer strokes and more pressure. When the dough is the desired size, gently loosen it from the board with a spatula. Fold in half, carefully lift into the pie plate, and unfold. Trim the edges. If using waxed paper, simply peel off the top layer of paper, invert dough over pie plate, and peel off remaining layer of paper.

Roll out the top crust. After filling the pie, lay the top crust over it and trim so that it hangs over the pie plate ½ inch. Fold the excess under the bottom crust and seal by pressing with tines of a fork all the way around the edge of the crust. Slit the top crust in several places to allow steam to escape.

MAKES TWO 9-INCH CRUSTS OR ONE DOUBLE CRUST

## SEITAN BOURGUIGNONNE

*1 tablespoon light sesame oil,
    butter, or soy margarine
1 large onion, thinly sliced
8-10 mushrooms, sliced
    (optional)
1½-2 cups seitan, sliced
1½ tablespoons whole wheat
    flour or arrowroot powder
1 tablespoon shoyu
pinch white pepper
½ bay leaf
½ teaspoon thyme
1 cup dry red wine mixed with
    ⅓ cup water
6 ounces egg noodles or
    artichoke noodles (fettuccine
    or shells)
minced parsley for garnish*

This recipe is always a hit, even with those guests who are not familiar with natural foods. When I served it to my father, he raved about it and asked how I made the beef so tender!

Heat oil or butter in a skillet and sauté onions over low heat for 5 minutes. Add mushrooms and sauté together briefly, then add seitan and brown lightly. Sprinkle with flour or arrowroot and toss to coat evenly and roast slightly. Add shoyu, pepper and herbs, and wine mixture to just cover the seitan. Stir gently then simmer, covered, for 20-30 minutes.

Cook the noodles according to directions on the package. After rinsing and draining, divide noodles and place in individual serving bowls. Cover with a generous portion of Bourguignonne and garnish with parsley.

SERVES 3

# SEITAN SUKIYAKI

This simple, attractive, one-dish meal is cooked and served in a large cast iron or stainless steel skillet. Vary the vegetables according to the season and availability, but keep in mind an attractive variety of colors. The following is just one possibility.

Place water, kombu, and shoyu in a large skillet and bring to a boil. Add vegetables, starting with the ones that require the longest cooking time. For example, in this recipe, place the carrots, squash, cabbage, and seitan in the skillet, arranging them so each variety is separate, not mixed with the others, and so colors are attractive; for example, separate squash and carrots, both "yellow" vegetables, with cabbage or seitan.

Cover and simmer until vegetables are nearly tender. Add tofu, cover, and simmer for about 5 minutes more. Add watercress for just the last minute of cooking. Uncover skillet and serve immediately by placing it in the center of the table. Provide diners with small individual bowls of your choice of the two dip sauces given below.

SERVES 4

*2 cups water*
*4-inch piece kombu (optional)*
*2 tablespoons shoyu*
*1 large carrot, cut into ¼-inch diagonal slices*
*several slices winter squash (acorn, butternut, or buttercup)*
*¼ head cabbage, cut into 4-5 wedges*
*2 cups seitan, sliced or cut into bite-sized pieces*
*½ pound tofu, cut into ¾-inch cubes*
*1 bunch (6 cups loosely packed) watercress or other bright, leafy green*

## MISO-TAHINI DIP

Blend all ingredients until smooth.

*¼ cup mellow white miso*
*3 tablespoons tahini*
*2 tablespoons lemon juice*
*¼ cup water*
*1-inch knob of fresh ginger, peeled and sliced*

## SHOYU-GINGER DIP

Simmer first 3 ingredients together for 1-2 minutes, remove from heat, and add ginger.

*1 cup kombu stock or water*
*shoyu to taste (approximately 1½ tablespoons)*
*1 tablespoon mirin*
*1 tablespoon peeled and grated ginger*

*1 cup pinto beans or navy
    beans*
*4-inch piece kombu (optional)*
*4½ cups water*
*1 teaspoon unrefined vegetable
    oil (light sesame, safflower,
    or corn)*
*1-2 cloves garlic, minced*
*1 onion, thinly sliced*
*1 rib celery, thinly sliced
    (optional)*
*1 carrot, chopped*
*1½ cups seitan, chopped*
*½ cup (dry measure) elbow
    noodles*
*½ teaspoon sea salt*
*1 bay leaf*
*½ teaspoon oregano*
*barley or red (rice) miso to
    taste (approximately 2 table-
    spoons)*

## SEITAN PASTA E FAGIOLI

This is a variation on traditional Italian pasta and bean stew. Though, of course, not a usual part of the recipe, seitan is a great addition to this hearty dish. Besides lending rich flavor, it adds plenty of protein to enhance that of the beans.

Soak beans in water to cover for 3 hours or overnight. Discard soaking water and combine beans with kombu and 4½ cups fresh water in pressure cooker. Boil, uncovered, for 10 minutes. Skim off any foam that rises to the surface. Cover, bring to pressure, lower heat, and cook for 1 hour. (If pot-boiling, add more water as needed and simmer until beans are completely tender—about 2 hours.)

Meanwhile, heat oil in a skillet and sauté garlic and onion for 2-3 minutes. Add celery, carrot, and seitan and sauté for 2-3 minutes more. Reduce heat to very low, cover, and cook for 10 minutes more. Add a *little* water if necessary to prevent scorching.

Parboil noodles in lightly salted water for about 5 minutes or until they just begin to soften. Immediately drain, rinse under cold running water until thoroughly cool, drain again, and set aside. (Noodles should be undercooked.)

When beans are cooked and pressure has returned to normal, add salt, bay leaf, oregano, and vegetable-seitan mixture. Simmer for 15 minutes, add parboiled noodles, and simmer for 5 minutes more. Turn off heat, dissolve miso in 2 tablespoons water, add to pot, stir, cover, and let sit briefly before serving.

This hearty stew goes well with corn bread, or other whole grain breads, and cole slaw.

# FU GLUTEN CAKES

An excellent source of easily digestible vegetable protein, *fu* was developed centuries ago by Buddhist monks, probably as a meat substitute, and today is still popular in the Orient. A "cake" of fu resembles a crisp, light biscuit. When cooked, it readily softens and enhances the flavors of other ingredients with its light wheat flavor.

The first step in making fu is the same as for seitan: wheat flour is mixed with water and kneaded to activate the wheat's natural gluten, then rinsed to remove the starch and bran. But next the pure, protein-rich gluten that remains is mixed with more flour, wrapped around a pole in 4 layers, and toasted in an oven after each layer is added. The fu is then lightly steamed to soften its texture and leaven it. Finally it is sliced and dried.

It is difficult to make fu at home, but there are several types of commercially manufactured Japanese fu available in Oriental markets and natural foods stores. The most common of these are *kuruma*, *zeni*, *zenryu*, and *shonai* fu. In Japanese kuruma means "wheel" and zeni, "coin." Both are doughnut shaped, but kuruma fu is much larger. Zenryu fu is an intermediate-sized, doughnut-shaped whole wheat variety. While all the other types are a combination of wheat gluten and unbleached white flour, zenryu fu is made with half gluten flour and half whole wheat flour. Shonai fu, also called *ita fu,* is a thin, flat variety that is especially good in miso soup. It may be broken into small pieces and added dry to the soup.

To reconstitute, soak fu in lukewarm water for 5 to 10 minutes. When it is soft, gently squeeze out excess water and add the fu to stews, casseroles, beans, and simmered vegetable dishes. For a clear soup, simmer whole cakes of fu for 15 minutes in a vegetable or kombu stock seasoned with natural soy sauce and serve with a sprinkle of minced scallion. Add fu to hearty stews during the last 15 minutes of cooking to let it absorb the full flavor of the ingredients. When camping or traveling, add fu to soups and one-pot meals—it is the perfect lightweight, high-protein food.

*8 cups kombu-bonito or
    kombu-shiitake stock (see
    page 143)*
*6 pieces kuruma fu or 18
    pieces zeni fu*
*1 teaspoon sea salt*
*1 tablespoon mirin*
*2 tablespoons shoyu or tamari*
*3 large collard or bok choy
    leaves or several turnip or
    spinach leaves*
*1 cup scallion, cut into ½-inch
    lengths*

# CLEAR SOUP WITH FU

Clear soups are simple and elegant. Though they may be served anytime, their lightness makes them especially appealing in warm weather or as an accompaniment to large, festive meals.

While preparing the stock, soak the fu in lukewarm water for 10 minutes, then gently squeeze out excess moisture between the palms of your hands. Add the fu to the simmering stock along with the salt, mirin, and shoyu or tamari. Simmer for 5-10 minutes, then add scallions and simmer for just 3-5 minutes more.

Meanwhile, parboil the greens in a separate pot of lightly salted water until just tender, then immediately drain and toss to cool quickly and prevent further cooking. Spinach becomes tender in just 30-60 seconds and collards take 5-7 minutes, so watch the cooking greens carefully. If overcooked they will lose their color, and the visual effect of the soup will suffer. Slice the greens and set aside.

Carefully place 1 piece of kuruma fu or 3 pieces of zeni fu in each bowl. Add a small mound of greens, then cover with the broth. Serve hot!

**SERVES 6**

# FU-BEAN SOUP

*2 cups pinto beans (or kidney,
    azuki, or navy beans)*
*6-inch piece kombu (optional)*
*9 cups water*
*1 bay leaf*
*1½ teaspoons sea salt*
*1 large onion, thinly sliced,
    or leek, sliced diagonally ¼
    inch thick*
*1 large carrot, diced*
*1 rib celery, sliced diagonally
    ⅛ inch thick (optional)*
*5-6 rounds kuruma fu or 8-10
    zenryu fu or 12 rounds zeni
    fu, broken into bite-sized
    pieces*
*3 tablespoons barley miso or
    red (rice) miso*

Soak beans for 3 hours or overnight, drain, and discard soaking water. Combine beans with the 9 cups water and, if desired, kombu in a pressure cooker. Bring to a boil and simmer, uncovered, for 10 minutes, then bring to pressure, lower heat, and cook for 50-60 minutes. (If pot-boiling you will need to add more water occasionally. Cook for 2-3 hours, until beans are tender, then proceed.) Reduce pressure and uncover.

Break bay leaf into 2-3 pieces and add to beans along with salt, vegetables, and fu. (It isn't necessary to presoak the fu here.) Simmer for 20 minutes more, then remove from heat. Dissolve the miso in 2 tablespoons water and add. Let rest briefly before serving. If desired, garnish with minced parsley or scallion.

**SERVES 6-8**

# FU STEW

Combine water and kombu in a large saucepan and bring to a simmer, uncovered, over medium heat. As soon as it begins to boil remove kombu and reserve for another use. Slice leek on the diagonal, ¼ inch thick. Peel rutabaga and cut into ½-inch cubes. Heat oil in a skillet and sauté leek for a minute. Add rutabaga and a small pinch of salt, sauté briefly, then lower heat, cover, and cook for 5-10 minutes. Cut carrot and potato into large chunks, add to skillet, toss, cover, and let cook for 10 minutes more. Soak fu in lukewarm water for 10 minutes, then cut into bite-sized pieces.

Add fu to soup stock along with the partially cooked vegetables, green beans, bay leaf, rosemary, and salt. Simmer for about 20 minutes or until vegetables are tender. Add shoyu and simmer for 1 minute more. Remove from heat. Dissolve the kuzu or arrowroot in 3 tablespoons water and add to stew while stirring briskly. Return to heat and simmer for 1-2 minutes or until broth is thick and clear. Serve hot.

SERVES 4

*4 cups water*
*6-inch piece kombu*
*1 leek*
*1 small rutabaga*
*1-2 teaspoons unrefined vege-*
*table oil (light sesame, saf-*
*flower, or corn)*
*1 large carrot*
*1 potato (optional)*
*12 pieces zeni fu or 8 pieces*
*zenryu fu or 4 pieces*
*kuruma fu*
*10-12 green beans, cut into*
*1-inch lengths*
*½ bay leaf*
*small pinch rosemary*
*(optional)*
*½ teaspoon sea salt*
*2 tablespoons shoyu*
*3 tablespoons kuzu or*
*arrowroot powder*

# HATO MUGI ("JOB'S TEARS")

*Hato mugi* resembles barley, but it is actually a member of the rice family. An easily digestible whole grain with only the tough outer husk removed, hato mugi contains less vitamin $B_1$ than brown rice, but approximately twice as much protein, iron, vitamin $B_2$ and fat, and slightly more calcium.

Hato mugi has long been respected in the Far East, where it was originally used by the Chinese for medicinal purposes. Since ancient times Oriental medicine practitioners have recommended hato mugi for strengthening the stomach and nervous system, purifying the blood, and restoring health. Since it is so effective in helping the body to discharge toxins, people who are sick and weak, and women who are pregnant, nursing a baby, or menstruating should eat it sparingly.

This nutritious and health-giving food is most commonly cooked in combination with brown rice or brown rice and azuki beans. A good proportion is about 20 percent hato mugi (1 part hato mugi to 4 parts rice). Pressure cook or boil as you would for plain brown rice (see pages 77-78), or follow the recipe for Fluffy Brown Rice with Hato Mugi given below. Hato mugi can also be cooked with rice and 7-10 parts water to 1 part grains until very soft, then seasoned with umeboshi or miso to make *o-kayu* ("soft rice"). This Japanese folk remedy is still commonly used to restore strength in cases of colds, flu, or digestive disorders.

Hato mugi adds flavor and body to soups and stews that require lengthy cooking. It should be added at or near the beginning of the cooking time. Try using it in place of up to half the barley in Mushroom-Barley Stew (see page 111). If hato mugi is washed and soaked for several hours or overnight, cooking time will be reduced. Besides its use as a food, it is often roasted and used with roasted barley for a tea. Hato mugi tea is available in some natural foods stores. It is delicious served hot, and when chilled it makes a refreshing summer drink.

## FLUFFY BROWN RICE WITH HATO MUGI

*2 cups brown rice*
*½ cup hato mugi*
*½ teaspoon sea salt*
*5 cups water*

Although this combination of brown rice and hato mugi may be prepared in any way you usually cook brown rice, roasting the grains first results in a light, fluffy texture. After cooking, the individual grains are more separate than in regular boiled or pressure-cooked rice.

Combine the grains in a pot or bowl and wash them by adding cold water, stirring, then draining. Repeat several times until the rinse water is clear. Drain well.

Place a large un-oiled skillet over medium heat and pour in the washed grains. Stir constantly until the grains are golden brown (in a cast iron skillet it takes 10-15 minutes). Meanwhile, combine water and salt in a heavy pot with a tight-fitting lid, and bring to a boil. For a dry, fluffy result, it is important that the water is boiling when you add the grain. *Slowly* add the roasted grain to the boiling water to prevent it from boiling over. Let it boil rapidly for 1 minute, then lower heat, cover, and simmer for 50 minutes to 1 hour. Do not remove the lid while the grain is cooking. For best results, simmer over medium-low heat for the first 15 minutes, then reduce heat to very low for the remainder of cooking time. As you transfer the grain to a serving bowl, lightly toss and cut through any clumps with the side of a rice paddle or wooden spoon.

This dish is excellent served with Hearty Gravy or Kuzu Sauce. Leftovers are excellent in Ginger Fried Rice.

SERVES 5

# SPLIT PEA SOUP WITH HATO MUGI

This thick, hearty, warming soup is especially satisfying on a cold day.

Wash peas and hato mugi and combine them along with 8 cups water in a large pot. If desired for flavor, add the kombu. Bring to a boil and skim off any foam that rises to the surface, then lower heat and simmer with the lid ajar until the peas are tender (1-1¼ hours). Check occasionally and add more water as necessary. (It generally takes about 10 cups of water total, but adding it all at the beginning might result in a too-thin soup.)

Cut the onion in half from top to bottom, then slice it into thin half moons. If using a leek, slice it through halfway lengthwise and wash it well to remove dirt that may be trapped between the layers, then slice it thinly on the diagonal. Heat the oil in a medium-sized skillet and sauté onion or leek for 2-3 minutes. Add the carrot and celery and a small pinch of the salt and sauté for a few minutes more. Add a *little* water if necessary to prevent scorching, then cover, and cook over very low heat for 10 minutes. Remove from heat and uncover.

When the peas are tender, add sautéed vegetables and remaining salt and simmer soup for 20 minutes more. Add a little more water, if necessary, and stir frequently to prevent scorching. (If the bottom does burn, carefully pour the soup into another pot without scraping the burned portion.) Add herbs, if desired, and shoyu or miso. If using miso, dissolve it in a little water before adding it to the soup. Simmer for 2 minutes more. Garnish with parsley and serve hot.

Leftovers taste even better the next day, but be careful not to burn the soup when reheating. Split pea soup becomes very thick as it cools, then thins again when reheated. I find it best to add just a little water and a little more shoyu or miso before warming the leftovers.

SERVES 6

*2 cups green split peas*
*⅓ cup hato mugi*
*3-inch piece kombu (optional)*
*1 large onion or leek*
*1-2 teaspoons light sesame or corn oil*
*1 large carrot, diced*
*1 rib celery, thinly sliced*
*1½-2 teaspoons sea salt*
*1 bay leaf*
*½ teaspoon dried basil (optional)*
*¼ teaspoon ground or whole celery seed (optional)*
*1 tablespoon shoyu or 2 tablespoons red or barley miso (or to taste)*
*minced parsley for garnish*

# RICE SYRUP

Pastries were introduced to Japan by Portuguese and Dutch traders in the 1500s. There was nothing comparable among Japanese sweets until then. Even today most Japanese do not make Western-style pastries in their homes—their household ovens are not suited to it. Pastries are readily available from bakeries, however, and are commonly given as gifts. Although rice syrup (*mizu ame*) was used throughout Japan to make sweets, today it is not easy to find in Japan. Except for brands sold in natural foods stores, rice syrup that can be found almost always contains added sugar.

Fortunately, most rice syrup found in the U.S. is a delicious, mildly-flavored natural sweetener made from only rice, water, and a little sprouted rice or whole barley. The natural malting process involves drying and crushing the sprouted grain and mixing it with a large amount of soft-cooked rice. The enzymes from the malted grain ''digest'' the carbohydrates in the cooked rice, converting them into natural sugars. The resultant sweet mash is then strained, and the liquid is boiled down to a thick syrup.

While some brands of rice syrup are still traditionally made by the natural malting process, others, including some available in natural foods stores, are now being made by adding enzymes to the cooked rice to convert the carbohydrates to sugars. Check the list of ingredients on the jar label and choose one that includes ''sprouted barley,'' ''malted barley,'' ''sprouted rice,'' or ''malted rice.'' Since enzymes are not required to be listed, brands made with added enzymes may list rice and water as the only ingredients. Rice syrup is usually found only in natural foods stores. When it can be found in Oriental markets, it often contains added sugar.

The stiffness of rice syrup varies according to the brand and the temperature at which you store it. If the syrup is too stiff to pour, place the uncovered jar in a saucepan with two inches of water and simmer for a minute or two or until the syrup is warm and pours easily.

Rice syrup does not have the overly sweet, sharp flavor of sugar and honey. Since the more complex sugars contained in rice syrup are digested more slowly and enter the bloodstream steadily over a longer period of time, there is less likelihood that they will upset the body's blood sugar balance.

Creative macrobiotic and natural foods cooks have found that rice syrup is an excellent sweetener, and are using it in baked goods for a perfect marriage of East and West.

Whole, natural ingredients lend a much fuller flavor than those that have been highly refined and, as is often the case, laced with additives and preservatives. Natural desserts are somewhat less sweet, but more flavorful than those made from de-natured ingredients and white sugar. For the recipes here, if you prefer a sweeter taste increase the amount of rice syrup or substitute part with maple syrup or honey. A lighter texture can be achieved by increasing the leavening or substituting unbleached white for some of the whole wheat flour.

Though I don't feel it's necessary in baking to eliminate leavening agents entirely, it is possible to use less and still get good results. Choose a preservative-free brand of yeast, such as Red Star, and an aluminum-free baking powder. For those concerned with reducing their salt intake, there are low-sodium baking powders available. Your pastries made from whole grain flour and a moderate amount of leavening will not be as light as highly leavened refined white flour pastries, but you will have the satisfaction of serving delicious desserts that are much more nutritious.

## ALMOND COOKIES

Although I often think of cookies as too plain to serve to guests, these have a little fancier, more ''professional'' appearance and a wonderful flavor as well.

Preheat oven to 350° F. Toast ¾ cup of the almonds in a dry skillet, stirring constantly over medium heat until they begin to brown (about 5 minutes). In a blender, grind toasted almonds until finely chopped to a meal. In a medium-sized bowl beat oil and syrup together. Add egg, vanilla, and almond extract and beat well. Add baking soda, salt, almond meal, and 1 cup of the flour, and mix. Add remaining ½ cup flour a little at a time. The dough should be very stiff. If necessary, add a little more flour.

Drop dough by rounded teaspoonfuls onto lightly oiled cookie sheets. Press cookies with a fork to about ½-inch thickness. Press an almond into the center of each cookie. Bake for 12-15 minutes or until bottoms are golden. Remove and cool on a wire rack.

MAKES 24 TWO-INCH COOKIES

*1 cup almonds*
*¼ cup unrefined corn,*
*    sesame, or safflower oil*
*½ cup rice syrup*
*1 egg, slightly beaten*
*1 teaspoon vanilla*
*⅛ teaspoon almond extract*
*    (optional)*
*¼ teaspoon baking soda*
*¼ teaspoon sea salt*
*1½ cups (approximately)*
*    whole wheat pastry flour*

## TOLL HOUSE COOKIES

Any present or former fan of chocolate chip cookies will enjoy this wholesome version of that popular treat. Rice syrup gives cookies a crunchy texture, unlike honey, which tends to make them soft and cake-like.

Preheat oven to 375° F. and lightly oil two cookie sheets. Combine oil, rice syrup, and vanilla in a medium-sized mixing bowl. Add egg and mix well. Add salt and baking soda, then oats and wheat germ. Gradually mix in the flour until you have a stiff dough. Fold in the carob chips and walnuts, then drop the dough onto the oiled cookie sheets by slightly rounded teaspoonfuls. Allow room for expansion. Bake for 10-15 minutes, then immediately place cookies on wire racks to cool. Store cookies in an airtight container when thoroughly cool.

Though this is rather unorthodox, I like to bake all drop cookies for 10-12 minutes, then flip and bake for 2-3 minutes more.

MAKES ABOUT 24 TWO-INCH COOKIES

*⅓ cup corn oil*
*⅔ cup rice syrup*
*1 teaspoon vanilla*
*1 egg, lightly beaten*
*    (optional)*
*pinch sea salt*
*¼ teaspoon baking soda*
*½ cup rolled oats*
*¼ cup wheat germ (or*
*    increase flour to 1½ cups)*
*1⅓ cups whole wheat pastry*
*    flour*
*⅓ cup carob chips*
*½ cup chopped walnuts*

*⅓ cup corn oil*
*⅔ cup rice syrup*
*1 teaspoon vanilla*
*1 egg, lightly beaten*
*pinch sea salt*
*¼ teaspoon baking soda*
*¼ teaspoon ground cloves*
*½ teaspoon cinnamon*
*1 teaspoon ground ginger*
*1¾ cups whole wheat pastry*
  *flour*
*½ cup raisins*

## RAISIN SPICE COOKIES

Preheat oven to 375° F. and oil two cookie sheets. Combine oil, rice syrup, and vanilla in a medium-sized mixing bowl. Add egg and beat well. Add salt, baking soda, and spices. Gradually mix in the flour to form a stiff dough. (The mixing will take some effort.) Fold in raisins, then drop the dough onto the oiled cookie sheets by slightly rounded teaspoonfuls. Allow room for expansion. Bake for 10-15 minutes, then place cookies on wire racks to cool.

If you like your cookies on the crunchy side, bake them for 10-12 minutes, then flip and bake them for about 3 minutes more.

MAKES ABOUT 24 TWO-INCH COOKIES

*¼ cup corn, light sesame, or*
  *safflower oil*
*⅔ cup rice syrup*
*1 teaspoon vanilla*
*1 egg, slightly beaten*
  *(optional)*
*¾ cup soy milk, almond milk*
  *(see recipe on p. 41), or*
  *water*
*2 cups whole wheat pastry*
  *flour*
*¼ teaspoon sea salt*
*1 teaspoon baking soda*

## VANILLA CAKE

Preheat oven to 350° F. and oil a 9" x 9" or 13" x 7" baking pan. Combine the oil, syrup, and vanilla in a medium-sized bowl. Add egg and beat well. (If omitting the egg, increase liquid to 1 cup.) Add soy milk and mix thoroughly. Sift the dry ingredients together, stir to distribute salt and baking soda evenly, then add dry ingredients to wet. The batter should be thin enough to pour. If too thick, add a little more soy milk, almond milk, or water. Pour batter into baking pan, shake pan gently to spread batter evenly to the corners of the pan, and bake for 30-40 minutes.

When the cake is done it should pull away from the sides of the pan and spring back when the top is lightly pressed. Cool the pan on a wire rack. When cake is cool, top with your favorite frosting or ladle Fresh Fruit Topping (see recipe page 185) over each slice before serving.

## BLUEBERRY CAKE

Proceed as for Vanilla Cake, combining ¾ teaspoon cinnamon with dry ingredients and folding ½ pint washed and stemmed blueberries into the batter before baking.

This cake is especially good with Walnut Topping (recipe follows). Evenly distribute the topping over the batter before baking.

# WALNUT TOPPING

Try this simple and delicious topping on cakes, cupcakes, and muffins.

Heat the oil in a small skillet and add nuts. Stir and roast until nuts are fragrant. Remove from heat and add syrup and cinnamon. Sprinkle on top of batter before baking.

*1 tablespoon corn, light*
*    sesame, or safflower oil*
*⅔ cup chopped walnuts*
*2 tablespoons rice syrup*
*½ teaspoon cinnamon*

# FRENCH APPLE CRISP

Combine raisins and water in a small saucepan and simmer for 10-15 minutes. Pour raisin cooking liquid into measuring cup and add water, if necessary, to equal ½ cup. Peel, quarter, remove cores, and slice apples. Set them aside. Combine next eight ingredients to make a crumbly mixture. In another bowl combine apples, raisins, and rice syrup. Mix well. (Use the larger amount of syrup if apples are tart.)

Arrange half the apple mixture in a baking pan or casserole dish, sprinkle half the raisin water over and top with half of the rolled oat mixture. Repeat layers. Cover and bake at 350° F. for 25 minutes. Remove cover and bake for 20 minutes more.

SERVES 8

*¼ cup raisins*
*1 cup water*
*6-8 apples*
*1½ cups rolled oats*
*¼ cup whole wheat pastry*
*    flour*
*¼ cup sesame seeds*
*¼ cup chopped walnuts*
*¼ cup corn or light sesame*
*    oil*
*½ teaspoon cinnamon*
*¼ teaspoon sea salt*
*¼ teaspoon nutmeg (optional)*
*⅓ to ½ cup rice syrup*
*½ cup raisin cooking water*

# CINNAMON ROLLS

This is a basic sweet dough that can be used in a variety of ways.

Dissolve yeast in the tepid water and let sit until frothy (for 5-10 minutes). Meanwhile, beat oil, salt, and syrup together. Mix in egg, if using. Add water, then yeast, and mix well. Add flour one cup at a time, blending vigorously. Add just enough flour so it isn't sticky, but the dough should be soft. Knead for 5 minutes. Add a little more flour if dough becomes sticky while kneading. Place dough in an oiled bowl and turn it once to coat with oil (this keeps it from drying out while rising). Cover the bowl with a damp towel and set in a warm place.

When the dough has doubled in size (after about 1½ hours), punch it down, turn it out onto a lightly floured board and knead briefly, adding more flour if dough is sticky.

For cinnamon rolls, roll out dough into a large rectangle about ⅓-inch-thick. Combine syrup and cinnamon and dribble over

*½ tablespoon active dry yeast*
*¼ cup tepid water (105° F.)*
*¼ cup unrefined corn or light*
*    sesame oil*
*½ teaspoon sea salt*
*¼ cup rice syrup*
*1 egg, slightly beaten*
*    (optional)*
*1 cup lukewarm water*
*5-5½ cups whole wheat pastry*
*    flour*
*½ cup rice syrup*
*1 teaspoon cinnamon*
*⅓ cup raisins*

dough. Sprinkle on raisins. Roll the dough into a cylinder starting at one long edge. Pinch to seal seam. Slice into 1-inch-thick rounds and lay rolls flat on a lightly oiled cookie sheet, allowing at least one inch between them for expansion. Let rise in a warm place until almost doubled in size (about 40 minutes). Preheat oven to 350° F. and bake for 20-25 minutes.

To make Sticky Buns, dribble a little rice syrup over the rolls before baking.

MAKES 18 ROLLS

## GLAZED SWEET ROLLS

*2 tablespoons kuzu*
*¼ cup water*
*½ cup rice syrup*
*1 teaspoon lightly grated*
*orange or lemon rind*
*(preferably organic)*

Follow directions for sweet dough as in Cinnamon Rolls.

After the dough has risen to double in size, punch down and knead on a lightly-floured board just until smooth. Pinch off pieces of dough and shape into smooth balls about 1½ inches in diameter. Space 2 inches apart on lightly oiled baking sheets, cover with a slightly damp towel, and allow to rise in a warm place until doubled in size (30-40 minutes). Place in a preheated 425° F. oven and bake for 15 minutes. Cool on wire racks, then place rolls on a platter.

For glaze, crush lumps of kuzu into a coarse powder before measuring. Thoroughly dissolve kuzu in the water, and combine with warmed syrup and citrus peel in a small saucepan. Bring to a boil while stirring constantly. Simmer for 1-2 minutes, allow to cool for 10-15 minutes, then dribble glaze over buns while syrup is still warm.

MAKES 2 DOZEN

## HOT CROSS BUNS

Follow directions for sweet dough as in Cinnamon Rolls, but add 1½ teaspoons allspice when mixing oil and syrup and knead 1 cup of raisins into the dough after the first rising. Shape pieces of dough into balls 1½ inches in diameter. Space them 2 inches apart on lightly oiled baking sheets, cover with a slightly damp towel, and allow to rise in a warm place for 30-40 minutes. With a sharp knife make ¼-inch deep crosses on top of each bun. Place in a preheated 425° F. oven and bake for 15 minutes. Cool on wire racks, then place buns on a platter and lightly glaze as for Sweet Rolls.

MAKES 2 DOZEN

# DOUGHNUTS

Follow directions for sweet dough as in Cinnamon Rolls.

After the first rising, roll out the dough to ½-inch thickness, and cut doughnut shapes using a glass or a jar top for the outside dimension and a bottle top to punch out the holes. Allow doughnuts to rise for about 30 minutes, then deep fry in 350° F. oil until golden brown. Turn once or twice while frying to be sure they are evenly cooked. Remove, shake excess oil back into the pot, and place doughnuts on wire racks or on absorbent paper. Dip one side in maple syrup, or a mixture of toasted unsweetened coconut flakes and date sugar, or date sugar and cinnamon, or dip in maple syrup then in toasted coconut flakes. You can also glaze them as for Sweet Rolls.

(As always when deep-frying, do not add too many pieces at once. Overcrowding will cause the temperature of the oil to drop radically, resulting in oily, unevenly cooked doughnuts. Always remove all of one batch from the oil before adding more.)

# CORN-BUCKWHEAT BREAD

Preheat oven to 350° F. Combine dry ingredients. In a medium-sized bowl beat oil and rice syrup together well. Add vanilla and egg, if using, and mix thoroughly. Add water and beat until well blended. (If omitting egg, use the larger amount of water.) Fold dry ingredients into wet, mixing as little as possible. If necessary, add a little more water. (Batter should be thick but not stiff.) Pour into an oiled 11″ x 7″ or 8″ x 8″ baking pan and bake for 25-30 minutes. When done, a toothpick inserted into the center should come out clean, and the bread should pull away from the sides of the pan. Cool in the pan on a wire rack.

To make muffins, oil muffin tin, fill wells ¾ full, and bake at 400° F. for 15-20 minutes. Remove muffins from tin 5-10 minutes after removing tin from oven. With the addition of a little more water, this batter also makes scrumptious pancakes.

*1½ cups corn meal*
*½ cup whole wheat flour*
*¼ cup buckwheat flour*
*½ teaspoon sea salt*
*¼ teaspoon aluminum-free baking powder*
*1 teaspoon baking soda*
*¼ cup unrefined corn or light sesame oil*
*¼ cup rice syrup*
*1 egg (optional)*
*½ teaspoon vanilla (optional)*
*1 to 1¼ cups lukewarm water*

*¼ cup unrefined corn or light
    sesame oil
⅓ cup rice syrup
1 egg, lightly beaten (optional)
1½-1¾ cups water (or water
    reserved previously from
    cooking noodles )
2 cups whole wheat flour
⅓ cup buckwheat flour
½ teaspoon sea salt
1 teaspoon baking soda
¼ teaspoon aluminum-free
    baking powder*

## QUICK WHOLE WHEAT-BUCKWHEAT MUFFINS

Buckwheat flour adds a hearty flavor to these simple muffins. Served with soup and salad, they round out a perfect lunch.

Preheat oven to 400° F. and oil a muffin tin. Combine measured oil and syrup in a medium-sized bowl and beat well. Mix in the egg, add the water, and mix vigorously with a wire whisk or beat with an electric mixer for 1-2 minutes. (If omitting the egg, use the larger amount of water.)

In a separate bowl thoroughly mix all dry ingredients. Add dry ingredients to wet and mix with as few strokes as possible. Fill the muffin cups to within ¼ inch of the tops and bake for 20-25 minutes or until tops spring back when lightly pressed. Cool the pan on a wire rack for 5-10 minutes before removing the muffins. They are delicious fresh and warm, but store well if first allowed to cool completely.

MAKES 1 DOZEN

## RICE BRAN

Because of our consumption of refined grains, many of us in the West may be deficient in B vitamins. One good source of these essential vitamins is vegetables pickled in rice bran (*nuka*). Properly made, fresh rice bran pickles are mild and delicious, and enhance the appetite.

Pickles, especially rice bran pickles, are an excellent source of beneficial *Lactobacillus* bacteria, which aid in maintaining strong, healthy intestines. Because of their nutritional value, in traditional cultures it is considered important for a homemaker to know how to make a variety of tasty pickles.

Besides being high in B vitamins, particularly $B_1$ and niacin, rice bran is abundant in both linoleic acid and vitamin E, which work together in the body to reduce cholesterol. So, by all means add some lightly-toasted nuka to your favorite bread and muffin recipes. To toast, place bran in a dry skillet over medium-low heat. Stir constantly for just a few minutes until the bran releases a nutty fragrance.

Rice bran can be tied in a small drawstring bag and used in place of bath soap. Soap takes the oil out of the skin, but rice bran gently stimulates and cleans, and adds a little oil to dry skin. It is particularly good for babies. If you use a small sack of bran for washing dishes, you will notice its softening effect on your hands.

Rice bran is an excellent wood polish and cleansing agent. Tied in a dry cotton bag and used to wipe woodwork, over time the oil in the bran imparts a deep luster—a characteristic of Japanese temples.

## RICE BRAN MUFFINS

Warm a medium-sized skillet over low heat, add rice bran, and stir constantly for about 3 minutes. Immediately remove bran and set aside. If using raw wheat germ, toast it in the skillet by stirring constantly until it is golden-brown and fragrant. Remove from skillet and set aside.

Preheat oven to 400° F. and oil a muffin tin. Combine the ¼ cup oil and the rice syrup in a large mixing bowl, stir in water and egg, then salt, baking soda, bran, wheat germ, lemon peel, and cinnamon. Gradually add flour to make a thick but pourable batter. (With the egg it will probably take 1¼ cups of flour, otherwise about 1 cup.) Stir just until the batter is evenly moist, then fold in the raisins. Fill muffin tins ¾ full and bake for 20-25 minutes or until the tops of the muffins spring back when lightly pressed. Cool in tins on a wire rack for 5-10 minutes, then carefully remove muffins.

MAKES 10 LARGE MUFFINS

*½ cup rice bran, lightly toasted*
*¼ cup light sesame or corn oil*
*¼-⅓ cup rice syrup*
*1 cup water*
*1 egg, lightly beaten (optional)*
*¼ teaspoon sea salt*
*¾ teaspoon baking soda*
*½ cup wheat germ*
*1½ tablespoons lightly grated fresh or 2 teaspoons dried lemon peel*
*½ teaspoon cinnamon*
*1-1¼ cups whole wheat pastry flour*
*½ cup raisins*

## QUICK RICE BRAN PICKLES

This type of pickle tastes best in spring, summer and fall. Starting a batch of quick rice bran pickles means making a commitment of a couple minutes each day, since it is essential to thoroughly stir the mix every 24 hours. Also, you must add "tempering" vegetables each day for the first 7-10 days to prepare the medium for pickling. After that you can harvest delicious, nutritious pickles daily.

In a non-metal crock or tub, mix bran, salt, chili pepper, and kombu well by hand. Add koji, water, and eggshell and mix thoroughly. Insert 2 or 3 vegetables (see below), whole or in large pieces, at different levels in the mash (these needn't be top quality since they won't be eaten). Cover crock and put in a cool, dark place. After 24 hours, remove and discard the vegetables added the day before, mix the mash, and put more vegetables in. Continue this process every day for a week to 10 days. These first pickled vegetables will be sharp and salty and inedible, but they serve to "mellow" the mash in order to give you the delicious pickles you can begin harvesting soon.

Now you are ready to start making edible pickles.

Pickling cucumbers and young, tender daikon are especially good pickled in this medium but carrots, turnips, red radishes, green pepper, celery, and Chinese cabbage also make tasty pickles. Wash vegetables, pat dry, and insert in the mash whole or in large pieces. You can pack different types of vegetables

*2 pounds rice bran, sifted*
*¾ cup sea salt*
*3 dried red chili peppers, seeded and cut into small pieces*
*2 cups water, boiled then cooled*
*two 6-inch strips dry kombu, cut into small pieces*
*1½ cups koji, soaked 15 minutes in tepid water to just cover (or omit koji and substitute 1 cup beer for 1 cup water—do not boil beer)*
*1 crushed eggshell, inner membrane removed (eggshell is optional, but aids preserving)*

together, but they shouldn't be so crowded that they touch each other. Pickles will be ready in 1-4 days, depending on type and size.

To serve, remove pickles, rinse briefly, and slice. When mash becomes too wet, press a sieve into it and with a cloth soak up the liquid that enters it. Add a little more bran and salt. If proper care is taken, the mix will last for 3-6 months.

Each day when you harvest your pickles remember to mix the mash thoroughly to prevent it from souring or becoming moldy. And add more vegetables to ensure a continuous supply.

See Koji-Takuan Pickles (page 115) for another delicious and healthful rice bran pickle recipe.

*Itsuko Onozaki and Jan Belleme clean three giant bamboo shoots in preparation for cooking.*

I remember making a comment in Japan about the fact that I had seen many different fruits but no pears during the several months that we had been there. The answer was, simply, "They have not been in season." Although it is different in the cities, the principle of eating locally-grown vegetables and fruits in season is taken for granted in rural Japan. Land is in short supply even in the country, yet nearly everyone grows as much of their food as space permits.

In preparation for the cold winter months when fresh, locally-grown vegetables are hard to get, Japanese women put vegetables by in several ways. They prepare a variety of pickles from several different vegetables. They sun-dry some vegetables and fruits such as *kaki* (Japanese persimmons); and they store other vegetables—in the garden under a heavy mulch, in underground pits, in makeshift root cellars, or simply in a cool, well-ventilated place not subject to freezing temperatures.

Wild varieties are an important part of the ever-changing vegetable scenario. In spring, whenever there was a tea break at the Onozakis', or any informal gathering including older people, the conversation would inevitably turn to wild foods foraging. Someone had just spotted the first *fuki* (butterbur— a plant with the bitter taste characteristic of the wild greens of early spring). It wouldn't be long before the *zenmai* (fiddlehead ferns) and *take no ko* (bamboo shoots) appeared. "Keep your eyes open!" was the order of the day. No matter how busy Mrs. Onozaki was, she would take time to gather each of these precious foods in its own time, or she would make sure that someone else did.

Wild vegetables are so important to traditional Japanese cuisine that some standard holiday menus are centered around them. For example, wild mugwort (*yomogi*) is available by the end of February and homemade wild mugwort *mochi* is an integral part of the Girl's Day celebration, which falls on March 3rd.

Naturally, those vegetables freshly picked from the garden or foraged from the wild are more vital and delicious than store-bought. But when you buy vegetables, as most of us must, select those that look freshest and most alive. In winter we can eat in season by choosing those vegetables that are winter-hardy, store well, or have been naturally preserved by pickling or drying.

Many of the vegetables used in Japanese cooking are familiar to Americans. Several, such as corn, cabbage, and bell peppers, were probably introduced to Japan from America or Europe. Many others I have never seen being sold fresh in this country. Neither of these categories will be included here. Instead, I have chosen vegetables that are important in Japanese cooking and, if not well-known, are at least available here. Some were selected both for their flavor and for their healthful qualities. All the following vegetables are sold in many Oriental and natural foods stores and most can be found in some of the bigger supermarkets.

## SHIITAKE (LENTINUS EDODES)

*Shiitake*, Japanese forest mushrooms, are one of the Orient's most exotic and delicious foods. Their distinctive taste lends a gourmet flair to almost any dish. Though fresh shiitake are still a rare and high-priced find in markets in this country, this may change as North Americans try their hand at cultivation. There are already a few commercial growers of shiitake in the United States, and small-scale mushroom farming is becoming popular. My husband and I have been growing shiitake for several years and have found our area of western North Carolina to be well-suited to this rewarding and exciting hobby.

Besides being a delicious and versatile vegetable, shiitake has a long history of use as an important folk medicine. Recently scientists have published remarkable findings that largely verify the main tenets of shiitake folklore.

The use of shiitake—which derives its name from the Shii tree (*Quercus cuspidata*), an oak of central and southern Japan upon which the mushroom most frequently grows—probably dates back to ancient China before the spread of rice cultivation, at a time when most daily food was picked wild in the forest. Gradually, perhaps instinctively at first, early food foragers must have noticed the relationship between eating shiitake and relief from specific ailments. This knowledge was passed on to future generations, and a folklore surrounding shiitake evolved. As culture developed and healing became more specialized, herbalists began concentrating shiitake's medicinal components by boiling or slow-cooking to make potent teas and pastes. It was found that the high temperature of ordinary cooking does not destroy shiitake's healing qualities—quite the contrary, cooking enhances them, making a concentrated medicine for the treatment of flu, heart disease, high blood pressure, obesity, and problems related to sexual dysfunction and aging.

By the fourteenth century shiitake had become part of the largely vegetarian diets of China, Korea, and Japan. With an understanding of the shiitake life cycle, cultivation techniques slowly developed. During the past quarter of the present century, aided by modern laboratory techniques, the cultivation of shiitake has become Japan's leading forest industry, with an annual production of about 100,000 metric tons of mushrooms.

Each year in the spring and fall, hardwood logs are cut, dried to just the right degree, and inoculated with shiitake spawn and placed in a damp, shady area to develop for about two years. After this preparatory period, every spring and fall dozens of mushroom caps push up almost in unison through the bark of

*Top, a shiitake grower drills holes in oak logs. Bottom, the logs are inoculated by hammering wood plugs of shiitake spawn into the holes.*

each log, sometimes almost covering the log's surface. The mushrooms are gathered and dried or sold fresh at local markets. Traditionally, shiitake were sun-dried. Now they are almost always dried by machine—in large commercial situations gas-fueled hot air ovens are used, and on a smaller scale, food dehydrators.

The harvesting time of shiitake is very important. If the mushroom is left on the log too long it will completely open and shed its spores. The resulting thin, dark, flat mushroom is inferior in both taste and medicinal qualities. Picked at just the right time, shiitake are still a little closed and have thick, fleshy, slightly rounded caps full of spores. These are prized for their excellent taste and health-giving qualities.

Some Japanese families supplement their rice farming with shiitake cultivation. John and I worked with one such family, the Watanabes. In our visits to the Watanabe home, we participated in many aspects of shiitake farming and enjoyed several fine meals of traditional Japanese dishes, including shiitake prepared in a variety of ways. Our favorites were baked fresh shiitake, shiitake tempura, and shiitake miso soup.

After returning to the United States our interest in shiitake continued, and we wondered whether modern science had discovered the healing powers of this mushroom. We later learned that scientists both here and in Japan have actually been conducting sophisticated experiments using shiitake. The studies, about thirty in all, focus on shiitake's ability to combat virally-induced diseases, and their ability to rapidly lower blood cholesterol. These two qualities of shiitake strike at the heart of modern civilization's most dread spectres: cancer and heart disease.

Two of the most dramatic studies were performed on animals but have obvious human application. At the National Cancer Research Center in Tokyo, mice suffering from sarcoma, a type of virally-induced cancer, were treated with small doses of shiitake over short periods of time. The results, published in *Cancer Research* (November, 1970), showed that about six out of ten mice had complete tumor regression. At slightly higher concentrations shiitake was 100 percent effective—all mice showed tumor regression.

Similar studies have shown that animals given shiitake extract reject repeated attempts at tumor transplantation. It is now believed that shiitake cause the body to reject foreign substances. The key to this mechanism seems to be the shiitake spore itself. Once in the digestive organs, each spore is thought to release a tiny harmless virus particle. This virus stimulates the production of interferon, an intercellular messenger that travels to neighboring healthy cells and warns of viral diseases, including some forms of cancer.

The second area of current medical investigation is shiitake's amazing ability to rapidly lower blood cholesterol. Since cholesterol is linked to many serious diseases such as atherosclerosis and stroke, scientists have been working to isolate and identify the active agent in shiitake mushrooms. This substance, now called eritadenine, was given to rats on a high-cholesterol diet and, as reported in the *Journal of Nutrition* (1966), their blood cholesterol rapidly dropped 25 to 45 percent.

The person most responsible for stimulating scientific interest in shiitake mushrooms is Dr. Kisaku Mori of Japan. Dr. Mori established the Institute of Mushroom Research in 1936 and, until his death, worked with scientists from around the world to document the medicinal effects of shiitake. Using sophisticated analytical techniques, Mori found shiitake high in many enzymes and vitamins not usually occurring in plants. His findings, published in *Mushrooms as Health Foods (Shiitake Kinkoko*, Japan Publications, 1974), were extensive. Working for years with human subjects, he discovered that shiitake was effective for a long list of ailments including cancer, high blood pressure, sexual problems, excess cholesterol, gallstones, hyperacidity and stomach ulcers, diabetes, vitamin deficiencies, anemia, and the common cold.

Though shiitake are expensive, we feel the rich flavor and vitality they add to a meal more than make up for the cost. Shiitake are delicious simmered in a seasoned broth, in sautéed or stir-fried dishes, noodle broths, soups, stews, fried rice or noodles, sauces and gravies. To bring out shiitake's full flavor, lightly season with shoyu and, if desired, mirin and garlic or ginger. When using shiitake in steamed or boiled dishes such as sukiyaki, they should first be simmered in broth seasoned with shoyu and mirin.

I am including one of our favorite recipes for fresh shiitake in case you are lucky enough to find them in your local natural foods store or supermarket. Select fresh mushrooms with thick caps. Though the tops are usually medium to dark brown and smooth, the variety with whitish creases in the caps are delicious. Thin, limp shiitake with upturned caps are of poor quality. Check the color of the underside, too. If fresh, it will be cream-colored, not brownish.

Though the texture of reconstituted dried shiitake cannot compare with that of the fresh mushrooms, shiitake's exquisite flavor is even more concentrated with drying. Dried shiitake are readily available in Asian markets and natural foods stores, and are quickly becoming a common item in supermarkets. They are available packaged whole in a variety of grades, and also sliced or in pieces. Though more expensive, large thick whole mushrooms whose caps are turned under are by far superior in flavor as well as nutritional and medicinal value. Stored in an airtight container in a cool, dry place, dried shiitake keep almost indefinitely.

To reconstitute, submerge dried shiitake in water for at least two to three hours, and preferably overnight. (Since they float,

*Top, shiitake at the Watanabe shiitake farm in Yaita, Japan is ready to be picked. Bottom, Itsuko picks shiitake from some old shiitake logs discarded in the forest.*

you will need to weigh them down with a saucer or other suitable object.) Once rehydrated, cut off and discard stems or reserve them for making soup stock, and use only the caps. The shiitake soaking water makes a wonderfully rich stock for soups, stews, sauces, and gravies. Used with their soaking water, these mushrooms make a superb miso soup (see recipe page 8).

## BAKED FRESH SHIITAKE

15 average-sized shiitake (2½ to 4 inches in diameter)

1½ tablespoons shoyu

1½ tablespoons dry white wine, sake, or mirin

2 teaspoons unrefined light sesame or toasted sesame oil

¾ cup water or kombu stock

Each spring and fall we check our shiitake logs daily, eagerly awaiting the mushrooms' biannual appearance. Though we enjoy dried shiitake year-round, for this wonderful treat there is no substitute for tender, succulent, fresh shiitake.

Preheat oven to 425° F. Remove stems from shiitake. If they are very dry, submerge them in water for 15-20 minutes. Using a sharp knife, lightly score caps with an "X." Combine remaining ingredients and mix well. Place shiitake, caps up, in a dry baking pan and pour 1 tablespoon of seasoning liquid over each mushroom.

Bake shiitake for 40 minutes. About every 10 minutes turn and baste each mushroom in the liquid in the pan. (You may need to tilt the pan so the liquid goes to one end.) If desired, sprinkle with a little juice of grated fresh ginger one minute before removing from the oven. Baste again just before serving so that caps are moist. Serve 3 large or 5 smaller shiitake per person.

SERVES 3-5

## MUSHROOM GRAVY

4 dried shiitake

2 cups water

1 tablespoon Italian olive or light sesame oil

1 clove garlic, minced (optional)

4 tablespoons whole wheat or unbleached white flour

½ teaspoon sea salt

¼ bay leaf (optional)

2-3 teaspoons shoyu

2 teaspoons mirin (optional)

Submerge shiitake in the water and soak for at least 2 hours. Cut off and discard stems, and dice caps. Heat oil in a small skillet, add garlic and shiitake, and sauté for 2-3 minutes. Add flour and stir constantly for 1-2 minutes. Slowly add the shiitake soaking water while stirring briskly. Add salt and, if desired, bay leaf and bring to a simmer, stirring occasionally. Simmer for 15 minutes. Add shoyu and mirin and simmer for 2 minutes more. Delicious over grains, "burgers," and grain and vegetable casseroles.

MAKES 1⅔ CUPS

## MUSHROOM-BARLEY STEW

At its best on cold fall or winter days, this thick, warming stew is hearty enough to be a meal in itself.

Wash barley and place in a large pot along with shiitake, water and, if desired, kombu. Use a small plate or bowl to keep mushrooms submerged. Soak for 3 hours. Remove kombu and reserve for another use. Remove and slice shiitake (discard stems). Return shiitake to pot, bring to a boil, and add salt and bay leaf. Reduce heat, cover, and let simmer.

Meanwhile, heat oil in a skillet and sauté onion until translucent. Add carrot and celery and sauté for 5 minutes. Remove from heat and set aside. After simmering soup for 1 hour or so, add oregano, sautéed vegetables, and a little more water if necessary. Simmer until vegetables are tender (about 15 minutes). Remove from heat. Dilute the miso in a little water and add to soup. Serve hot, garnished with minced parsley or scallion if desired.

**SERVES 4**

*½ cup barley*
*6 dried shiitake*
*7 cups water*
*6-inch piece kombu (optional)*
*1 teaspoon sea salt*
*1 small bay leaf*
*1 teaspoon unrefined vegetable oil*
*1 onion, sliced*
*1 carrot, sliced*
*1 rib celery, sliced*
*¼ teaspoon oregano (optional)*
*2 tablespoons (or to taste) red or barley miso*

## EGG DROP SOUP

This is a nutritious and strengthening soup that is quick and simple to prepare.

There are two methods for making kombu-shiitake stock. The first is to soak the shiitake and a 6-inch piece of kombu together in 6 cups of water for 2-3 hours. Remove shiitake and kombu, squeezing excess water from shiitake. Cut off and discard stems. Thinly slice caps and return them to the soaking water, which is now the stock to be cooked. Set kombu aside and reserve for another use.

The second method is to soak the shiitake only, then slice and return to soaking water along with kombu. Bring this just to a simmer, uncovered, over medium heat, then remove kombu.

Add salt, leek, and mirin to simmering stock. Cook for ten minutes, then add greens and simmer just until they are tender (5-10 minutes). Add shoyu and simmer for one minute more. If you are not ready to serve the soup, remove pot from heat and set aside with lid ajar. Just before serving, bring soup to a low simmer over medium heat and slowly dribble the beaten eggs into the pot while stirring the soup with a gentle circular motion. Simmer for one minute only, then serve. Garnish with a sprinkle of finely minced scallion.

**SERVES 4**

*3-4 dried shiitake*
*6-inch piece kombu*
*6 cups water*
*½ teaspoon sea salt*
*1 leek, cut into ½-inch-thick diagonal slices (optional)*
*1 teaspoon mirin (optional)*
*2 cups chopped greens (kale, mustard, collards, turnip, bok choy, etc.)*
*1-1½ tablespoons shoyu*
*2 eggs, beaten well*
*minced scallion for garnish*

*In rural Japan, daikon dry in the autumn sun. Naturally dried daikon are said to make the finest pickles.*

## DAIKON (RAPHANUS SATIVUS)

The two Japanese characters that make up the word daikon (Japanese radish) mean "great root." Although the great roots typically weigh three to five pounds and measure eighteen inches long, one variety can grow to over 100 pounds!

Pickled, raw, dried, or cooked, the leaves and roots of daikon have long been one of Japan's most prized and widely used vegetables. Folk healers and scientists alike have noted the outstanding nutritional and medicinal qualities of raw and pickled daikon. Simply steamed with a little soy sauce, or elegantly prepared in the temple tradition with white miso sauce, the flavor of cooked daikon root is truly unique and delicious.

Raw daikon is used throughout Japan to complement the taste of oily or raw foods and, more importantly, to aid in their digestion. Laboratory analysis has shown that the juice of raw daikon is abundant in digestive enzymes similar to those found in the human digestive tract. These enzymes—diastase, amylase, and esterase—help transform complex carbohydrates, fats, and proteins into their readily assimilable components. Traditional Japanese restaurants serve grated daikon (daikon *oroshi*) in tempura dip to help digest oils, or shredded daikon with raw fish to help digest the protein. Grated daikon is a wonderful aid to people with a weak digestive system. It is important, however, to use grated daikon immediately. In just thirty minutes nearly 50 percent of its enzymes are lost.

The enzymatic action of daikon juice has recently gained the attention of scientists in Japan. At Tokyo's College of Pharmacy, researchers have discovered that daikon juice actually inhibits the formation of dangerous chemicals in the body. Nitrosamines, a type of carcinogen, can form in the stomach from chemicals present in both natural and processed foods. Daikon juice contains substances identified as "phenolic compounds" that can block this potentially dangerous reaction. Thus, a diet including raw daikon may reduce the risk of cancer.

My personal experience with raw daikon shows its effectiveness as a diuretic and decongestant. As a diuretic, raw daikon promotes the discharge of excess water by the kidneys. The result is increased urination and gradual reduction of the swelling condition known as edema. As a decongestant, the enzymes in daikon juice seem to help dissolve mucus and phlegm in the respiratory system and facilitate their discharge from the body.

Daikon, whether dried, raw, pickled, or in combination with other ingredients in various tonics, is useful in treating a truly extensive list of ailments. Books on Oriental medicine, such as Michio Kushi's *Natural Healing Through Macrobiotics* (Japan Publications, 1978) and Noboru Muramoto's *Healing Ourselves* (Avon, 1973) contain details on the use of daikon in traditional folk medicine.

For fresh use, be sure to select daikon that are firm and crisp. Limp roots with withered skins are past their prime and are likely to be dry inside. Daikon are almost always available in Oriental food stores and are commonly sold in natural foods stores and supermarkets.

When using it as a cooked vegetable, keep in mind that daikon has dense flesh and must be cooked well. Daikon's flavor is sweetest when it is completely tender. You can test whether it is done by inserting a toothpick or skewer into the thickest part of the vegetable. It should pierce the flesh easily, with little resistance.

Daikon is also available dried. Some dried daikon (also called *kiriboshi* daikon) is still being made by a traditional process carried out only in the winter months. Fresh daikon root is simply shredded, then allowed to dry thoroughly in the sun. Drying gives daikon a sweet, mellow taste and preserves most of its nutritional value. Stored in a sealed package in a cool, dry place, dried daikon keeps well, thus providing a good supplement to a winter diet.

To reconstitute dried daikon, soak it in lukewarm water for 10-15 minutes if you are planning to boil it, 30-60 minutes if sautéeing or pickling. Remove daikon, squeeze out excess water, chop, and add to soups and stews or sauté alone or with other vegetables.

## DAIKON ROUNDS WITH MISO SAUCE

Here is a simple, delicious, and attractive way to serve daikon. Though peeling is not generally necessary or recommended, this particular dish will look best if you lightly peel the daikon.

Cut a 6-inch length of root into ½-inch-thick rounds and steam or boil them in lightly salted water until soft. Be sure they are completely tender. (This dish should be served hot, so prepare miso sauce while daikon is cooking.) Any of the several sauces in the Miso section will work well. Try Piquant Miso-Ginger Sauce thinned with water to desired consistency, White Sauce, or Sweetened Miso Sauce. If using White Sauce in this recipe, reverse the quantities of white miso and tahini, using 3 tablespoons mellow miso and 2 tablespoons tahini.

Arrange 3 daikon rounds in each individual serving bowl or small plate. Neatly spread miso sauce over each round. If desired, garnish with a parsley or watercress sprig or a few toasted black sesame seeds. Or use a more exotic garnish—in early spring wild violets are perfect. You can even eat the flowers!

SERVES 4

4-inch piece kombu
1 medium-sized daikon root,
    cut into medium bite-sized
    chunks
1 large carrot, cut into large
    bite-sized chunks
water to almost cover vege-
    tables
pinch sea salt
2-3 teaspoons shoyu

## SIMMERED DAIKON AND CARROTS

This simple dish brings out the natural sweetness of the vegetables.

Depending on the size of the daikon, it may be easier to slice it
lengthwise in half or quarters before cutting into chunks.   Cut
carrots larger than daikon since they cook more quickly.   Place
kombu in a medium-sized pot, place vegetables on top, and add
water to almost cover.   Bring to a boil, add salt and shoyu, then
lower heat and gently simmer until vegetables are tender.
Remove from broth and serve hot.

SERVES 4

## DAIKON OROSHI (GRATED DAIKON)

As mentioned previously, grated raw daikon is often served with
tempura and fish since it helps in the digestion of oils and protein.   The Japanese generally use a ceramic or porcelain grater
for this purpose (see page 198), but any type that can grate the
vegetable finely will do.   There should be a fair amount of juice
created and only small particles, none large enough to sink your
teeth into.   Always grate  daikon just before serving, never in
advance.

Grated daikon has too strong a flavor to be eaten as is.   When
served with fish, shoyu (to taste) is often added.   Usually when
served with tempura or other fried foods, or in dips for *nabe*
(simmered mixed vegetables and seafood) or *sukiyaki*, grated
daikon is added to a kombu, kombu-bonito, or kombu-shiitake
stock seasoned with shoyu and sometimes mirin or sake.   The
daikon is always added after the broth is finished and has cooled
considerably.

1 cup kombu stock or water
1½ tablespoons shoyu
1 tablespoon mirin
¼ cup grated daikon
2 teaspoons peeled and grated
    fresh ginger (optional)

## DIP SAUCE

This delicious, multipurpose dipping sauce can be made in just a
few minutes.   The grated daikon makes it especially appropriate
for fish or fried foods such as tempura, but this sauce can be
used to add flavor to dishes such as sukiyaki and baked or pan-
fried mochi as well.

Combine first three ingredients in a saucepan and simmer for one
minute.   Allow to cool to lukewarm or room temperature.   Just
before serving, grate daikon and, if desired, ginger and add to
dip.

MAKES 1⅓ CUPS

# VEGETABLE MEDLEY

Soak daikon in lukewarm water for 30-60 minutes. Remove, squeeze out excess water, and chop. Reserve soaking water. Cut carrot into matchsticks or red pepper into thin slices. Heat oil and sauté daikon for 1-2 minutes. Add carrot or pepper and sauté briefly, then add scallions and sauté for two minutes more. Add a small pinch of salt, the mirin, and ¼ cup daikon soaking water. Cover and simmer for 5-10 minutes. Add greens and shoyu and simmer for a few minutes more. Add a little more daikon soaking water if necessary to prevent scorching. Greens should be tender but still colorful.

SERVES 3

*1 cup dried daikon*
*1 carrot or ½ sweet red pepper*
*1 teaspoon unrefined sesame, safflower, or corn oil*
*3-4 scallions, cut into ½-inch lengths*
*small pinch sea salt*
*2 teaspoons mirin (optional)*
*approximately ¼-½ cup daikon soaking water*
*4 cups sliced greens (such as kale, turnip or mustard greens, bok choy)*
*2 teaspoons shoyu (or to taste)*

# KOJI TAKUAN PICKLES

Many of the healthful properties of raw daikon are preserved and sometimes even amplified by the pickling process. Although there are many ways to pickle daikon, the *takuan*, or rice-bran daikon pickle, is legendary for its characteristic taste, smell, and nutritional benefits. Although its odor is at first unusual to some Westerners, its daily consumption, particularly the sweeter homemade variety, can become "habit forming," especially for those with low-level vitamin B deficiency.

Developed by vegetarian monks during Japan's feudal period, takuan are a rich source of B vitamins as well as microorganisms which, in the small and large intestines, aid digestion, synthesize vitamins, and inhibit the growth of undesirable bacteria. Rice bran (*nuka*), the main ingredient in the pickling medium of takuan, is particularly high in thiamine and niacin. Analysis of koji takuan, made using the recipe that follows, shows that a four-ounce serving contains nearly 50 percent of the daily requirement of niacin. In contrast, salt-pickled daikon contained an insignificant amount of this important B vitamin.

Takuan also contain large amounts of *lactobacilli* bacteria which, as explained in the Pickle section, are important to the digestion of grains and vegetables. It has been determined that one ounce of sweet koji takuan contains about 800,000 *lactobacilli*. Eating takuan regularly is an excellent way to maintain these beneficial bacteria.

*approximately 40 daikon*
*8 pounds rice bran*
*5 pounds rice koji*
*2 pounds sea salt*
*2½ cups raw soybeans*
*15 dried red chili peppers (a natural preservative), seeded and cut into ½-inch pieces*
*2 handfuls dry kombu, cut into small pieces*
*dried peel from 8-10 oranges or tangerines (peel and allow to dry for 1 week), broken into small pieces.*

Takuan are available in some Oriental and natural foods stores. However, the Oriental food store varieties usually contain a yellow dye for appearance and are either pasteurized or have added preservatives. Some contain sugar and others are salt-pickled daikon that are made without rice bran. The natural foods store varieties are of higher quality. However, because of the long distance they must travel, these pickles are either very salty or they have been pasteurized. Pasteurization not only destroys useful microorganisms, but also most of the enzymes, which are heat sensitive.

A common practice in this country is to soak store-bought takuan in water for a few hours or overnight to reduce their saltiness. This does remove much of the salt, but since takuan's vitamins, enzymes, and microorganisms are all water-soluble, they leach out of the pickle into the soaking water. Depending on the length of soaking and the amount of water, much of takuan's nutritional value can be lost.

The solution, of course, is to make your own takuan pickles from high-quality ingredients. This can be an exciting family adventure as well as a great learning experience for everyone. Although making delicious takuan depends more on experience than on knowledge of microbiology, a basic understanding of the process can help avoid failure. Takuan pickling, like making sauerkraut or cucumber pickles, is technically called "lactic acid fermentation." The key points for making this type of pickle successfully are discussed in the pickle section. Reread the paragraph on lactic acid fermentation before making takuan.

Takuan are traditionally made in the fall, when the weather has become cool. In rural Japan one can still see rows of brilliant white daikon, hanging from their leaves, drying in the autumn sun. When dry, the daikon are placed in a rice bran mix for varying lengths of time, depending on the recipe. There is one record of takuan being pickled for 313 years! (Although long aging gives takuan a deep, rich flavor, you won't have to wait that long.) The following technique results, in just two to three months, in a delicious takuan with a subtle sweetness suited to American tastes. This pickle, Koji Takuan, is much less salty and is higher in *lactobacilli* than standard Japanese takuan. Koji Takuan should be made and aged in the fall and eaten throughout winter and early spring.

This recipe can be halved or doubled, according to your needs. Simply adjust the quantity of the mix ingredients and the size of the container.

Scrub daikon and hang, with leaves intact, in a cool, dry, well-ventilated place, such as a protected porch for 1-2 weeks. They should not touch each other and must be brought in at night if freezing temperatures are expected. You should be able to bend the daikon into a semicircle when they are dry enough. Do not let them get too dry. Slice off the top of the root, just below where the leaves attach. Cut leaf stems about two inches above this junction and discard the section. (It contains too much dirt, which might contaminate the pickles.) Cut off and discard any shriveled root tips, and set the leaves aside. For pickling you will need a large (about 5-gallon), preferably wide, leakproof wooden, stoneware, or plastic crock or pail.

By hand thoroughly mix all other ingredients together. Sprinkle a little salt in your pickling container and cover the bottom with a thin layer of mix. Tightly pack one layer of whole daikon roots side by side on top of mix. Add enough mix to just cover the daikon. Continue alternating layers of daikon and mix until all vegetables are used. Cover the top layer generously with mix (about a ⅔- to ¾-inch layer) and sprinkle with a small handful of sea salt.

Next, lay the dried daikon leaves on top. Cover the leaves with a sheet of plastic, then with a flat, strong lid that fits inside the crock. Place two heavy rocks or other weights, each about equal to the weight of the daikon, on top of the lid. It is essential to age the pickles in a cool, dark place such as a basement, shed, or attic (40° to 60° F. is ideal). Freezing temperatures will not hurt the pickles, but prolonged exposure to extreme cold will slow fermentation considerably. After several days, when liquid rises up above the lid, remove one of the rocks. The pickles will be ready to eat in 2-3 months.

Mature Koji Takuan are light yellow throughout. To test, remove and rinse one pickle and cut it in half. If the color is uniform and the flavor is mildly salty with sweet undertones, you may begin enjoying them daily. Remove a few days supply of takuan from the pickling container, then replace lid and rocks. Unlike saltier takuan, these will not keep in warm weather, so if you have any left in the spring, remove from the mash and refrigerate in a covered container. To serve, quickly rinse the bran mix off and slice the pickled daikon thinly on the diagonal.

Chinese cabbage can be substituted for the daikon in Koji Takuan. Use 10-12 pounds of Chinese cabbage (4 small- to average-size heads) and reduce the quantity of all mix ingredients by 50 percent. The raw soybeans can be eliminated.

Combine mix ingredients. Wash the heads of cabbage and cut each lengthwise into sixths. (Slice only up through the core, then pull the sections apart by hand.) Cut away all the core or leave a thin strip of core to hold the sections together. Pat dry. Sprinkle mix ¼-inch thick over the bottom of the crock. Add a single layer of cabbage sections, packed tightly together. Knead the cabbage briefly with the heel of your hand to soften it and make it lay flat when pressed. Add mix to almost cover the cabbage. Continue alternating layers of cabbage and mix until all the cabbage is used. Completely cover the top layer with mixture and sprinkle with a tablespoon of sea salt.

Cover the contents of the crock with a piece of plastic, then with a flat, strong lid that fits inside the crock. Continue as for Koji Takuan. These pickles will be ready to eat in just one month. Remove a section of cabbage from the crock, rinse it and cut into small pieces to serve.

## HOKKAIDO PUMPKIN
## (CURCURBITA MOSCHATA)

Interestingly, this delicious vegetable originated in the U.S. Though not originally or exclusively grown in Hokkaido, Japan's northernmost island, once cultivation began there, Hokkaido-raised pumpkins quickly became prized for their sweet, rich flavor. Eventually this popular vegetable became commonly known in the U.S. as "Hokkaido pumpkin."

*Kabocha*, as it is called in Japan, is a winter squash. It might have been dubbed "pumpkin" in this country because of the bright red-orange skin color of one of the two most popular varieties. Orange Hokkaido is a beautiful, teardrop-shaped squash with smooth-textured flesh. It is delicious baked, simmered, mashed, in pies, and sliced, batter-dipped, and deep-fried as a tempura vegetable. Sometimes it is marketed in the U.S. under the names Baby Red Hubbard and Red Kuri.

Green Hokkaido has a rich, sweet, yellow flesh similar in flavor to buttercup squash, but with a drier texture. At most about eight inches in diameter it is a little smaller than buttercup, with a ribbed and rounded shape and a gray-green, slightly waxy skin. Green Hokkaido is excellent baked, stuffed, mashed, or sliced and used in tempura. Its texture is flakier than Orange Hokkaido, and it needs careful attention when simmering or steaming or it will begin to fall apart if cooked too long.

Hokkaido Pumpkin may be sold as "Japanese Squash." If you cannot find either of these varieties, substitute buttercup or acorn squash in the recipes that follow.

## MILLET-PUMPKIN LOAF

This bright yellow and orange loaf is simple to prepare and attractive, especially when served with contrasting foods such as lightly steamed greens and azuki beans or hijiki.

Wash millet well in several changes of rinse water. Combine millet, water, salt, and pumpkin in pressure cooker. Bring up to

*2 cups millet*
*4 cups water*
*½ teaspoon sea salt*
*2½ to 3 cups seeded, peeled, and diced Hokkaido pumpkin*

pressure, lower heat, and cook for 20-25 minutes. (If pot-boiling, use 7½ cups water and ¾ teaspoon salt. Bring to a boil, lower heat, cover, and simmer for 30-40 minutes.) Remove from heat, allow pressure to return to normal, then pour or scoop the mixture into two standard-size loaf pans. (If desired, mash lightly with a potato masher before filling pans.) Allow to rest for at least 20-30 minutes before slicing. The loaf will become firm as it rests and cools.

Serve with Kuzu Sauce (page 183).

SERVES 6-8

## BAKED HOKKAIDO PUMPKIN

Another simple dish, this method of cooking brings out the pumpkin's full flavor and sweetness. Preheat oven to 400° F. Cut pumpkin in half from top to bottom and scoop out seeds. Depending on the size of the vegetable, number of people being served, and how quickly you want it to cook, cut each half into 3 or 4 wedges. Rub the flesh of each piece with a small pinch of sea salt, then rub with unrefined vegetable oil to lightly coat (light sesame oil is best). Wrap the wedges in aluminum foil individually or in pairs. (They will cook a little more quickly if wrapped individually.)

Place on a baking sheet and bake for 30-40 minutes or until tender. To test for doneness, pierce the thickest part of the flesh with a skewer, toothpick, or chopstick. It should be soft but not mushy. To avoid overcooking, check several times and remove from the oven and unwrap as soon as pumpkin is completely tender.

SERVES 6-8

## SIMMERED PUMPKIN

Place kombu in the bottom of a medium-sized saucepan, top with pumpkin chunks, add water to almost cover, and bring to a simmer. Add salt and shoyu and simmer gently just until pumpkin is tender. Remove from broth and serve.

SERVES 4-6

*4-inch piece kombu*
*½ to 1 Hokkaido pumpkin,*
   *peeled and cut into large*
   *bite-sized chunks*
*water to cover*
*small pinch sea salt*
*1-2 teaspoons shoyu*

## PUMPKIN FLOWERS

This beautiful addition to a meal is easy to make.

Use leftover cooked pumpkin, or steam or bake raw pumpkin until tender. If still in the skin, scrape the flesh out with a spoon. Mash to remove any lumps. When smooth, place a rounded teaspoonful in the center of a double-layer square of cheesecloth. Gather the corners of the cheesecloth and hold them tightly just above the pumpkin ball with one hand while you give the ball a gentle half-twist with your other hand. Carefully unwrap and place on a serving plate or arrange three "flowers" in each small individual serving bowl.

## CHINESE CABBAGE
## (BRASSICA CAMPESTRIS)

Chinese cabbage is one of the most commonly used vegetables in Oriental cooking. Its distinct, slightly sweet flavor is milder than that of Western cabbage, and its crisp texture more tender. The Japanese enjoy it lightly boiled, in soups and stews, in a type of one-pot cooking called *nabemono,* and pickled in a variety of ways. The tender inside leaves are also good steamed, in pressed salads, and added to stir-fried dishes toward the end of cooking. It is delicious in tossed salads. This distinctive green is high in vitamin C and vitamin A.

A cool weather crop, Chinese cabbage is usually eaten in Japan from late summer to early winter, though in some areas a smaller crop is planted in the spring and harvested in early summer. Chinese cabbage forms a large, compact, cylindrical head with pale-green, wrinkled leaves. It is available in most supermarkets, as well as in Oriental and natural food stores, and is sometimes sold under the name "nappa."

## CHINESE CABBAGE ROUNDS

Simple yet appealing, this is especially good on a warm day. In cooler weather it can provide a light, refreshing complement to a hearty entree.

Fill a wide pot halfway with water, add about ¼ teaspoon sea salt, and bring to a boil. Add half the cabbage leaves and simmer for 3-5 minutes or until just tender. You may need to poke the leaves under the water occasionally to ensure even cooking. Remove and immediately drain the leaves in a colander or bamboo basket. Fan or toss gently to cool quickly. Cook the rest of the leaves.

Pick up 3 leaves, *gently* squeeze to remove excess water, and stack them neatly, spread out in the same direction on top of each other on a cutting board. Slice the leaves crosswise into 1¼-inch wide strips. Roll the strips to form a cylinder. Gently squeeze, then stand the rolls cut side up. Continue until all the leaves are cut and rolled. Arrange the rounds on a serving platter or place 2-3 each on small individual serving plates or in bowls. Sprinkle each roll with a few drops of ume-su or a combination of equal parts lemon juice and shoyu or tamari. Serve at room temperature.

SERVES 4-5

*12 large outer leaves of Chinese cabbage approximately 1 tablespoon ume su or 2 teaspoons lemon juice and 2 teaspoons shoyu or tamari*

## PRESSED CHINESE CABBAGE SALAD

This combination of vegetables is just one possibility; use whatever salad vegetables you have on hand along with the Chinese cabbage. Thinly sliced green bell pepper and fresh, tender green beans cut on the diagonal into very thin, 1¼-inch long strips are good options.

Cut the cabbage leaves in half lengthwise, then thinly slice crosswise. If using pickling cucumbers, slice them into thin rounds. Regular cucumbers from the grocery store are usually waxed and often contain large seeds, so peel, cut in half lengthwise, and scrape out the seeds before slicing.

Combine all ingredients in a salad press or mixing bowl and toss well. If using a bowl, place a plate (right side up) or other flat round object on top of the vegetables. Unless you are using a straight-sided container, there should be at least ½ inch between the edge of the plate and the bowl all the way around so that even after liquid is pressed out of the vegetables and the mound shrinks, the plate will not be touching the sides of the bowl. Place a 5-6 pound weight, such as a gallon jar filled with grains, beans, or water, on top of the plate. Press for 1-2 hours, then gently squeeze the vegetables with your hands and pour off any excess liquid.

*½ head Chinese cabbage, thinly sliced (5 cups, tightly-packed)*
*5-6 red radishes, thinly sliced*
*1 carrot, slivered*
*2 pickling cucumbers or 1 regular cucumber*
*2 level teaspoons peeled and finely minced fresh ginger*
*½ teaspoon sea salt*

Serve with your favorite salad dressing. You can use any of the dressings included in this book, but creamy ones such as Miso-Tofu Salad Dressing or Ume-Tofu Dressing, and oil and vinegar types such as Italian Dressing or the one given in the recipe for Parboiled Salad with Japanese Dressing complement this pressed salad particularly well.

SERVES 5

## KIMUCHI (KOREAN-STYLE CHINESE CABBAGE PICKLES)

*1 large or 2 small heads
Chinese cabbage
3 tablespoons sea salt
1 small carrot, slivered
1 teaspoon minced garlic
⅓ cup minced scallion
1½-2 teaspoons cayenne
pepper powder
½ apple, peeled, cored, and
grated coarsely
1½ teaspoons sea salt
1-2 teaspoons finely minced
peeled fresh ginger
⅔ cup water*

These pickles start off spicy and seem to get even hotter as they sit. They are good served with sake or beer, or served sparingly with rice or other grains. This recipe and the next were learned from a Japanese friend who has a seemingly endless repertoire of pickle recipes for all seasons and occasions.

If the cabbage heads are small, cut them in half lengthwise; if large, cut into quarters. Cut only through the tough core, then separate by gently pulling the halves apart. Rub the 3 table-spoons of salt into the cabbage, concentrating on the thicker bottom portion and using less on the upper leaves. Place the cabbage in a bowl, cover with a plate (right side up) or other appropriate pressing lid and put a 5 pound weight on top. Press for 8-10 hours (not longer). If desired, briefly rinse the cabbage to remove excess salt, then *gently* squeeze out excess liquid. Cut the cabbage into approximately 1-inch square chunks and set aside.

Combine and mix all remaining ingredients. Use the larger amount of cayenne only if you like a very hot taste. Add the mixture to the cabbage and toss well. Put the mixture into a wide-mouthed jar, cover, and let sit in a cool place for 3-5 days. After this time the pickles will be ready to eat and will keep for at least 2 weeks if refrigerated. Do not rinse these before serving.

# QUICK MIXED VEGETABLE PICKLES

These light, refreshing pickles are served mainly in spring and early or late summer. (Cabbage is a cool weather crop, so in many regions it is not available in mid-summer.) Since these pickles keep only about a week, it is best to make frequent small batches.

Cut the cabbage into 1-inch square pieces. If the lemon is not organic, lightly peel it then cut the quarter in half or thirds and thinly slice. Remove the seeds and membranes from the green pepper, cut lengthwise, then thinly slice crosswise. If using a pickling cucumber, simply slice it. Regular cucumbers are usually waxed and often contain large seeds, so they should be peeled, cut in half lengthwise, and seeded before slicing.

Combine all ingredients in a salad press or other suitable container and press as for Pressed Chinese Cabbage Salad with a weight of approximately 3 pounds. These pickles will be ready to eat after 12-24 hours and are best if eaten within 5-7 days. Refrigerate and keep under pressure until all the pickles are eaten.

*½ large head Chinese cabbage*
*¼ lemon*
*½ green bell pepper*
*½ carrot, slivered*
*½ apple, peeled, cored, quartered, and thinly sliced*
*¼ red onion, thinly sliced*
*1 pickling cucumber or ½ regular cucumber*
*5-6 red radishes, thinly sliced*
*1 teaspoon finely minced fresh ginger*
*1 tablespoon sea salt*
*1-2 pinches crushed or powdered red pepper (optional)*

## NABEMONO

10 cups kombu or kombu-
shiitake stock (see page 143)
½ large or 1 whole small head
Chinese cabbage
1½ pounds fresh white fish fillet (snapper, grouper, sea
bass, cod, or tile fish work
well)
two 8-ounce packages udon
noodles
2 large carrots, sliced on the
diagonal ⅛-inch thick
6 cups (loosely-packed) spinach, washed and sliced into
1-inch wide strips
1-1½ pounds fresh tofu, cut
into 1-inch cubes
Seasonings and Garnishes:
shoyu
1 tablespoon peeled and finely
grated fresh ginger
(optional)
½ lemon, cut into wedges, or
1 tablespoon finely minced
lemon rind
½ cup finely minced scallion
⅔ cup finely grated daikon
(optional)

*Nabemono*, "things in a pot," is a popular style of Japanese cooking. Ingredients can be varied endlessly according to availability and personal preference.

Even today, the Japanese make efficient use of energy and in winter prefer to warm their bodies rather than their homes. This one-pot cooking method, prepared at the table—traditionally in a kettle suspended from the rafters over an open fire and now most commonly over a portable gas burner—warms the spirit as well as the body. It fosters good cheer and is a simple, leisurely meal that takes little time to prepare. The following is one typical assortment of ingredients. Other popular choices include deep-fried tofu, daikon, oysters, shrimp or chicken, and baked mochi added at the end in place of the noodles.

Prepare the kombu or kombu-shiitake stock. Wash, quarter, and core the Chinese cabbage, then slice it crosswise into 1-inch wide strips. Rinse the fish, pat dry, sprinkle lightly with sea salt, and slice it crosswise on the diagonal into 1½-inch wide strips. Parboil the noodles for just 4-5 minutes in plenty of unsalted water (see directions on page 62). They should be undercooked or they will become too limp when reheated. Drain, rinse under cold water until thoroughly cool, then drain again and set aside. Cut the other vegetables and the tofu. Prepare the garnishes and place them in small individual bowls. (If organic lemons are not available, lemon wedges are preferred over the lemon rind.) Arrange the vegetables, fish, and tofu attractively on one or two large platters.

Place a portable gas or electric burner in the center of the table, or use a large electric pot or skillet. If using a burner, a large flameproof earthenware Japanese casserole called a *donabe* is most attractive, but a stainless steel pot or cast iron Dutch oven will be fine. Place the shoyu and garnishes on the table along with a ladle and a slotted spoon for removing broth and ingredients from the pot.

Bring the kombu stock to a gentle simmer and begin adding the ingredients, a few of each at a time. Since the fish adds a rich flavor to the broth, some of it should be added at the beginning of cooking along with ingredients that require the longest cooking. Chinese cabbage, spinach, and tofu require little cooking—not more than a couple of minutes. The foods should be removed and eaten as soon as they are tender, so don't add too much of any one ingredient at once.

Each diner ladles a little of the broth into his soup bowl and adds shoyu to taste as well as his choice of any or all of the garnishes. Then, using the slotted spoon or a pair of long cooking chopsticks, each person serves himself from the pot. After everyone fills their bowls, add more ingredients to the pot. Continue until everything has been eaten, then add about half the noodles and simmer just until cooked through but not mushy—a minute or two should suffice. Cook the rest of the noodles if anyone is still hungry. Otherwise, they may be saved and used the following day.

SERVES 4-5

# BURDOCK (GOBO)

The burdock plant's long, slender tap root has a pleasant, crunchy texture and earthy flavor. Native to northern China and Siberia, burdock (*Articum lappa*) is cultivated mainly in Japan, where it has been an important vegetable since at least the 10th century.

Highly regarded by ancient practitioners of Oriental medicine, burdock was thought of as a strengthening food-medicine, and was commonly eaten as a blood purifier. It was prescribed to hasten recovery from sickness as well as for relief from arthritis and diseases of the skin. In addition to its healing qualities, burdock is a good source of B vitamins.

Whether you know it by name or not you have probably seen wild burdock, since it grows almost everywhere in this country except in the southernmost states. The large, heart-shaped green leaves and thick stalks resemble rhubarb. In its second year of growth, this biennial sends up a tall stalk that bears flowers, followed by the familiar prickly burrs that cling so tenaciously to clothing and animal fur.

All that is needed to gather this ubiquitous wild vegetable is determination and a small spade. Since the roots become fibrous in the second year, select first-year plants—those having no flower stalks. Even these are best gathered before the end of summer. If you can find a patch of burdock growing on a hillside or in sandy soil, it will be much easier to dig. Dig carefully so as not to injure the root, and deeply enough so you can pull it up without breaking it. Wild burdock has a shorter root and stronger flavor than the cultivated variety. More fibrous, it requires longer cooking.

Though still a rare garden vegetable in the U.S., more and more people are beginning to cultivate burdock. As long as the soil is deeply worked, it is easy to grow. Seeds are available from several major seed companies as well as from smaller companies that specialize in Oriental vegetables.

When you buy fresh burdock root (in natural foods stores, Oriental markets, and some supermarkets), look for firm, unbroken roots with taut skin. Slender roots tend to be more tender and less fibrous than thick ones. Avoid floppy roots or dry, brittle ones with wrinkled skins.

To prepare, scrub the root thoroughly but lightly with a stiff vegetable brush and remove any rootlets. It is best not to peel burdock except for overly tough roots, since the skin contains much of the flavor and nutritional value. Burdock's whitish flesh quickly becomes dark after being sliced. To avoid discoloration and eliminate the slightly bitter taste, immediately immerse sliced burdock in cold water for about 15 minutes or until ready to use.

Since burdock combines well with oil, it is often sautéed alone or with other vegetables, or deep-fried as tempura. It is also good simmered in a seasoned broth. Burdock requires lengthy cooking. When combining it with other vegetables in sautéed or simmered dishes, be sure to add burdock first and cook until it starts to become tender before adding other ingredients.

## KINPIRA

*3 burdock roots (each approximately 12 inches long)*
*2 large carrots*
*2 teaspoons light or dark sesame oil*
*¼ teaspoon sea salt*
*2 tablespoons mirin*
*1 tablespoon shoyu*
*small pinch cayenne or Japanese 7-spice (optional)*

A traditional Japanese side dish, this is my favorite way to prepare burdock. Kinpira is most appealing during the late fall and winter months.

Scrub burdock well, cut into thin, 2-inch long julienne strips, and immediately submerge in cold water. Cut carrots similarly, but a little thicker. Heat oil in a skillet or heavy sauce pan, drain burdock, and sauté over medium heat for several minutes. Lower heat, add a *little* water if necessary to prevent scorching, cover and cook for 10-15 minutes or until burdock is nearly tender. Add carrots, salt, and one tablespoon mirin, and sauté briefly. Cover and let cook, but check often to be sure vegetables are not sticking. When burdock and carrots are cooked dry, add one tablespoon shoyu, another tablespoon mirin, and a small pinch of cayenne or Japanese 7-spice. Toss, cover, and cook briefly until tender, adding 2 tablespoons water if necessary.

SERVES 4

# VEGETABLE SOUP WITH DUMPLINGS

Prepare stock. (I prefer kombu-shiitake stock. Use 3 or 4 dried shiitake and follow the directions for making kombu-shiitake stock under Kombu Dashi on page 143.) Slice shiitake caps thinly and set aside for use in the soup.

Scrub burdock, slice it thinly on the diagonal, then immediately submerge slices in cold water. Cut carrot in half lengthwise, then thinly slice halves on the diagonal. Heat oil in a medium-sized skillet and lightly brown the ginger. (There's no need to peel the ginger since it will be removed and discarded.) Drain the burdock well, add it to the skillet and sauté for 5 minutes. Add carrots and sauté briefly. Add shiitake and sauté for another minute. Add 2 tablespoons water and continue sautéeing for a few minutes more. Remove ginger.

Add salt and the sautéed vegetables to simmering stock and cook until burdock is just tender (it should still be slightly crunchy, but not tough or raw-tasting). Add shoyu, scallions, and greens, bring back to a boil, then add dumplings. Cook uncovered until dumplings rise to the surface, then lower heat, cover, and let simmer *gently* for 10 minutes. Serve hot.

SERVES 4

*7 cups kombu-shiitake,
    kombu, or vegetable stock*
*1 burdock root*
*1 large carrot*
*1 teaspoon light sesame oil*
*one or two ⅛-inch thick
    slices fresh ginger*
*½ teaspoon sea salt*
*1½-2 tablespoons shoyu*
*4 scallions cut into ½-inch
    lengths*
*1½-2 cups chopped greens*
*dumplings (recipe follows)*

# DUMPLINGS

Thoroughly mix vegetables, flours, and salt in a small bowl. Add boiling stock or water and mix just until flour is moistened. The mixture should be stiff, but not completely dry. (Though these dumplings are easy to make, if your dough is too wet they will fall apart. It should be firm enough so you can pinch off pieces of dough with your fingers, but not quite as stiff as bread dough.) When adding to soups, as in the above recipe, drop the batter into the boiling liquid by rounded teaspoonfuls and simmer for about 10 minutes or until they no longer taste dough-y or raw. If adding to thick soups, stews, or casseroles, cook dumplings first in lightly salted boiling water until done, then add to the other ingredients for the last two minutes of cooking.

*2-3 teaspoons grated onion or
    2 tablespoons minced scal-
    lion*
*1 tablespoon minced parsley
    or celery leaves*
*½ cup unbleached white flour*
*½ cup whole wheat flour (or
    rice, sweet rice, barley, or
    oat flour)*
*⅛ teaspoon sea salt*
*¾ cup boiling vegetable or
    kombu stock or water*

# HOW TO TEMPURA

ABOUT TEMPURA: Tempura is the delicious style of cooking in which foods such as vegetables and seafoods are dipped in batter and deep-fried.

One of the most well-known and popular "Japanese" foods, tempura was first introduced to Japan by Portuguese traders and missionaries. It caught on quickly with the Japanese, who refined the batter to a delicate crispness and accompanied it with flavor-enhancing dipping sauces. Though it is not difficult to make, there are several tips that help ensure a crisp, light, delicious tempura.

THE OIL: Use a light, cold-pressed vegetable oil (such as safflower or sunflower oil), which does not have a strong taste. Up to about ten percent toasted or light sesame oil can be added to give the oil an especially good flavor. The oil should be neither too shallow nor too deep in the pot—a depth of about three inches is generally good, but if frying large foods, you may need more oil. It should be at least twice as deep as the thickness of the food being deep-fried.

The temperature of the oil is critical. Different foods require different temperatures. For example, fish and tofu are fried at the relatively high temperature of 350-360° F. At this temperature a drop of batter will not sink into the oil, but will dance on the surface. Most vegetables are best fried at 320-340° F. At 320° a drop of batter will sink to the bottom of the oil, then immediately rise to the surface. At 340° F. a drop of batter will sink only about halfway before rising.

Keeping the proper temperature of oil constant is an important key to even frying and a light result. If the oil is too hot, the batter will burn before the inside of the food is cooked. If not hot enough, the food will absorb too much oil as it cooks. To help keep the oil temperature constant, do not add too many ingredients to the pot at once. It should never be crowded. Leave half to two-thirds of the surface area of the oil uncovered. Avoid adding cold foods to the hot oil. Ingredients should be at or near room temperature.

If properly stored, and not overheated to smoking, oil can be reused about three times. After it has cooled considerably, strain the oil with cheesecloth or a paper filter into a container with a tight lid. Store in a cool, dark place. Exposure to air, sunlight, and metal causes oil to deteriorate and become rancid quickly. When reusing, you can add a little new oil to freshen it.

THE BATTER: Overmixing the batter is one of the most common mistakes in making tempura. Lightly combine the ingredients, leaving lumps and even some dry, unmixed flour at the surface. Chopsticks are the best tool for this job, but a fork can be used.  Prepare the batter just before frying.

THE FOODS:  Most vegetables, fish, and seafoods can be tempura-ed.  Use fresh ingredients and make sure their surfaces are as dry as possible before dipping in the batter.  This prevents the oil from splattering.  Ingredients that have been soaked or parboiled before frying should be thoroughly drained, patted dry, then rolled in flour before coating with batter.  Rolling any food in flour will help the batter to adhere.

Pieces of fish or seafood will cook in 2-3 minutes.  Tough or thick vegetables may take 3-4 minutes, others should be done with about 2 minutes of frying.  Very delicate foods such as nori require only a few seconds.  Gently slide batter-covered ingredients into the oil and turn occasionally while frying.  When cooked, pick out the pieces with long cooking chopsticks and gently shake excess oil back into the pan.  Draining on a wire rack placed over a baking sheet or absorbent paper is ideal since it allows for air circulation, but placing the items directly on the paper is fine.  Do not lay them so they are touching each other.  Always remove all of one batch before adding more to the oil.

SERVING:  Tempura should be served immediately, while still hot and crisp.  Serve with Dip Sauce (page 114).  Tempura goes well with soup, especially miso soup, and rice and pickles.  Ginger pickles or light daikon pickles are especially delicious accompaniments and also help digest the oil.

## CARROT-BURDOCK TEMPURA

Please read About Tempura before you begin.

Burdock is a tough vegetable, so it must be cut thinly or it will not become tender.  After cutting, immediately soak pieces in water for 15-20 minutes.  Drain well, pat as dry as possible, then toss in flour.  Cut carrots.

Heat the oil to 330°-340° F.  Lightly combine the egg and water.  Add the flour, being careful not to overmix.  For this recipe the batter will be fairly thick.  Drop ¼ each of the carrots and burdock into the batter and gently toss to coat.  With your fingers pick up the vegetables in small bundles (about 8 sticks per bundle) and carefully slide them into the oil.  Do not crowd the pot.  Turning occasionally, cook for about 4 minutes.  Remove and briefly drain on a wire rack or absorbent paper.  Test one to be sure burdock is tender.  Continue until all the vegetables are cooked.  Serve hot with Dip Sauce.

**SERVES 4**

*2 cups burdock, lightly pared and cut into thin 2½" x ⅛"x ¼" julienne strips*
*2 cups carrot, cut into julienne strips, 2½" x ¼" x ¼"*
*oil for deep frying*

BATTER:
*1 egg, lightly beaten*
*1 cup ice cold water*
*approximately 1 cup unbleached white flour*

DIP SAUCE:
*see page 114*

## JINENJO (YAMAIMO OR "MOUNTAIN YAM," DIOSCORIA SPECIES)

One late summer evening a year or so after returning to the U.S. from Japan, John and I were relaxing on the porch of an old inn near our home. Suddenly John's distant look changed to alert disbelief. Climbing up the support beam next to us were long vines with the heart-shaped leaves and distinctive aerial tubers of *yamaimo*, the mountain yam we had thought grew only in Japan.

Prized by the Japanese for its exceptional strengthening and medicinal properties, this venerable plant is surrounded by a wealth of lore. Though the wild variety, in Japan specifically called *jinenjo*, is the most potent and flavorful, there are several cultivated varieties that possess the same properties but to a lesser degree. Yamaimo is the general term used in Japan for both wild and cultivated types. Americans usually call both the wild and the cultivated types "jinenjo." Specific names given to cultivated varieties include *nagaimo* ("long potato"), *yamatoimo* or *ichoimo* ("5 finger-potato"), and *tororoimo* (after the popular Japanese dish made with this type). The related one we found growing at the inn is referred to here in the southeastern U.S. as "wild yam" or "colic root."

The slightly hairy, beige tubers of the cultivated varieties typically grow to 2-3 feet in length, but wild jinenjo have been known to grow to 45 feet long! Jinenjo's flavor is mild, but the flesh has a sticky, mucilaginous quality that some Westerners have difficulty getting used to.

In Japan jinenjo is most commonly eaten raw in the form of *tororo* (see page 133). The root is peeled, finely grated, and mixed with a shoyu or miso-seasoned broth, sometimes with added bonito flakes, toasted slivered nori, and/or raw egg. This mixture is usually served over cooked barley, rice, or a combination of the two. By far the most common use of jinenjo in Japan is in tororo, but it is also used in many cooked dishes as a binder to hold the other ingredients together. Many people enjoy this vegetable thinly sliced and deep-fried like potato chips. Sprinkle the chips with a little sea salt after frying and serve while still crisp.

Raw jinenjo is an excellent digestive aid. It contains several times more diastase than daikon, which is a good source of this important starch-digesting enzyme.

In addition to its value as a digestive aid, jinenjo is a strengthening food that increases stamina. Traditionally it was considered to be a food only for men. Until recently, Japanese women rarely ate jinenjo for fear of becoming too masculine. Grated, then dried and powdered, it was used in traditional Oriental medicine for the treatment of such conditions as fatigue, weakness, low body temperature, and impotence.

Though they commonly acknowledge it, scientists in Japan have yet to document the secret to jinenjo's strengthening quality, and opinions vary widely. Some believe it lies in the sticky substance, a combination of globin (protein) and mannan (sugar). Others attribute it to the abundance of digestive enzymes, which enable accompanying foods to be quickly broken down and assimilated.

Jinenjo is one of the few plants that contain alantoin. Also abundant in comfrey, alantoin is responsible for both plants' effectiveness in cases of stomach ulcers, duodenitis, and asthma. Jinenjo is also the best plant source of arginine, an amino acid that plays an important role in the creation of new cells in the body and is integral to the proper functioning of the nervous system.

After discovering the wild yam at the inn and returning home with pockets full of the aerial tubers to plant, we wondered whether the Cherokee Indians who inhabited this area of North Carolina had made use of this vegetable that the Japanese hold in such high esteem. We did some research and found that wild yam was used by Native Americans and early European Americans as a source of both food and medicine. Used mainly for its rejuvenating effect, to treat such digestive problems as colic, bowel spasms, flatulence, and irregularity, and to prevent miscarriage and ease labor, its medicinal attributes paralleled those of its Eastern relative.

It is difficult to find jinenjo except in Japanese markets in large cities and in some natural foods stores. Oriental markets in smaller cities regularly order from large distributors and may be able to get some for you if you request it. Remember that it may be sold as "jinenjo," "yamaimo," "nagaimo," and "mountain yam."

If you live in an area where jinenjo is difficult to obtain, you may wish to grow your own. You will need one or two tubers to get started. If necessary, special order them in early spring from an Oriental market in your nearest large city. Since planting instructions are not readily available in English, I have included the following information, which was gathered from Japanese friends and substantiated by personal experience.

Jinenjo grows in temperate climates. The southwestern U.S. is probably too dry, and far northern areas may be too cold, although it is reported to grow even in areas of Japan with heavy snowfall. Shorter growing seasons in the north could affect time to maturity.

Both cultivated and wild varieties of jinenjo are perennials. They can be propagated either by "root cuttings" or by planting the largest of the aerial tubers that form in late summer. You must prepare a deep, loose, well-drained, and fertile seed bed and be prepared to wait.

Our first experiment was to plant cut sections from mature jinenjo we bought in an Oriental market. First we cut each root into 1½-2-inch-long sections. Then we made mounds supported by overturned plastic containers with the bottoms cut out, planted the cuttings lying sideways four inches deep, and provided support for the long vines, which is said to increase yields. After the vines had died back at the end of the first year of growth, we dug one up and were disappointed at its unimpressive size. We left the rest in the ground and by the end of the second year they were still not exactly record-breaking, but at least they were usable. Those harvested after the third year were of fairly good size. Jinenjo will continue to grow, but after the third year they are very deep and hard to dig.

The first year before the leaves yellowed we gathered the aerial tubers from the vines. They look exactly like miniature yams and even have the sticky substance inside. We stored them cool and dry over the winter, and in spring planted these as well as the ones we had collected from the wild yams. Aerial tubers take a year longer to mature than cuttings, but they do eventually achieve a respectable size.

In terms of both nutritional and medicinal value, the best time to harvest your jinenjo is from early December to early March, after the vines have died back and the weather has become cold, and before they sprout again in spring. They must be carefully dug to minimize damage to the brittle tubers.

## MOUNTAIN YAM BURGERS

*1 cup finely grated jinenjo*
*⅔ cup finely grated carrot*
*½ cup finely minced scallion*
*3 level tablespoons mellow white or mellow barley miso, thinned in 1 tablespoon water*
*1-1¼ cups (approximately) whole wheat or unbleached white flour*
*additional flour for dusting patties*
*2 teaspoons light sesame or corn oil*

We enjoy these burgers hot and unadorned, but you may like them topped with a sauce or gravy, a sprinkle of shoyu, or a dab of butter.

In a medium-sized mixing bowl combine the first four ingredients well. Add the flour a little at a time until the mixture is stiff enough to form patties. Moisten your hands with a little water or vegetable oil before making the patties, then flour your hands and dust both sides of each patty with flour.

Heat the oil in a large skillet, add the patties, cover the pan, and cook over low heat until golden brown. Flip and cook until golden on the other side. Serve hot.

MAKES TEN 2½-3-INCH BURGERS

# RICE BURGERS

This recipe is a variation on a common Japanese theme. The method of cooking and the vegetables and seasonings used vary from region to region in Japan. Usually made from leftovers, rice burgers are considered plain country fare, not something the Japanese would serve to guests, but they are certainly delicious and practical. Rice burgers are commonly included in box lunches, and farmers take several out to the fields to eat with pickles and tea under the shade of a tree during their lunch break.

In a medium-sized mixing bowl combine the rice and miso, then add the next three ingredients and mix well. Add the flour a little at a time until you have a fairly dry, not too sticky mixture, but one that holds its shape well. Moisten your hands with a little water or vegetable oil before making patties. If they are quite sticky, lightly dust both sides with flour before cooking.

Heat the oil in a large skillet, add the patties, cover the pan, and cook over low heat until golden brown. Flip and cook until golden on the other side. Serve hot as is or, if desired, with a sprinkle of shoyu or a dab of butter.

If you are making a large quantity, it may be easier to bake them. Place the burgers on a lightly oiled baking sheet and cook in a preheated 375° F. oven until golden brown on the bottom. Turn and cook until the other side is golden.

MAKES 6-7 3-INCH BURGERS

*2½ cups cooked brown or white rice*
*3 level tablespoons mellow white miso or 2 level table-spoons red (rice) or barley (mugi) miso*
*2 scallions, finely minced*
*⅓ cup finely minced parsley*
*2 tablespoons peeled and finely grated jinenjo*
*¼ cup (approximately) whole wheat or unbleached white flour*
*1-2 teaspoons light sesame or corn oil*

# TORORO

In some parts of Japan this traditional preparation, highly regarded for its strength-giving properties, is served on the third day of the New Year. After the excesses of the first two days, the meal on the evening of the third is kept very simple, with sometimes just a bowl of barley or rice topped with *tororo* and a side dish of pickles. According to folklore, eating tororo on this day will prevent a stroke throughout the year. Though traditionally made with jinenjo that grows wild in the mountains, today many people use one of the related cultivated varieties.

Prepare the stock, add the salt and shoyu, and simmer briefly. Place the grated jinenjo in a suribachi or mortar and grind it vigorously. (It should develop a stretchy quality so that a long, slippery strand forms when you spoon some out.) Add the soup a little at a time to the jinenjo, mixing well after each addition, just until you have a thick, pourable sauce that maintains its cohesive stretchiness. Serve over rice or barley or a combination of the two, and garnish with the nori.

SERVES 4

*1 cup (approximately) kombu-shiitake, kombu-bonito, or kombu stock (see page 143)*
*⅛ teaspoon sea salt*
*1 teaspoon shoyu*
*2 cups peeled and finely grated jinenjo*
*¼ sheet of nori, toasted and slivered*

## JINENJO JULIENNE

Here's another simple way, besides Tororo, to get the advantages of eating this vegetable raw. If you object to the texture of grated jinenjo you may prefer this method of preparation. Besides jinenjo, all you need is shoyu or *ume-su* and, if desired, brown rice vinegar or mirin. This dish should be served in small amounts, so don't prepare too much. About ¼ cup per person is enough.

Peel the jinenjo and cut it into julienne strips about 2 inches long, ¼ inch wide, and very thin. For a seasoning, combine equal parts shoyu and water and, if desired, ⅓ part brown rice vinegar. Ume-su also goes well with jinenjo. It can simply be diluted with water to taste (about 1:1). For this dish, I particularly like ume-su combined with mirin. Mix two parts ume-su with one part mirin, or try equal parts ume-su and water mixed with ½ part mirin.

To serve, place a small mound of jinenjo neatly on small individual plates or bowls. Sprinkle about one teaspoon of whichever seasoning you choose over the top. If desired, garnish with a few toasted sesame seeds or bonito flakes.

## LOTUS ROOT (RENKON)

The lotus is an exotic plant that grows in muddy ponds or paddies in tropical climates. The rhizomes, which form fat links, are planted in the mud under water; new leaves emerge from them, the stems elongating so that the first two or three leaves float on top of the water. The stem continues to grow, and subsequent leaves stand above the water. The showy, fragrant flowers, usually pink or rose-colored but sometimes white, bloom in late summer.

The rhizome, or "root," of the lotus has been a delicacy in Oriental cooking for over a millenium. Its mild flavor combines well with most other vegetables, and its crunchy texture is appealing in stir-fried dishes or thinly sliced and deep-fried with or without batter. In Japan it is also enjoyed in vinegared specialties and simmered dishes. When the root is sliced into rounds, the several small tunnels that run the length of each link create a decorative pattern that can lend an artful touch to a meal.

Besides its use as a food, all parts of the lotus plant—seeds, leaves, and flowers as well as the root—have long been respected in the East for their medicinal properties. In Oriental medicine lotus seeds are eaten to increase energy and vitality and to aid digestion. Containing 20 percent protein, the seeds are also nourishing. Though the entire rhizome can be used medicinally, the portion where the links join has the greatest effect. Small doses of the juice extracted from raw, finely grated lotus root is prescribed for lung-related ailments such as tuberculosis, asthma, and coughing, for heart disease, and to increase energy and neutralize toxins. Tea made from the grated and dried joint portion is also said to be effective. Combined with the juice of grated ginger, lotus root juice is said to be good for enteritis (inflammation of the intestine).

Harvested only in fall and winter, fresh lotus root is difficult to find even when it is in season, though it seems to be becoming more common in Oriental markets, especially those in large cities. When shopping for lotus root, select firm, cream-colored or grayish-white rhizomes with no bruises, blemishes, or soft spots. Whole links store relatively well in a cool, dark place, but use any cut portion within 2-3 days. If the inside surface of the tunnels is dark, it is past its prime. The flesh should be an attractive ivory color. To prevent the color from becoming dark after the root is sliced, it should be immediately and completely submerged in lightly salted water or water with a little vinegar or lemon juice added (a teaspoon of vinegar to two cups of water is enough). To maintain the bright color, let the cut pieces rest in the water for 30 minutes before cooking.

If you are unable to find fresh lotus root, look for packages of dried sliced lotus in your natural foods store. Dried lotus sold in Oriental markets is likely to be bleached, so be sure the label says "unbleached" before purchasing. Though it lacks much of the visual appeal of fresh, dried lotus root is convenient and easy to use and can be substituted for fresh in many recipes, including most sautéed, stir-fried, and simmered dishes. To reconstitute, simply soak dried lotus for two hours, then drain.

## STIR-FRIED VEGETABLES WITH PLUM SAUCE

If using dried lotus slices, soak them for two hours. If using fresh lotus, scrub well and thinly slice, then immediately submerge the slices in lightly vinegared water and let stand for 30 minutes. Combine the kombu and water in a small saucepan, bring to a simmer, uncovered, over medium heat, then remove kombu and reserve it for another use. Remove broth from heat. Cut the Chinese cabbage in half again lengthwise, then core it and slice the leaves crosswise into 1-inch wide strips. (The core can be used if very thinly sliced.) Quarter the red pepper, remove and discard seeds and inner membranes, and thinly slice on the diagonal. Remove tips and strings from snow peas.

Heat the oil over medium heat in a wok or large skillet. Drain the lotus root and sauté it briefly. Add red pepper, then Chinese cabbage, then scallions, sautéeing for one minute after each addition. Add a pinch of salt, lower heat, cover, and simmer for 5

*¾-1 cup dried or 1½ cups thinly sliced fresh lotus root*
*4-inch piece kombu*
*1 cup water*
*½ head Chinese cabbage*
*1 red bell pepper*
*20 snow peas*
*2-3 teaspoons light sesame oil*
*3-4 scallions, cut into 1-inch lengths*
*pinch sea salt*
*1½ tablespoons umeboshi paste or minced umeboshi plum*
*1 tablespoon mirin*
*1½ tablespoons kuzu*

minutes. Add snow peas and toss and cook for one minute more. Uncover and remove from heat.

Add the umeboshi and mirin to the kombu stock and blend or mix well. Dissolve the kuzu in 2 tablespoons cold water and add to the stock. Add the stock to the vegetables and bring to a boil over medium heat while stirring gently. Simmer for 1-2 minutes or until sauce thickens. Serve as a vegetable side dish or over noodles such as somen or bifun.

This dish is delicious with shrimp. Peel and devein 16 medium or large shrimp and cut each into 2-3 bite-sized pieces. Add shrimp just before adding the snow peas.

SERVES 4

## LOTUS ROOT WITH CARROT AND BURDOCK

¾ cup dried or 1½ cups fresh
   lotus root pieces
18 inches (approximately) burdock root
2 large carrots
2-3 teaspoons light or dark
   (toasted) sesame oil
⅛ teaspoon sea salt
2 tablespoons mirin (optional)
1½ tablespoons shoyu (use
   less if not using mirin)

If using dried lotus slices, soak them for 2 hours. Wash fresh lotus and thinly slice, then quarter the rounds. Immediately submerge fresh lotus pieces in lightly vinegared water and let stand for 30 minutes. Scrub burdock well, cut into julienne strips about the size of wooden matchsticks, and place in cold water to prevent discoloration. Cut carrots similarly, but a little larger than the burdock.

Heat oil in a skillet over medium heat. Drain burdock, and sauté it for 5 minutes, adding a teaspoon or two of water as needed to prevent scorching. Add carrot, then drained lotus root, and sauté briefly after each addition. Add the salt and 1 tablespoon of the mirin, toss, lower heat, cover, and simmer until just tender. (Check occasionally and add a little water if necessary to prevent scorching.) Add shoyu and the other tablespoon of mirin and cook for 1-2 minutes more.

SERVES 4

## ARAME WITH LOTUS ROOT

½ cup dried or 1 cup fresh
   lotus root pieces
1½ cups (dry measure) arame
1½ tablespoons light sesame
   oil
1 carrot
2 teaspoons mirin
2-3 teaspoons shoyu
minced parsley or scallion for
   garnish

If using dried lotus slices, soak for 2 hours. Wash fresh lotus, thinly slice, then quarter the rounds. Rinse arame and soak in 3 cups water for 5-10 minutes. Heat oil over medium heat in a skillet. Drain the lotus root, and sauté it briefly. Drain the arame, add to skillet, toss with lotus root, and sauté for 2-3 minutes. Add arame soaking water or fresh water to almost cover, bring to a boil, and simmer, covered, for 15 minutes.

Cut the carrot into ⅛-inch thick julienne strips, layer on top of arame, cover, and simmer for 5 minutes more. Add the mirin and 2 teaspoons shoyu, toss, and simmer for 2-3 minutes more. Remove cover. Add a little more shoyu if desired. If there is excess liquid in the pan evaporate it by cooking over medium-high heat for a few minutes, being careful not to scorch the vegetables. Place in a serving bowl and garnish with parsley or scallion.

SERVES 4

## LOTUS CHIPS

Wash lotus root and slice into rounds as thin as possible. Immediately submerge the slices in salted water (add ½ teaspoon sea salt for each cup water) and let stand for one hour. Drain thoroughly, then dry completely with a clean, absorbent kitchen towel. If desired, dust the slices with arrowroot powder or unbleached white flour. Deep-fry in unrefined vegetable oil heated to 325-340° F. for about two minutes or until crisp. Drain on absorbent paper or on a wire rack placed over a baking sheet. Sprinkle lightly with sea salt and serve.

Long before the development of agriculture, coastal peoples harvested a variety of nutritious vegetables from the sea. Today, sea vegetables are still appreciated in various regions of the world for their taste, versatility, and rich nutritional benefits. Before trying them, I remember thinking that eating "seaweeds" was rather odd, and thought they were probably quite unappetizing. I also supposed the different kinds all tasted about the same. However, I soon learned that properly prepared, high-quality sea vegetables are not only delicious but also provide a variety of delicious flavors and can be used to create dishes with beautiful contrasting colors and interesting textures.

Sea vegetables can enhance summer salads, light soups, hearty stews, pickles, and bean, vegetable, or grain dishes. One sea vegetable product, called *kanten* or agar, is used to make gelatin-like desserts, molded vegetable aspics, and cranberry sauce. In Japan, vegetables from the sea are as common to the traditional cuisine as garden vegetables. The typical Japanese breakfast, for example, may include dishes with three varieties of seaweed: *wakame* miso soup made from *kombu* stock, and toasted *nori* strips served with rice.

Sea vegetables are rich in essential minerals, vitamins, protein, and important trace elements that today are often lacking in our land vegetables because of soil demineralization. According to Doctors Seibin and Teruko Arasaki, authors of several books and articles on the seaweeds of Japan, "Sea vegetables contain more minerals than any other kind of food. . . . An extremely wide range of minerals accounts for from 7 to 38 percent of their dry weight. All the minerals required by human beings, including calcium, sodium, magnesium, potassium, iodine, iron, and zinc are present in sufficient amounts."[1]

Of the wide variety of minerals present, calcium, iron, and iodine, which are abundant in most types of seaweed, are of particular importance to people eating a non-dairy, grain-based vegetarian diet. For example, one-quarter cup of cooked *hijiki* contains over half the calcium in a cup of milk and more iron than eggs. *Aonori* (powdered green nori) has the highest iron content of all the edible sea vegetables; hijiki ranks second. Although iodine is, by nature, highly volatile and thus somewhat difficult to obtain, sea vegetables contain complex natural sugars that stabilize their iodine, making them an excellent source of this essential mineral.

In addition to being a rich source of minerals, sea vegetables contain an abundance of vitamins, including vitamins A (in the form of beta-carotene), $B_1$, $B_2$, $B_6$, $B_{12}$, niacin, vitamin C, pantothenic acid, and folic acid.[2] Along with some fermented soy foods such as tempeh, sea vegetables are one of the few vegetarian sources of $B_{12}$.

Although the commonly used sea vegetables are all high in protein, ranging from 10 to 48 percent of the dry weight, it has not yet been determined how much of the protein in sea vegetables can be used by the body. However, the small amount of research that has been done shows that the amino acid composition of sea vegetable protein is actually better than that of land vegetables.[3]

Besides their varied and concentrated nutritional value, sea vegetables offer other health benefits that provide even more reason for incorporating these gifts from the sea into our daily meals. For centuries Oriental medicine has recognized that sea vegetables contribute to general health, and especially to the health of the endocrine and nervous systems, resulting in thick healthy hair, soft skin, and a tolerance for stress. Studies have shown that sea vegetables are effective in reducing cholesterol and in helping to prevent atherosclerosis and hypertension.

Among other characteristics of sea vegetables currently being validated by medical research are their natural antibiotic and antitumoral effects. Recent surveys show that people living in geographic areas where sea vegetables are regularly included in the diet tend to live long, healthy lives.[4]

# KOMBU

Kombu is the Japanese name for several species of *Laminaria*, seaweeds that thrive in the pure, cold waters around Hokkaido, Japan's northernmost island. The wide, thick, leaf-like fronds are harvested with long hooks or forks between July and September, then spread out to dry. Top quality Japanese kombu is blackish-brown and quite thick and flat. When well dried, it is stiff. (Several species of North American *Laminaria*, as well as North American wakame (*Alaria*), have begun to be harvested on our shores and are becoming available in natural foods stores. Cooking methods for these delicious indigenous seaweeds are the same as for the Japanese varieties, although some North American types may need longer cooking.)

Kombu is a good source of a wide range of essential vitamins and minerals, including calcium, iron, iodine, and vitamins A, $B_1$, $B_2$, C, $B_6$, $B_{12}$, and niacin. It is also a reliable source of numerous trace minerals.

Long valued in Japan for its medicinal properties as well as its culinary use, kombu extract, powder, or tea was often prescribed by folk healers in cases of hypertension. Scientific research has shown that laminine, an amino acid found in kombu, is the key to its success in reducing tension. Kombu is also attributed with lowering cholesterol and relieving water retention.

Although soaking is occasionally called for in specific recipes, in general do not soak, wash, or rinse kombu before using it since the various components that account for kombu's flavor are water soluble. Simply wipe the kombu lightly with a clean, damp cloth to remove any dirt or sand. Kombu can be used in a variety of ways to create delicious dishes for any season, from delicate clear soups and cooling pressed salads to hearty stews and bean dishes. In general, lighter, more delicate preparations call for shorter cooking time. Heartier winter dishes, on the other hand, often require lengthy baking, sautéeing or boiling in a more highly-seasoned liquid. Although kombu need not be soaked before use in most recipes, when soaking is called for, it is only necessary to soak until the kombu softens and opens up. Use the soaking water in the recipe, or save it for soup.

Kombu's most common and important use is in the preparation of *dashi*, Japan's multi-purpose stock for soups, stews, and sauces. Dashi appears simple, but it is integral to Japanese cooking since it is the first step in many traditional dishes—the flavor and quality of the stock helping to determine the taste of the finished dish. The method for making dashi is given below.

Kombu is also good sliced and used in soups and stews, and in vegetable and bean dishes. Using kombu in cooking beans is particularly recommended because it helps soften them, reduces cooking time, and makes beans easier to digest. The Japanese use kombu in various types of pickles as well, often simply to enhance the flavor of the brine or "mash," as in some recipes for rice bran pickles and Chinese cabbage pickles, and sometimes as one of the ingredients to be pickled. Kombu can also be cooked in a seasoned broth and used to wrap pieces of burdock or other vegetables for hors d'oeuvres.

A nutritious condiment can be made by roasting kombu and grinding it to a powder. Cut the kombu into small pieces and roast in an unoiled skillet, stirring constantly until very crisp. Grind into a coarse powder. (A *suribachi*, Japanese grinding bowl, is ideal for this purpose.) Add this powder as seasoning to soups, sprinkle it over grains, or toss it with cooked rice before serving.

# KOMBU DASHI

A subtle but delicious stock for soups, stews, sauces, boiled vegetables, and noodle broths can be quickly prepared using only kombu and water.

Combine 4-6 cups water and a 6-inch piece of dried kombu in a saucepan. Bring just to a simmer, uncovered, over medium heat, then immediately remove kombu. This technique gives the most delicate and delicious results. Long boiling releases some strong, unpleasant-tasting compounds into the water that can be over-powering in a simple vegetable soup or broth.

Another method is simply to soak the kombu for several hours, then remove. Reserve the kombu—it can be cooked with beans or vegetables or reused 2-3 times for making stock. If reusing the kombu to make stock, bring to a boil, then lower and simmer for 10-20 minutes. Lightly scoring the kombu will help release the amino acid responsible for its flavor-intensifying effect.

This basic stock can be varied by adding dried shiitake mush-rooms, bonito (dried fish flakes), or small dried fish (*niboshi*). Dried shiitake should be soaked for at least 2-3 hours if they are to be added to the dish. After soaking, cut off and discard stems, and slice caps and return them to the soaking water. If you are not adding the mushrooms themselves, soaking time can be shortened. Soak for 15-20 minutes, then bring the shiitake and soaking water to a boil and simmer for 15 minutes. Remove shiitake and reserve for another dish. In both cases use the soak-ing water and continue with kombu as above.

About ¼ cup freshly shaved bonito flakes, or one packet pre-shaved bonito, makes a delicious stock. After removing kombu add bonito and turn off heat. Let sit for 1-2 minutes, then strain broth, squeezing or pressing all liquid from flakes with the back of a spoon. Discard flakes. Stock made from niboshi (sun-dried sardines) is stronger than bonito stock. It is most commonly used in Japan for thick, rich soups and stews. Combine ¼ cup with 4 cups cooled kombu stock, bring quickly to a boil, then reduce heat and simmer for 5-10 minutes. Remove from heat and strain.

Several recipes in this book begin with either kombu or kombu-bonito stock. The former is most often used to add flavor and nutrition to simple vegetable soups and delicate dips, whereas the latter adds rich, hearty flavor to fish soups, stews, and noodle broths.

*5 cups kombu or kombu-bonito
    stock*
*1 teaspoon light sesame oil*
*1 leek, sliced thin*
*1 rib celery, sliced thin*
*1 large potato, diced*
*½ teaspoon sea salt*
*pinch white pepper (optional)*
*¼ cup dried dulse (or
    wakame)*
*1 tablespoon shoyu*
*3-4 tablespoons kuzu or
    arrowroot powder*

# DULSE CHOWDER

Dulse is a hardy sea vegetable abundant on the New England coast. Of all the commonly used edible sea vegetables, dulse has the highest iron content, is high in the essential amino acid lysine, and contains 25 percent protein. High-quality dulse is a deep reddish-purple.

Dulse has a slightly spicy flavor that livens up soups and salads. It is especially good in thick chowders with leeks, potatoes, and celery. Dulse combines well with oatmeal and onions in soups and porridge. It has a strong flavor, so be careful not to overpower other ingredients. Before using dulse soak it for about five minutes to reconstitute and make it easier to remove any bits of shells or sand that may be attached to the fronds.

Prepare stock (Kombu Dashi, as on page 143). Heat oil in skillet, add leek, celery, and potato, and sauté briefly. Add a few grains of salt, toss, cover, lower heat, and cook for 5-10 minutes. Add vegetables to stock along with ½ teaspoon sea salt and, if desired, the white pepper. Simmer for 10-15 minutes.

Meanwhile, soak the dulse or wakame in 1 cup water for 5-10 minutes. When potatoes are just tender, chop dulse and add to soup along with shoyu. Simmer briefly and remove from heat. Dissolve kuzu or arrowroot in 3 tablespoons water. (If using kuzu, crush lumps with the back of a spoon before measuring.) Add this thickener to the soup while stirring briskly. Return to heat and simmer for 1-2 minutes. Serve this thick and soothing soup hot. If desired, garnish each bowl with a little finely minced celery leaves or scallion.

**SERVES 4**

*7-inch piece kombu*
*1 cup water*
*1 onion*
*½ small head cabbage*
*2 carrots*
*½ butternut squash, peeled, or
    buttercup, unpeeled*
*1 tablespoon plus 1 teaspoon
    shoyu*

# HEARTY BAKED VEGETABLES

This warming dish, with its attractive fall colors, is especially appealing during autumn or winter.

Preheat oven to 375° F. Place kombu in a pie plate or small baking dish and soak for at least 10 minutes in one cup water, then cut it into 1-inch squares. Cut onion in half and each half into eighths. Slice cabbage into ¾-inch wedges. Cut carrots into small bite-sized chunks and squash into large bite-sized chunks (squash cooks more quickly). Place all vegetables in a baking pan or casserole. Add shoyu to kombu soaking water and pour over vegetables. Cover and bake until tender (about 50-60 minutes).

**SERVES 3-4**

# PRESSED SALAD

Cooling and tangy, this typically Japanese "salad" is a perfect addition to a summer lunch.

Cut pickling cucumbers into 1/8 -inch thick diagonal slices. (If using regular cucumbers, peel, cut in half lengthwise, and scrape out seeds before slicing.) Place radish and cucumber in a bowl, sprinkle with ½ teaspoon sea salt, toss, and let sit for 10 minutes. Rinse with cold water and gently squeeze out excess water.

Soak kombu until soft, then cut crosswise into fine threads with scissors. Add kombu and ginger to cucumber and radish and mix well. Combine remaining ingredients and slowly pour over vegetables. Place a small plate right side up on vegetables and press with a two-pound weight (such as a quart jar three-quarters filled with water). Set in a cool, dark place, or refrigerate, for three hours. Toss salad with a little of the liquid left in the pressing bowl and serve a few pieces each in small individual bowls.

SERVES 4

*3-4 pickling cucumbers or 2 regular cucumbers*
*4-5 red radishes, thinly sliced*
*½ teaspoon sea salt*
*3-inch piece kombu, cut in half lengthwise*
*½-inch section fresh ginger, peeled and grated*
*3 tablespoons brown rice vinegar*
*2 tablespoons mirin*
*¼ teaspoon shoyu or tamari*
*pinch sea salt*

# KOMBU ROLLS

In Japan, these attractive little "packages" are served on special occasions such as the New Year's meal.

Kombu varies in width. For this dish, choose thin fronds that will cook more quickly, and if pieces are more than four inches wide, cut in half lengthwise. Soak kombu in water to cover just until soft. Cut carrots into sticks ¼-inch by ¼-inch and as long as the kombu is wide. You will need one piece for each strip of kombu. If using burdock, it should be scrubbed well, then cut in thinner sticks (1/8-inch thick) since it takes longer to cook. After cutting, soak burdock in cold water for 10-15 minutes.

Soak kampyo for 10-15 minutes to soften. Tightly roll one piece of carrot or two pieces of burdock in each strip of kombu and fasten by tying a 6-inch strip of kampyo in a bow around the center. (Wrap kampyo around the roll twice. Tie a small bow and trim ends.) If kampyo is unavailable, you will have to improvise. Try piercing the roll through the center with a strong, sharp toothpick, or tie with string to hold rolls together while cooking, then remove strings and fasten with toothpicks before serving.

Place rolls in a small saucepan. Combine last four ingredients and pour over the rolls. Simmer gently until kombu is tender (about 20 minutes). Serve hot or at room temperature.

SERVES 4

*8 pieces kombu, each 5-6 inches long*
*1 large carrot*
*1 burdock root (optional)*
*kampyo (gourd strips), tooth-picks, or string (for fasten-ing rolls)*
*3 cups kombu stock or kombu soaking water*
*5 tablespoons shoyu*
*4 tablespoons mirin*
*2 tablespoons brown rice vinegar*

## NORI

Japanese nori (*Porphyra tenera*) is a sea vegetable that has been dried and pressed into thin sheets. Versatile and easy to prepare, nori is rich in protein and is abundant in a wide range of nutrients, most notably calcium and iron, and vitamins A, B, and C. At present the Japanese alone consume almost nine billion sheets per year. Nori is also quickly gaining worldwide popularity, due partly to the proliferation of successful sushi bars that offer various combinations of rice and vegetables or fish wrapped in nori. And children love it! Our two-year-old son never tires of rice wrapped in nori. These two foods are so closely associated in his mind that when he's hungry he asks for "nori-rice."

Lesser grades of nori are a dull, purplish-black; high-quality nori is greenish-black and has a natural, vibrant luster. Except for "Sushi Nori," which comes pretoasted, just before using, nori should be lightly toasted by holding the unfolded sheet first at one end, then at the other, and passing it briefly over a gas flame or electric burner until the color changes to a more brilliant green and it becomes crisp and fragrant. (Be careful—it is delicate and burns easily.)

Nori is most commonly used to wrap rice balls, Japanese "sandwiches," which are probably still the most common and popular addition to Japanese lunch boxes and picnic baskets. Nori is also used to wrap foods, as in Nori-Maki Sushi (see page 148). Cut in half lengthwise, then into 1½-inch strips, nori is delicious wrapped around mouthfuls of warm rice with dabs of umeboshi paste. Crumbled or cut into strips, nori can be used to garnish soups, grains, fried rice, or noodles.

Another variety of nori, called "aonori," or "green nori," (*Enteromorpha* species), is sold in flake form and used as a garnish. This type is richest in iron and protein.

## RICE BALLS

*4 sheets nori*
*4 cups freshly cooked rice*
*4 umeboshi plums, or about 2*
  *teaspoons umeboshi paste*

Rice balls are tasty and convenient at any time and can be made in a variety of interesting ways. They are perfect for lunchboxes and picnic baskets, and since they keep well they are ideal for traveling.

Toast nori as above, fold, and carefully tear in half. Tear each half into halves. Moisten your hands in lightly salted water and gently but firmly form about ½ cup rice into a ball, cylinder, or triangle shape. Continue until all 8 are formed. Wet your hands as necessary to prevent sticking, but use as little water as possible.

Press your index finger into the center of the rice ball and insert ½ umeboshi plum, or about ¼ teaspoon umeboshi paste. (For variety, use substitutes such as minced pickles, or bonito flakes lightly dampened with shoyu.) Seal hole, then press ball to flatten slightly. The surface of the ball may be rubbed very lightly with umeboshi or miso.

Wrap a ball of rice with 2 squares of the nori—one on the top and one on the bottom. At first it may look a little ragged; set it down, wrap the others, then come back to the first and gently pack it as you would a snowball until the nori sticks neatly to the rice.

Umeboshi helps preserve the rice and aids its digestion. Rice balls keep best if wrapped in wax paper, then in paper. Do not wrap in plastic or store in an airtight container. (In Japan almost everything you buy is wrapped in paper, even a single croissant from a bakery. Japanese women use this leftover paper to wrap rice balls.)

MAKES 8

 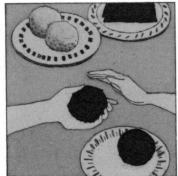

# NOODLE ROLLS

Noodle rolls require a delicate hand but are not difficult to make. When patiently and skillfully prepared, the reward is a beautiful, elegant, and delicious main dish that bespeaks order and simplicity.

Divide uncooked noodles into 3 equal bundles. Tie each bundle firmly with several turns of string about ³/₈ -inch from one end. (Do not tie both ends.) Drop noodle bundles into a large pot of boiling water and cook until just tender. Remove and plunge into cold water. Change water once, then drain. Being sure to

*1 package thin soba or somen noodles*
*3 sheets nori*

DIPPING SAUCE:
*1 tablespoon shoyu*
*1 tablespoon water or soup stock*
*1 teaspoon mirin (optional)*
*1 teaspoon (approximately) wasabi paste*

keep the 3 bundles separate and the noodles in each bundle parallel, spread noodles out on a clean, dry towel to drain. Cut off each uncooked portion of noodles at string end and discard it.

Toast nori as on page 146. Place toasted side down on a sushi mat, small towel, or counter, and spread one bundle of noodles over it so the noodles lie across the nori from side to side. Leave uncovered ½ inch of the nori at the bottom and 1½ inches at the top. Roll as firmly as possible and let the roll rest on its seam. Repeat with the other 2 bundles of noodles and sheets of nori. Using a sharp knife and cleaning the blade after each cut, carefully slice the rolls in half, and each half into 3 equal pieces. Combine Dipping Sauce ingredients. Place Noodle Roll pieces cut side up on a platter and serve accompanied by individual small saucers of dipping sauce.

Wasabi, Japanese horseradish, is usually sold as a powder. Add just a few drops of water at a time until you have a paste. Wasabi is strong, so start by adding a small amount to the sauce, and adjust to individual tastes.

SERVES 2-3

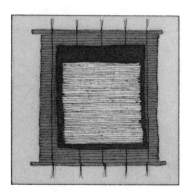
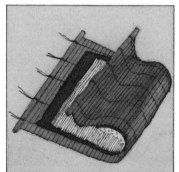

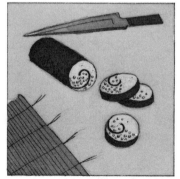

# NORI-MAKI (NORI ROLLS WITH RICE)

One of our favorite everyday "roll" fillings is half brown rice and half sweet brown rice cooked together. (Follow directions for preparing brown rice on page 77.) Sushi Rice (page 79) makes delicious "treat" nori-maki, and is the rice used in most of modern Japan's nori-maki.

Toast nori briefly (unless using sushi nori, which is pretoasted). Place nori, toasted side down, on a sushi mat or countertop. Spread about 1½ cups cooked rice evenly over nori, leaving uncovered 1½ inches nori at the top and ½ inch at the bottom.

Various ingredients can be used for the center of nori rolls. A most simple yet delicious roll can be made using only umeboshi paste—rub umeboshi in a line from left to right across the center of the rice. If desired, vegetables such as thin cucumber strips and/or parboiled carrot strips can be placed next to the umeboshi paste. Shiso (beefsteak) leaves, which come pickled with umeboshi plums, or shiso *senmai* (whole pickled shiso leaves) are especially good.

Starting at the edge closest to you, gently but firmly roll into a tight cylinder. Let the roll rest on its seam. (If necessary, dampen the top edge of the uncovered nori to seal the roll.) Cut the roll in half, and each half into four pieces. Clean knife between cuttings.

Other center ingredients, such as pickles; natto mixed with a little shoyu and minced scallion; sauerkraut; avocado; or very fresh raw salt-water fish and wasabi, provide a variety of interesting tastes and textures. If using wasabi powder, add just a few drops of water to form a paste. It is strong, so rub only a thin layer across the rice. An innovative chef at an American Japanese restaurant invented the "California Roll," a delicious and attractive combination of wasabi, avocado, and strips of boiled crab rolled in nori and white rice.

Depending on the filling, you may or may not need a dipping sauce. More flavorful rolls can be enjoyed as is. Those made with wasabi and unseasoned vegetables or fish are best dipped in a mixture of 3 tablespoons kombu stock or water, 3 tablespoons shoyu, and 1 tablespoon mirin. Combine these ingredients in a small saucepan, simmer for 1 minute, then cool to room temperature. Serve dipping sauce in small individual shallow dishes.

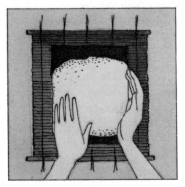
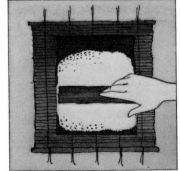

## WAKAME

Appreciated for its flavor and texture, wakame (*Undaria pinnatifida*) has long been a staple in the traditional Japanese diet. A dark green sea vegetable that grows at depths of about two meters, wakame thrives in cold, strong ocean currents. It is an important source of calcium and trace minerals. The taste and texture of different brands of wakame vary considerably. If you have been put off by the strong ocean flavor and relatively tough texture of one brand, ask for recommendations and try another. You may be surprised at how mild and delicious wakame can be.

Dried wakame must be reconstituted by soaking, in water to cover, for 10-15 minutes. Remove, squeeze out excess moisture, cut away any tough ribs, and slice. Wakame is especially good in soups and salads. It can also be added to stews and vegetable or bean dishes. Wakame is tender and should not be cooked for more than a couple of minutes.

You can make a nutritious condiment by toasting dried wakame (be careful—it burns easily) over a flame in a dry skillet or in the oven, then crumbling or grinding into a powder. Toasted sesame seeds may be added and ground with the toasted wakame. Sprinkle over grains, toss with cooked rice before serving, or add a little as seasoning to soups and salads.

*Alaria* is a North American sea vegetable closely related to Japanese wakame. Abundant in cold waters on both coasts, it is now being harvested, dried, packaged, and distributed nationally. Alaria is particularly mild-flavored. Although it requires slightly longer soaking and cooking time, it can be substituted for wakame in most recipes.

## WAKAME/WHITE MISO SOUP

*6 cups water*
*6-inch piece kombu*
*1 packet (¼ cup) bonito flakes (optional)*
*1 large carrot, sliced thin*
*12-inch section wakame*
*5-6 level tablespoons mellow white or mellow barley miso*

The golden color and light, sweet flavor of this nutritious soup make it an ideal choice during the warmer months.

Combine measured water and the kombu in a saucepan, bring just to a boil, and remove kombu. (Set kombu aside and re-use for soup stock, or cook with beans or root vegetables.) Add bonito, remove stock from heat, and let rest for 1-2 minutes. Strain to remove bonito and press flakes with the back of a spoon to return all liquid to stock. Discard flakes. Add carrot to stock and simmer for 10 minutes. Add scallion and simmer 5 minutes more.

Meanwhile, soak wakame for 10-15 minutes, cut away any tough ribs, and slice fronds into 1-inch pieces. Add to soup, simmer for 2 minutes, then turn off heat. Thin the miso in a little of the broth and add it to the soup. Let rest briefly before serving.

If desired, garnish with minced scallion.

This soup can be varied simply by substituting other vegetables such as turnip, potato, onion, leek, or greens. Try adding diced tofu. For an entirely different flavor, substitute 3-4 tablespoons barley or red (rice) miso for the mellow miso.

SERVES 4

## LENTIL SOUP

Served with whole grain bread, this thick, rich soup makes a satisfying lunch in the cooler seasons. It also goes well with rice or millet, pickles, and greens to make a nutritious full-course meal.

Wash lentils and combine with water in a large pot. Break bay leaf into 2-3 pieces and add. Bring to a boil, then lower heat and simmer for 30 minutes or until lentils are just tender. Meanwhile, heat the oil in a skillet, add onion and garlic, and sauté briefly. Add celery and carrot and sauté for 1-2 minutes. Toss with a small pinch of sea salt, cover, lower heat, and cook for 10 minutes.

Soak wakame in 2 cups water for 10-15 minutes. When soft, cut wakame into 1-inch pieces and set aside, reserving soaking water. When lentils are tender, add sautéed vegetables, wakame soaking water, salt, and oregano. Return to a simmer and cook for 15-20 minutes more. Add wakame 5 minutes before the end of cooking time. Remove from heat. Dissolve miso in a little water and add it to the soup. If desired, garnish each bowl with minced parsley.

SERVES 6-8

*2 cups green lentils*
*8 cups water*
*1 bay leaf*
*1 teaspoon light sesame oil*
*1 onion, sliced thin*
*1-2 cloves garlic, minced*
  *(optional)*
*1 rib celery, sliced thin*
*1 carrot, diced*
*⅓ to ½ cup (tightly packed)*
  *dried wakame*
*1½ teaspoons sea salt*
*½ teaspoon dried oregano*
  *(optional)*
*2 level tablespoons barley*
  *miso or red (rice) miso*

## WAKAME-CUCUMBER SALAD

This dish is especially refreshing on a summer day.

Slice cucumber, sprinkle with salt, toss, gently squeeze for one minute, and set aside. Soak wakame, drop into boiling water, then remove and immediately plunge it into cold water to brighten and set the color. Remove any tough ribs and chop wakame into 1-inch pieces. Wrap it in a clean towel to remove excess moisture.

Gently squeeze excess water from cucumbers and place them in a bowl with the wakame. Combine remaining ingredients, add to vegetables, and toss. For an elegant presentation, serve on a bed of lettuce and garnish with paper-thin slices of red radish and a light sprinkling of alfalfa sprouts.

SERVES 3

*1 cucumber, sliced thin*
*½ teaspoon sea salt*
*1 cup (soaked) wakame*
*2 tablespoons rice vinegar*
*2 teaspoons mirin*
*2 teaspoons shoyu*
*1 teaspoon water*

## WAKAME WITH CARROTS AND GINGER

*1½ cups soaked and sliced wakame*
*2 carrots, sliced thin on the diagonal*
*2 teaspoons tamari or shoyu*
*1 teaspoon juice squeezed from grated fresh ginger*

Place soaked and sliced wakame over sliced carrot in pot. Add enough wakame soaking water to almost cover, bring to a boil, lower flame, and simmer for 10 minutes or until vegetables are tender. Add shoyu, toss, and simmer, uncovered, for a few minutes more. If necessary, cook over high heat for the last few minutes to reduce excess liquid. Sprinkle ginger juice over vegetables, toss, and serve.

Leeks are a flavorful addition to this combination of vegetables. Slice a leek into ½-inch diagonals and sauté briefly in 1 teaspoon light sesame oil. Add carrots, then soaked and chopped wakame, sautéeing for 1-2 minutes after each addition. Add 1 cup wakame soaking water, cover pan, and simmer for 10 minutes. Add 1 teaspoon ginger juice and tamari or shoyu to taste (2-3 teaspoons) and cook for 1 minute more.

SERVES 3

## HIJIKI AND ARAME

When properly cooked and presented, hijiki is very attractive. Its shimmering black color adds vivid contrast and beauty to any meal. When planning a meal including hijiki, try to use deep orange colors such as carrots, winter squash, or pumpkin, along with bright greens such as lightly steamed broccoli or watercress. Hijiki salad, topped with a creamy white tofu dressing and a sprinkle of finely minced green onion or parsley, presents an attractive contrast of colors, particularly appealing on a hot summer day.

Hijiki, which in Japanese means "bearer of wealth and beauty," has a balancing effect on blood sugar levels and encourages good facial coloring and thick, healthy hair. Like most other seaweeds, hijiki contains all the nutritional minerals and is especially high in calcium and iron. It is also abundant in protein and many of the essential vitamins.

Although hijiki (*Hizikia fusiforme*) and arame (*Eisenia bicyclis*) are both dark brown sea grasses that are easy to cook and can be used in many of the same ways, there are a few important differences. Hijiki is thicker, somewhat coarser, and has a strong ocean flavor. Arame is the shredded form of a wide-leaf sea grass. Its considerably milder aroma and taste make it a good choice for anyone just beginning to use sea vegetables. Both should be rinsed quickly but carefully to remove foreign matter such as sand and shells, then soaked in water to cover. However, because of the difference in texture, soak hijiki for 10 minutes and the more delicate arame for 5 minutes.

Longer soaking leaches out important nutrients and makes these vegetables waterlogged and therefore less able to absorb the flavor of the seasonings you use. Take into consideration that soaking increases the dried volume by about four times. If you use the soaking water in cooking, pour it carefully so as not to disturb any sand or shells that have sunk to the bottom. Keep back a small amount in the bowl and discard it. Using the soaking water results in a somewhat stronger flavor and decreases the need for added salt or shoyu. In the recipes that follow, fresh water was used, so if you choose to use soaking water, cut the amount of shoyu in half, and add more if needed.

For general preparation, squeeze out excess water after soaking and sauté the sea vegetable in a little oil for a few minutes. Add soaking water or fresh water to almost cover, and simmer until tender and most of the liquid is absorbed (about 40 minutes for hijiki and 25 minutes for arame). Finally, season with shoyu and, if desired, mirin, and cook for a few minutes more. Both hijiki and arame are delicious sautéed with sweet vegetables such as carrots, slow-cooked onions, lotus root, shiitake mushrooms, or dried daikon radish, or with deep-fried fresh tofu or dried tofu. A little chopped hijiki or arame can be combined with cooked rice, millet, or barley, or with fried rice. They are also good in salads, especially with a tofu dressing.

The recipes below are for hijiki. Simply make the above-mentioned adjustments in soaking and cooking time if you wish to substitute arame.

*4-5 dried shiitake mushrooms*
*1¼ cups dry hijiki (or arame)*
*1½ teaspoons sesame oil*
*4 pieces dried tofu*
*1½-2 tablespoons shoyu (use lesser amount if soaking water rather than fresh is added for cooking)*
*2 teaspoons mirin*
*1 carrot, sliced thin on the diagonal*
*2-3 tablespoons minced parsley*

## HIJIKI WITH SHIITAKE, CARROT, AND DRIED TOFU

This is our favorite hijiki recipe. The colorful combination of hijiki, carrots, and parsley is delicious and beautiful. Dried tofu supplies additional concentrated protein and an interesting taste and texture, and mirin lightens the flavor and provides a mild sweetness.

Soak shiitake for at least 2 hours, then remove and discard stems and thinly slice caps. Wash and soak hijiki. Heat oil in a skillet or heavy saucepan, add sliced shiitake, and sauté briefly. Drain hijiki; add to pan and sauté briefly. Add soaking water from hijiki and/or shiitake or fresh water to almost cover. Bring to a boil, lower heat, and let simmer, covered.

Meanwhile, soak dried tofu for 5 minutes, then squeeze out excess water. Dice tofu, add it to the pan, and toss. Simmer for 30 minutes. Add shoyu and mirin, and toss. Place carrots on top of hijiki mixture, cover pot, and let cook for 10 minutes. Toss. If any liquid remains, cook uncovered over medium heat for a few minutes until nearly dry. Sprinkle parsley over, cover, and steam for 1 minute.

**SERVES 4-5**

## HIJIKI WITH SUNFLOWER SEEDS

This variation on the previous recipe includes the rich flavor and high nutritive value of sunflower seeds. It also has a delightfully crunchy texture.

Slice 1 large onion into thin half-moons. Heat the oil and sauté the onion for 2-3 minutes with a small pinch of sea salt. Cover pan and cook onions over very low heat for 15-20 minutes. Add soaked and drained hijiki and proceed as for the above recipe, omitting the shiitake and dried tofu.

To serve, garnish individual portions with minced parsley and toasted sunflower seeds. (To toast seeds, place them in a dry skillet over medium heat and stir constantly just until golden brown and fragrant—about 5 minutes.) For interesting contrast, use white bowls or plates to accent hijiki's deep black color.

**SERVES 4-5**

## HIJIKI SALAD WITH TOFU DRESSING

In this dish the light-colored, cool, and creamy dressing nicely complements the hijiki.

Boil 1¼ cups (dry measure) washed and soaked hijiki in 5 cups water for 25 minutes. If desired, add 1 tablespoon shoyu and 1 teaspoon mirin to cooking water. Drain hijiki and allow to cool to room temperature, or chill slightly. Serve over lettuce leaves with Tofu Sesamiso Dressing (page 187) or Miso-Tofu Salad Dressing (page 10), or nest a spoonful on tossed green salad. Garnish with a little finely minced green onion or parsley.

SERVES 4-5

## KANTEN

This is the Japanese Jello. A vegetable "gelatin" made from several varieties of red seaweed, kanten (also commonly known as agar) is easy to use (and contains absolutely no calories!). It comes prepackaged, in bars, flakes, or powder. Even without refrigeration, kanten sets quickly as it cools, and seals in the natural flavor and sweetness of any fruits and vegetables used. Light and refreshingly cool, kanten dishes are especially popular in summer. In any season kanten can be used with vegetables and stock to make molded aspics, as a substitute for pectin in jams and jellies, in cranberry sauce, and in desserts such as puddings and pie fillings.

Kanten is harvested and processed only in the coldest winter months. After the seaweed is cooked, it is allowed to harden into a dense gelatin, then cut into squares and spread on mats to freeze-dry naturally. Over a period of about ten days, moisture in the gelatin freezes at night and forms ice on the surface, then thaws during the day, until all the moisture is gone and only the light, flaky bars of pure kanten remain. Kanten flakes are produced by simply shredding the bars. Although kanten also comes in powder form, this product is made by more modern processing methods in large factories, so I recommend using bars or flakes.

To use kanten bars, tear them into several pieces and soak them in water for 30-60 minutes. Remove, squeeze out excess water, and place kanten in a saucepan with liquid (fruit juice or vegetable broth, according to the dish you are making) that is cold or at room temperature. Bring to a simmer over medium heat without stirring. Once it begins to simmer, stir occasionally until the kanten dissolves (about 2-3 minutes). The texture will be best if you simmer the mixture for no more than 3-4 minutes. Prepackaged flakes need not be soaked. Simply sprinkle the measured amount over the liquid before heating and proceed as for bars.

The amount of kanten needed varies according to the type of liquid and the other ingredients being jelled, so follow recipes carefully until you have gained some experience with this product. In any recipe, flakes can be substituted for bars, and vice-versa. The jelling strength of one bar of kanten is equivalent to two slightly rounded tablespoons of flakes.

## APPLE-BERRY COOLER

*4 cups juice (apple, apple-raspberry, or apple-strawberry)*
*small pinch sea salt*
*4 slightly rounded tablespoons kanten flakes, or 2 bars kanten*
*2 cups fresh berries (raspberries, strawberries, blackberries, or blueberries)*

Kanten makes an especially good summer dessert since it is light and cooling and requires little time and heat to prepare.

Pour juice into a saucepan and add salt. Sprinkle in kanten. (If using bars, follow directions given above.) Bring to a simmer over medium heat without stirring. When it begins to simmer, occasionally stir gently. Simmer 3 minutes, then remove from heat. Pour over fresh whole or sliced berries in a casserole dish or mold. Refrigerate or set in a cool place, uncovered. The kanten should be firm in 1-2 hours.

For a delightful variation, add 1-2 teaspoons juice from grated fresh ginger and 2 tablespoons lemon juice to the mixture after removing from heat.

SERVES 6

## BLUEBERRY KANTEN IN HONEYDEW

*3 cups apple juice*
*small pinch sea salt*
*4 slightly rounded tablespoons kanten flakes*
*1 cup blueberries*
*2 honeydew melons (or cantaloupes)*

Here is another quick and simple fruit gelatin, but with an elegant presentation.

Combine juice and salt in saucepan, sprinkle kanten on and bring to a boil without stirring. When boiling, gently stir to dissolve kanten, then add blueberries and cook for 5 minutes. Remove from heat.

Pour kanten into a bowl and refrigerate until slightly gelled (about 40 minutes), then stir to evenly distribute berries.

Cut melons in half and scoop out seeds. Pour out any juice and pat melon dry with paper towel or clean dish cloth. Fill melon halves with the kanten. (Pour any remaining kanten into dessert cups or a small bowl.) Refrigerate until completely set. Slice into wedges to serve.

SERVES 6-8

# BANANA CREME PIE

Sensuously cool and creamy, wonderfully rich and delicious, this pie is sure to be a hit.

Prepare your favorite pie crust or follow the recipe for a single whole wheat pie crust on page 88. Prebake (at 375° F. for 15-20 minutes or until crisp) and allow to cool before filling.

To prepare almond milk, drop ½ cup almonds into boiling water to cover. Boil for 10 seconds, turn off heat, and let sit for 2-3 minutes. Drain, and remove skins. Combine almonds with 2 cups cold water, ⅛ teaspoon sea salt, ½ tablespoon light sesame or corn oil, and 2 tablespoons rice syrup or 1 tablespoon honey in blender and blend for 1-2 minutes. Strain through cheesecloth, squeezing out all liquid, and store refrigerated in a covered container. Use strained almond meal for Bob's Coconut-Amazake Macaroons or for Almond Cookies. Almond milk will keep for about 6 days in the refrigerator.

To make vanilla pudding/pie filling, combine maple syrup, 1¾ cups almond milk and ⅛ teaspoon sea salt in a small saucepan. Sprinkle kanten flakes over and bring to a simmer over medium heat without stirring. Simmer for 1 minute. Thoroughly dissolve the arrowroot or kuzu in the remaining ¼ cup almond milk and add to the pudding while stirring briskly. Return to a simmer and cook for 1-2 minutes. Remove from heat and mix in vanilla and, if desired, butter.

Slice 2 bananas and place in prebaked pie shell. Slice the third and fold into pudding. Pour pudding into pie shell, garnish with toasted unsweetened coconut (toast in a dry skillet, stirring constantly, until golden) or toasted slivered almonds. Chill the pie for at least 1-2 hours (until firm) before serving.

*1 pie shell (prebaked)*
*2 cups almond milk (see recipe this page)*
*¼ cup maple syrup*
*⅛ teaspoon sea salt*
*2 level tablespoons kanten flakes*
*2 tablespoons arrowroot powder or 1½ tablespoons kuzu*
*1 teaspoon vanilla extract*
*1 tablespoon butter (optional)*
*3 ripe bananas*
*2-3 tablespoons toasted unsweetened coconut or toasted slivered almonds*

# CAROB PUDDING/PIE FILLING

Follow directions for vanilla pudding in Banana Creme Pie recipe, but blend 2-3 tablespoons carob powder into the 1¾ cup almond milk before heating. Reduce maple syrup to 3 tablespoons, and vanilla to ½ teaspoon. Chill in small dessert cups or pour into prebaked and cooled pie shell, and garnish as for Banana Creme Pie.

Carob powder is derived from the seed pods of a Mediterranean tree. It has a flavor similar to chocolate but does not have a high fat content.

PUDDING SERVES 4-5

*1 cup raisins*
*3½ cups apple or apple-*
   *cranberry juice*
*2 cups cranberries, washed*
*pinch sea salt*
*4 level tablespoons kanten*
   *flakes*
*2 tablespoons kuzu*

## CRANBERRY SAUCE

Simmer raisins in 1 cup of the juice for 10 minutes. Add remaining juice, cranberries, and salt. Sprinkle kanten flakes over and bring to a simmer without stirring. When simmering, stir occasionally until kanten is dissolved. Simmer for 10 minutes (cranberries will rise to the surface and pop). Remove from heat.

Crush lumps of kuzu before measuring and dissolve it in 2 tablespoons water. Add kuzu to pot while stirring briskly. Return to heat and simmer for 2 minutes. Pour into a bowl or mold and allow to set.

SERVES 8

[1]Arasake, S. & Arasake, T., *Vegetables from the Sea.* Tokyo: Japan Publishers, Inc., 1983, p. 45.
[2]*Ibid, p. 46.*
[3]*Ibid, p. 39.*
[4]*Ibid, p. 60.*

A superficial look at traditional Japanese food might suggest that beans are an insignificant part of the diet. Dishes such as thick bean soups and baked beans never appear. Occasionally, on special holidays, a small side dish of black beans is served, and rice or sweet rice is sometimes cooked with the addition of about 10 percent beans. For instance, azuki-rice is served for the celebration of a birth or other festive event.

A closer look will show, however, that beans are a part of almost every Japanese meal. Soybeans fermented in a variety of ways or processed as tofu and its residue byproduct *okara* are an important source of protein and other nutrients in the grain-based, mainly vegetarian traditional Japanese diet. Among the fermented soy products, miso and shoyu are of particular importance. Both are used daily. Though less central, *natto*, another fermented soyfood, is often served with rice. These foods are discussed in detail in the Fermented Foods section of this book.

It is common for beans to have a prominent place in cultures whose traditional diet is centered around grains. And what has been intuitively understood for thousands of years has recently been rediscovered by scientific research. That is, that neither beans nor whole grains contain all the essential amino acids ("building blocks" of protein). However, the amino acids in beans complement those in grains—when eaten together they provide an abundance of high-quality protein in proper proportions for ready assimilation. In addition, beans are a rich source of calcium, iron, the B vitamins thiamine, riboflavin, and niacin, complex carbohydrates, fiber, and fat.

Beans are also flavorful and versatile. They can be eaten hot in hearty winter dishes or enjoyed in summer salads. The same bean can take on different personalities depending on whether it is seasoned with salt, shoyu, or miso, or marinated in a blend of oil, vinegar, and herbs. Beans can be combined with grains, noodles, and land or sea vegetables in soups and stews, side dishes, salads, and casseroles. Leftover beans can be reheated, or mashed and made into savory spreads, with vegetables and herbs such as minced onion or scallion, garlic, parsley, celery, lemon, and cayenne. Bean spreads are especially good on chapati or crackers with lettuce and alfalfa sprouts.

Beans are often difficult to digest, but several measures can be taken to reduce their gas-forming tendency. First, except for azuki beans and lentils, beans should be soaked for at least several hours or overnight. Since they expand considerably when soaked, use three times as much water as beans. Another method is to bring the beans to a boil then soak for two hours. I have been told that some of the elements that create gas are water soluble, so I always discard the soaking water. Cook beans, except for azukis, with a piece of kombu since it aids digestibility as well as decreases cooking time by helping to soften them.

Whether pressure cooking or simmering, begin by boiling the beans in an uncovered pot for about ten minutes. Skim off any foam that rises to the surface, then cover and continue cooking until beans are tender. Long, slow cooking is best. Never add salt, shoyu, or miso to beans before they are tender, or their cooking will be slowed considerably. When the beans are tender, salt should be added to aid digestion and enhance flavor.

There are other factors besides cooking method that affect how your intestines will receive beans. Eat a reasonably small volume and chew well. Serve beans for lunch or as an early dinner so you will have plenty of time to digest them before sleeping. Finally, when serving beans, always be aware of the other ingredients in that dish and in the entire meal. In general, keep things simple. Beans and sweets are an especially troublesome digestive combination. So it is best not to eat fruit or dessert for at least an hour or two after a meal that includes beans.

## AZUKI BEANS

Azuki beans have long been highly regarded in Japan for their rich nutritional and strengthening qualities. Like other legumes, the small, red azukis are a good source of vitamins, minerals, and protein.

For centuries azuki beans have been used in the Orient as a folk remedy for kidney problems. Traditional medicine recommends the use of azukis cooked with pumpkin or squash to help restore and maintain proper blood sugar balance.

Although soaking most beans reduces the cooking time, it isn't essential to soak azuki beans. If pressure cooking, wash beans, add 2½ to 2¾ cups water for each cup of beans, bring up to pressure, then turn heat down and cook for 50 minutes to an hour. Let pressure come down, add ¼ teaspoon sea salt, a little more water if necessary to keep the beans moist, and simmer for 10-15 minutes more. Pot boiling takes almost twice as long as pressure cooking, but results in a slightly sweeter flavor. You will need to add more water for pot boiling. Start with water to cover the beans and occasionally add cold water to cover as liquid is absorbed. The beans will cook faster this way than if all the water is added at the beginning.

*Always add salt, shoyu, or miso to all varieties of beans only after they are tender.*

## AZUKI SOUP

*1 cup azuki beans*
*5 cups water*
*1 onion, sliced or diced*
*½ bay leaf*
*pinch rosemary (optional)*
*1 rib celery, sliced (optional)*
*1½ cups diced carrot, or*
   *peeled and diced winter*
   *squash*
*½ teaspoon sea salt*
*½ cup minced parsley*
   *(optional)*
*1 tablespoon shoyu, or 1*
   *rounded tablespoon miso*
   *thinned in a little water*

Wash beans and combine with water, onion, bay leaf, and rosemary in pressure cooker. Bring to pressure, reduce flame, and cook for 50 minutes. Reduce pressure, add celery, carrot or squash, salt, and, if necessary, a little more water, and simmer for 20 minutes. Add parsley (reserving a little for garnish) and shoyu or miso, and simmer for two minutes more.

If pot-boiling instead of pressure cooking, simmer for about 2½ hours, adding more water as needed. Add celery, carrot or squash, and salt when beans are just tender, and continue as above.

## AZUKI RICE

*⅓ cup azuki beans*
*2 cups brown rice*
*3¼ cups water*
*2 pinches sea salt*
*2 tablespoons toasted sesame*
   *seeds and/or minced pars-*
   *ley, for garnish*

Azuki beans go particularly well with brown rice, and the combination supplies a good balance of all essential amino acids. The water reserved from parboiling azuki beans adds color to this festive dish.

Wash beans, combine with 1½ cups water in a saucepan, and bring to a boil. Simmer, uncovered, for 10-15 minutes, then let cool to lukewarm. Wash the rice and place in a pressure cooker. Drain beans and add water to bean liquid to equal 3¼ cups. Add beans and water to rice, along with the salt. Bring to pressure, reduce flame, and cook for 50 minutes to one hour. Allow pressure to return to normal. (If you are pot-boiling Azuki Rice, parboil beans in 2 cups water for 30-40 minutes. Drain beans. Add water to bean liquid to equal 4¼ cups liquid and combine with rice, beans, and salt. Cook, covered, over medium-low flame for one hour after it begins to boil.) The amount of water needed for either cooking method will vary slightly depending on variety of rice and type of pot used.

Remove cover, toss, and garnish with parsley and/or toasted sesame seeds.

For variation, substitute ½ cup barley or ½ cup sweet brown rice for ½ cup of the rice.

**SERVES 4**

# BAKED AZUKI-SQUASH MEDLEY

This recipe brings out azukis' full flavor and sweetness. If possible, use organic squash—it is more flavorful.

For this recipe, soak beans for two to three hours, then discard soaking water. Place beans in a pressure cooker with water to cover and bring to boil, uncovered. Drain beans and discard liquid (this removes azukis' slightly bitter taste). Add 2½ cups cold water, and the herbs. Bring to pressure, lower heat, and cook for 45-50 minutes (or use pot-boiling method).

Meanwhile, slice onion thinly and sauté in the oil until translucent and limp. Add squash and a small pinch of sea salt and sauté briefly. Lower heat, cover, and cook until squash is somewhat softened but not completely tender. (Check frequently and, if necessary, add only enough water to prevent scorching.) Uncover and set aside.

Preheat oven to 375° F. Combine in a casserole dish cooked beans, vegetables, and miso thinned in two tablespoons water. Cover and bake for 30-40 minutes. Serve garnished with chopped parsley.

SERVES 5-6

*1 cup azuki beans*
*2½ cups water*
*½ bay leaf*
*pinch dried rosemary*
*1 teaspoon light sesame oil*
*1 large onion*
*2½ cups bite-sized pieces winter squash (peeled butternut or acorn, or buttercup)*
*pinch sea salt*
*2 level tablespoons red miso*

# NOODLE-BEAN SALAD

Light, colorful, and nutritious, this is a good way to get beans into your diet in summer when hot soups and heavier dishes are unappetizing.

Bring salt and measured water to a rolling boil and gradually add noodles so as not to completely stop the boiling. Stir until water returns to a rapid boil to prevent noodles from sticking to the bottom of the pan. Cook until just tender (7-10 minutes), then immediately drain and cool thoroughly under cold running water. Drain and set aside.

While noodles are cooking, wash and cut vegetables. Blend dressing ingredients until smooth. Combine beans, noodles, and vegetables in a large bowl (reserving a little of the parsley), add dressing, and mix well. Garnish with remaining parsley. Serve at room temperature or slightly chilled.

SERVES 4-6

*1 cup cooked azuki beans*
*2 cups dry noodles (such as elbows, small shells, spirals)*
*½ teaspoon sea salt*
*10 cups water*
*½ cup minced scallion*
*⅓ cup minced parsley*
*¾ cup celery, sliced thin*
*¾ cup green pepper, seeded and diced*

DRESSING:
*2-3 level tablespoons mellow white miso*
*3 tablespoons tahini*
*2 tablespoons lemon juice*
*4-5 tablespoons water*
*pinch garlic powder (or 1 clove minced fresh) and/or tarragon (optional)*

## BLACK SOYBEANS

With 35 to 40 percent protein content, soybeans have become known as "the meat of the East." Black soybeans are almost identical in nutritional composition to yellow soybeans, but they are easier to digest than yellow soybeans and much tastier. In Japan the rich, sweet flavor of black soybeans is combined with rice or cooked alone as a side dish. They are also delicious with onion, carrot, and celery in a hearty soup.

Except for Black Soybeans and Rice, these beans should always be soaked for 10 to 12 hours before cooking and should be boiled rather than pressure cooked since the skins loosen easily and can clog your pressure cooker valve.

## BLACK BEANS

*1 cup black soybeans*
*4-5 cups water*
*¼ teaspoon sea salt*
*2 teaspoons shoyu*

Various traditional foods, each symbolizing a hope for the New Year, are always included in the first meal of the year in Japan. Boiled black soybeans, representing health, are an important part of this special and elaborate dinner.

Soak beans in 3 cups water for 10-12 hours, then drain, combine with 4-5 cups fresh water in a saucepan, and bring to a boil. Allow to boil uncovered for a few minutes, and skim off any foam that rises to the surface. Lower heat, cover, and simmer until beans are tender (about 3-4 hours). Add water as needed to keep beans just covered. When tender, add salt, and simmer uncovered to reduce liquid. When there is just a little "bottom juice" left, add shoyu, gently shake the pot to stir, and simmer for a few minutes more, being careful not to scorch. Remove from heat, shake the pot to coat beans with the small amount of remaining liquid, and serve.

Although there is certainly something to be said for long, slow cooking of beans, Black Beans can be made in less than half the time if you have an Ohsawa Ceramic Cooking Pot. This wonderful invention fits inside a pressure cooker and allows the beans to cook in just an hour. Since the ceramic pot is covered, you don't have to worry about the bean skins loosening and clogging the pressure cooker valve. Combine the soaked beans and 1¾ cups water in the ceramic pot and place 4 cups water in your pressure cooker. Place the ceramic pot inside the pressure cooker, bring to pressure, and cook for 60-70 minutes. Remove from heat, allow pressure to return to normal, then transfer beans and their cooking liquid to a saucepan, add the salt, and proceed as described above. Ohsawa Pots are now being distributed in this country, and can be found at some natural foods shops that carry macrobiotic supplies.

*SERVES 4*

# BLACK BEAN SOUP

For a savory black bean soup, simply follow the recipe for Black Beans, adding more water or stock to soup consistency. When beans are tender, add ½ teaspoon sea salt and, if desired, vegetables such as sliced celery, carrot, and onion or leek. Simmer until vegetables are tender (about 20 minutes), add shoyu to taste, and cook for a few minutes more. This soup is especially attractive and delicious garnished with a thin round of fresh lemon and a sprig of parsley.

SERVES 4

# BLACK SOYBEANS AND RICE

This delicious and satisfying dish is simple to prepare and provides plenty of high-quality complete protein.

*⅓ cup black soybeans*
*1 ½ cups brown rice*
*½ cup sweet brown rice (or*
*  use 2 cups brown rice)*
*approximately 2 ¾ cups water*
*¼ teaspoon sea salt*

Wash beans, drain, and roast in a dry skillet over medium heat. Stir constantly for 5-10 minutes, or until skins begin to crack and pop.

Wash rices and drain well. Add beans to rice in pressure cooker and mix. Add water and salt. (The exact amount of water needed may vary slightly according to the type of pressure cooker and variety of rice you are using.) Bring to pressure, then lower heat and cook for one hour. Turn off and allow pressure to return to normal, then remove cover, toss, and serve. (For pot-boiling, you will need to precook the beans before cooking with the rice. Add water to cover the roasted beans and simmer for 2-3 hours, adding water as necessary, or until they begin to be tender. Drain beans and add enough water to their liquid to equal about 3 ¼ cups. Add beans, liquid, and salt to rice, cover tightly, and simmer for one hour or until all liquid is absorbed and rice and beans are tender.)

If desired, garnish with a sprig of parsley, and serve with *gomashio* (see page 188) on the side.

SERVES 4-5

## TOFU

Tofu (soybean curd) is one of the most well-known Japanese foods in the West. Versatile, nutritious, economical, and available almost everywhere, it has a mild, unimposing flavor of its own and an ability to absorb other flavors well. Some of the most popular ways of enjoying tofu are the simplest, taking but a few minutes to prepare. Tofu is equally at home in all styles of cooking from the plainest to the most beautiful and elegant.

Tofu's long and honorable history began with its development in China more than two thousand years ago. It gradually became a popular and important source of protein throughout the East. After being brought to Japan in the eighth century, probably by Buddhist monks, tofu quickly became an integral part of the vegetarian cuisine served in Japanese temples. Though the basic process for making tofu remained the same, the Japanese modified the dense, relatively dry Chinese variety by making it more delicate and tender, with the consistency of a firm custard. By the fifteenth century, tofu had become a common item in the diet of all classes of Japanese people. Commercial production of tofu began in the U.S. about a century ago, in Chinese and Japanese communities. In the last twenty years or so it has been rapidly gaining in popularity, especially among health-conscious people.

As more Westerners become aware of the health dangers of an overconsumption of dairy products, meat, and eggs, they are turning to tofu as an excellent source of easily digestible protein. According to William Shurtleff, author with Akiko Aoyagi of *The Book of Tofu* (Ballantine Books, 1979), the usable protein supplied by an eight-ounce serving of tofu is equivalent to that of two eggs—over 25 percent of the recommended adult daily protein requirement. Tofu is a particularly important food in a grain-centered diet since it is abundant in lysine, an essential amino acid that many grains and grain products contain only small amounts of. Conversely, tofu is deficient in those amino acids that most grains are high in. This complementary relationship means that tofu and grains eaten together in the same meal provide considerably more usable protein than they would if served separately.

Another advantage that tofu has over many other high-protein foods is its digestibility. In *The Book of Tofu* Shurtleff and Aoyagi point out that tofu's digestion rate of 95 percent greatly exceeds that of cooked whole soybeans (68 percent) because the soybeans' crude fiber and water-soluble carbohydrates are removed during the tofu-making process.

Tofu is an excellent source of calcium and a good source of several other minerals and vitamins—most notably iron, several B vitamins, and vitamin E. I was surprised to learn that the type of tofu most commonly sold in this country contains 23 percent more calcium by weight than dairy milk. And as a diet food, tofu is hard to beat. Highly nutritious yet low in calories,

carbohydrates, and saturated fats and completely free of
cholesterol, tofu is an excellent substitute for meat, eggs, and
dairy products. Tofu also helps the body break down and eliminate fat deposits because it has a high concentration of linoleic
acid, an essential polyunsaturated fatty acid that emulsifies stored
cholesterol and fatty acids. Also, many protein-rich foods are
acid-forming, but tofu contributes to an alkaline condition in the
body, which is important to maintaining health and well-being.
With all this going for it, it is no wonder that tofu has become so
popular.

In Japan there are thousands of family-operated tofu shops
as well as many large, modern factories making various types of
tofu. Even today it is usual for fresh tofu to be delivered daily
or on request to homes in a shop owner's locality. In the small
community where we lived there were two tofu shops. I
remember the wife of one of the shop owners driving up on a
motor scooter to deliver tofu and its related products. When I
was sent to the shop to pick up some deep-fried tofu for the
evening meal, I was surprised to find available many types of
tofu and tofu products. They ranged from the smooth and shiny,
delicate *kinu* ("silk") tofu to the firm, lightly-broiled *yakidofu*,
to golden-brown, deep-fried tofu in a variety of sizes and shapes.
Since my Japanese was not yet nearly fluent enough to ask the
numerous questions that came to mind, much less to understand
the answers, I knew my curiosity would have to be satisfied gradually by watching, tasting, and finally by asking and listening.

Over time it became clear to me that *momen* ("cotton") tofu
is the most versatile and commonly used variety in Japan and by
far the most available in the U.S. It is often referred to as "regular" tofu. The making of this and all other types begins with
the soaking, draining, and grinding of soybeans. The ground
beans are gently simmered in water. Straining the liquid and
pressing the bean pulp until it is dry yields soy "milk." A
coagulant is then added to the soy milk to separate the curds and
whey. The next step differentiates regular tofu from silk tofu.
To make regular tofu, the curds are poured into cotton-lined
molds that are perforated for drainage. The curds are pressed
until they take block, or "cake" shape and become firm.
Finally the cakes are soaked in cold water to maintain freshness
and make them a little more firm.

Silk tofu differs from regular in that it is made from a
thicker, richer soymilk that is neither strained nor pressed. The
soymilk is simply mixed with a coagulant and allowed to take
shape in molds that have no holes for drainage. Since the curds
and whey are not separated, silk tofu has a higher water content
and, consequently, a much softer, smoother consistency. The two
types are similar in appearance, but silk tofu has a smoother,
glossier exterior. Prized for its delicate, creamy texture, and
slightly sweeter flavor, this light, sensuous delicacy is in great
demand in Japan during the hot, humid summers, when it is used

mainly in Chilled Tofu (see page 173). Less versatile than regular tofu and less able to absorb flavors, silk tofu is also commonly used in Simmered Tofu (see page 174). In this country silk tofu is generally only available in some Oriental food stores.

Regular tofu, on the other hand, is readily available and can be used in countless ways. It is excellent in soups, one-pot dishes, and salad dressings. It can be used for mock fried chicken, scrambled "eggs," sandwich spreads, dips, creamy dressings, even desserts. Mixed with lemon juice, or in combination with lemon-tahini-miso-garlic, tofu can be made to resemble sour cream or soft cheese in both taste and appearance.

In Japan, grilled tofu (*yakidofu*) and deep-fried tofu (*age*) are common in many traditional Japanese dishes and are prepared daily at local tofu shops. Grilled tofu is simply regular tofu that has been pressed to extract excess water, then lightly broiled. Because of its firmer texture, grilled tofu keeps its shape well when sautéed or simmered in stews. To prepare it at home, simply press ½-inch thick slices of regular tofu as described in Pan-Fried Tofu Cutlets on page 171, then lightly broil until the skin is mottled but not scorched.

The two types of deep-fried regular tofu used in Japan both have a firm yet tender, meaty texture, hearty flavor and golden-brown color. After frying, tofu maintains freshness longer, absorbs flavors better and, because it has almost 50 percent less water than "raw" tofu, it contains nearly twice as much protein by weight. Thick deep-fried tofu, called *atsu-age* or *nama-age*, is made by frying 1-inch-thick slabs of pressed regular tofu in vegetable oil heated to 375°F. In just a few minutes the high temperature of the oil makes the surface of the tofu crisp and golden-brown, while the interior remains soft and white. This type is easy to make at home (see Deep-Fried Tofu, page 172).

Thin deep-fried tofu (*usu-age*) is difficult to make at home, but is available in some Japanese markets. It is made by first frying ¼-inch thick slices of pressed regular tofu in moderately hot oil for a relatively long time, then transferring them to a pot of hot (375°F.) oil for a short time. This method causes the tofu to expand and become porous inside. Although this type is better for making stuffed tofu "pouches," for most purposes, thin and thick deep-fried tofu can be used interchangeably.

There are a couple of important things to remember about tofu. First, it must be eaten while still fresh. In Japan it is usually eaten within a day or two after being made. That may not always be possible in this country, and properly stored it will keep for 5-7 days. Tofu must be refrigerated continuously. If you are shopping and have several errands to do, try to make your stop for tofu last so it won't have a chance to get warm before you get it home. Store the tofu covered with water—the more water you use, the longer it will stay fresh. To maximize shelflife, the water should be changed daily. If tofu develops a sour taste and odor, it should be discarded. If it is several days old, but not yet sour, it can be refreshed before use by parboiling for just a minute or two, or by deep-frying. Refrigerated in an airtight container, deep-fried tofu will keep for 7-10 days. Do not store deep-fried tofu in water. Preserving tofu by freezing results in a radical change to a drier, more spongy texture, so unless you are doing it for that purpose, it is not recommended.

Another thing to keep in mind is that tofu should not be cooked too long, in most cases not more than 5-10 minutes, or it will become porous and hard. When you are using it in soups and simmered dishes, add it at the last minute to just heat through.

Regular tofu is available almost everywhere—in natural foods stores, supermarkets, and Oriental food stores. Blocks, or "cakes," of tofu vary in size and weight, but generally weigh between ten and sixteen ounces. They are often packaged in water in small plastic tubs or in large bulk containers, though more and more manufacturers are vacuum packaging individual blocks in an attempt to extend shelflife.

When you shop for tofu, read the label for the type of coagulant used. Most tofu found in natural foods outlets, and some carried in supermarkets and Oriental markets, is made with "natural *nigari*" (bittern), the residue that remains after salt is extracted from sea water. Nigari is made up mostly of magnesium chloride, but it also contains various trace minerals. Tofu manufacturers who use natural nigari also often use organically grown soybeans and well water. Refined nigari is commonly listed on the label as "magnesium chloride." This nigari is usually the byproduct of an extensive chemical process. Occasionally you may find tofu made with lemon or lime juice, which gives the tofu a mildly tart flavor.

According to William Shurtleff, calcium sulfate, another commonly-used coagulant, is preferred over all others for three reasons. First, it is the most pure and natural. Calcium sulfate is a naturally-occurring mineral found in deep mines in this country, and there is no chemical processing involved. Second, the tofu made with calcium sulfate has three and a half times more calcium than that made with natural or refined nigari. Finally, tofu made with calcium sulfate costs less since the coagulant itself is less expensive and because it is easier to make tofu with it.

Since freshness is of the utmost importance, another point to be aware of when shopping for tofu is where it was made. While more grocers are beginning to order tofu from local suppliers, here on the East Coast it is still common to find tofu in supermarket chain stores that was made in California. More than likely, tofu shipped such a great distance will be spoiled before you even get it home, so try to find a good source of locally-made, or at least regionally-made, tofu. Natural foods stores tend to order from the nearest high-quality manufacturer. Sometimes the date of manufacture is stamped on the package. If not, find out when it is delivered—often it comes in on the same day or days each week—and plan your shopping accordingly.

The quality of tofu in Oriental food stores varies greatly, so read labels and ask questions. Though Japanese markets, especially those in metropolitan areas, carry a wider variety of tofu products, such as silk tofu and deep-fried tofu, this advantage must be weighed against the often inferior quality of the ingredients used. Chinese-style tofu is available in many Asian food stores. This type is similar to regular tofu, except that it is considerably more firm and dry as a result of being pressed with a heavier weight for a longer period of time. Its coagulant is usually calcium sulfate.

If you do not live in an area where fresh, good-quality tofu is available, try making it at home. There are several books that provide clear step-by-step directions. Even though it is not difficult, and the results are generally superior to what you can buy, at first it may seem like a lot of time and effort for a pound or so of tofu. Once you become accustomed to the process, however, you will find it easy and the rewards at table well worth the effort.

An added advantage to making tofu at home is that you are actually making two products at once. Called *okara* in Japanese, the soy pulp left after straining the liquid has many uses. Mixed with flour or cooked grain, vegetables, and seasonings, it can be made into burgers or croquettes. It is also good sautéed with vegetables and seasoned with shoyu and mirin, or added to breads or muffins. Some tofu manufacturers use it to make "soysage," a meatless mock sausage. Okara provides some nutrients as well as plenty of fiber. Its greatest benefit, though, is to nursing mothers. Okara has been eaten for centuries in Japan to enrich mothers' milk and stimulate its flow. It is also commonly fed to dairy cows for the same purpose (*The Book of Tofu*, p. 91). A few Oriental markets carry okara, and if you happen to live near a tofu shop you can get it fresh almost anytime.

Dried tofu (*koya-dofu*) is a product closely related to fresh tofu, but with some very different properties. When reconstituted it has a porous, spongy texture that enables it to absorb flavors especially well. It has an unrefrigerated shelflife of several months and an exceptionally high protein content.

Begin by trying the tofu recipes below and soon you will be thinking up your own interesting ways to use this versatile and nutritious food.

# BROILED TOFU WITH WALNUT-MISO TOPPING

This delicious, protein-rich entree is easy to prepare. Cut the block of tofu crosswise into six ½-inch-thick slices and lay them on one end of a clean, dry kitchen towel. Fold towel over tofu pieces and pat lightly to soak up surface liquid. Remove tofu from towel and place the slices on a lightly oiled cookie sheet or baking pan. Broil on one side until golden. Turn and broil on the other side.

Meanwhile, roast the nuts in a dry skillet over medium heat, stirring constantly, until crisp and fragrant. Grind the roasted nuts to a fairly fine meal in a suribachi or blender. Add the miso and mix thoroughly, then mix in the water or stock and, if desired, mirin or rice syrup. Spread a thin layer of topping on each slice of broiled tofu and broil for one minute more. Garnish with chopped chives or a sprig of parsley.

For a variation on this recipe, instead of walnut-miso use the sweet miso topping described in Mochi Dengaku. With the addition of a little more water, this topping turns into a savory sauce for noodles, grains, or steamed vegetables.

SERVES 3

*1 large block tofu (approximately 1 lb.)*
*½ cup walnuts*
*3 tablespoons mellow white or mellow barley miso*
*3 tablespoons water or stock*
*1-2 teaspoons mirin or 1 teaspoon rice syrup (optional)*

# PAN-FRIED TOFU CUTLETS

Cut the block of tofu into 4 slices crosswise. Lay the pieces at one end of a clean kitchen towel placed on a cutting board. Fold the towel over the top of the tofu and cover with a 4-5 pound flat object, such as another cutting board or a cookie sheet with a pot on top for added weight. Prop up one end of the bottom cutting board with a book to raise it an inch or two so that any moisture squeezed out of the tofu can drain off. Let it sit for about 10 minutes.

Place 1 tablespoon shoyu in a bowl or plate and gently roll the tofu slices in it to coat all surfaces. Drain off any excess shoyu. Combine flour and corn meal and roll the tofu in the mixture. Heat the oil in a skillet and fry tofu over medium heat until crisp and golden on both sides. If there is excess oil in the pan, blot dry between slices with a paper towel. Combine remaining 1½ tablespoons shoyu, the wine or sake (if using), and the mirin. Pour sauce over the tofu, then remove skillet from heat.

Use individual bowls or plates for serving. Garnish each slice with a little minced scallion and, if desired, finely grated ginger. Place a little of the liquid remaining in the pan around the tofu. Serve hot.

SERVES 4

*1 large block tofu (approximately 1 lb.)*
*2½ tablespoons shoyu*
*1 tablespoon whole wheat flour*
*2 tablespoons corn meal*
*1½ tablespoons light sesame, corn, or safflower oil*
*1 tablespoon dry white wine or sake, optional*
*2 teaspoons mirin (if omitting wine or sake, increase mirin to 1½ tablespoons)*
*1 scallion, finely minced*
*1 rounded teaspoon grated ginger (optional)*

*2 blocks tofu*
*¼ cup arrowroot powder*
  *(optional)*
*2-3 cups unrefined vegetable*
  *oil for deep-frying*

## DEEP-FRIED TOFU (AGE)

Properly fried, tofu should be crisp and golden on the outside and soft and tender, with a spongy texture, inside. Generally, deep-fried tofu is dowsed in boiling water to remove excess oil. Dip the pieces of deep-fried tofu in boiling water, then drain for a minute before using. If desired, pat them dry with paper towels.

In Japan, deep-fried tofu is commonly added to soups, especially miso soup, used in various simmered dishes, sautéed with hijiki or other vegetables, and floated on noodles in broth. A delicious variety of sushi, called "*inari zushi*" or "pouch" sushi is made by making a slit in a thin rectangular or triangular slice of deep-fried tofu, then simmering it in a seasoned broth and filling it with sushi (vinegared) rice. Deep-fried tofu is also adaptable to Western-style cooking. Try some in casseroles, stews, salads—especially grain, noodle, or chef's salads—and in sandwiches. A simple and delicious way to serve deep-fried tofu is freshly prepared, while still crisp and hot, with just a sprinkle of shoyu and a little minced scallion and finely grated ginger. When served this way, or when broiled after frying, the tofu should not be dowsed in water.

If the blocks of tofu are large (about one pound), cut them in half lengthwise, then into 3 or 4 crosswise slices about ¾-inch thick. Smaller blocks need not be cut lengthwise before slicing. Drain in a towel on a cutting board as in Pan-Fried Tofu Cutlets. Let drain for 30-40 minutes, then pat dry with another towel. If desired, roll the tofu in the arrowroot powder, which adds crispness (but can be a hindrance by making the frying tofu pieces stick together).

Tofu must be deep-fried at a relatively high temperature, so be sure the oil is very hot (375°F.) before you slip in the first few pieces. Keep them separated, turn occasionally, and fry until all surfaces of the tofu are golden brown (about 3 minutes). Remove all pieces from one batch and place on wire racks or absorbent paper before adding more tofu to the oil.

To store deep-fried tofu, allow it to cool completely, then wrap it in plastic wrap or in an airtight plastic bag and put it in the refrigerator or freezer. With freezing, the tofu becomes porous and even more able to absorb flavors, making it excellent for use in stews and sauces.

## DEEP-FRIED TOFU IN BROTH

One simple and delicious way to serve deep-fried tofu is topped with minced scallion and finely grated daikon and ginger in a shoyu-seasoned broth. To remove excess oil, dip the deep-fried tofu in boiling water for a few seconds or pour boiling water over it. Drain well before using. Follow the directions for Deep-Fried Mochi in Broth (page 83) exactly, but substitute tofu for the mochi and, if desired, garnish with a little grated ginger.

SERVES 3

## CHILLED TOFU

This simple dish is wonderfully cooling and refreshing. Light and nutritious, and involving little if any cooking, it makes an ideal addition to a summer lunch. The only catch is that the tofu must be absolutely fresh, which is no problem if you make your own or if your natural foods store has a regular supply of good quality, locally-made tofu. Find out what day the tofu is delivered to the store, make sure what you are buying is fresh and not left over from the last delivery, and use it within two days of delivery.

Blocks of tofu vary in size from about 10 ounces to 16 ounces. Cut smaller blocks in half crosswise, larger ones into thirds. If using the tofu the day it is delivered there should be no need to boil it first. However, by the next day I prefer to freshen it by dropping the pieces into rapidly boiling water for just one minute, then immediately transferring them to a large bowl of ice water.

Drain tofu well and place in individual serving bowls. Season each piece with shoyu or tamari to taste (½-1 tablespoon each) and garnish with a rounded teaspoon of minced scallion and ¼-½ teaspoon grated ginger.

3 tablespoons finely minced
　scallion
2 teaspoons finely grated fresh
　ginger
4-inch piece kombu
4½ cups water
pinch sea salt
2 pounds tofu

DIP SAUCE:
¼ cup kombu stock
⅓ cup shoyu or tamari
2 tablespoons mirin

## SIMMERED TOFU (YUDOFU)

The cool weather relative of Chilled Tofu, this light and elegant dish is almost as quick and easy to prepare. Simmered Tofu is one of the most popular ways to eat tofu in Japan. It can be cooked at the table in an electric skillet or over a gas or electric burner, or prepared on the stove and brought to the table piping hot in the pot or skillet.

Prepare the scallion and ginger and place them on the table as condiments.

Place kombu with the water and salt in a pot or skillet. Bring this just to a simmer, uncovered, over medium heat, then remove from heat. Cut the tofu into 1″ x 1½″ x 1½″ cubes.

For dip sauce, combine ¼ cup of the kombu broth with the shoyu or tamari and mirin in a small saucepan. Simmer the mixture gently for 30 to 60 seconds. Keep hot, but not boiling, until ready to serve, or reheat just before serving.

If you are cooking this dish at the table, place the pot of kombu stock on the portable burner, or transfer it to an electric skillet. Add the pieces of tofu and gently simmer just until the pieces rise to the surface (2-3 minutes). Turn off heat.

Ladle or pour the hot dipping sauce into small individual serving bowls and let each person add condiments to taste. Invite each person to help themselves to the tofu with chopsticks or a slotted serving spoon, and dip the tofu into the sauce before eating.

SERVES 4-5

## SIMMERED MARINATED TOFU AND SCALLIONS

MARINADE:
1½ cups water
¼ cup shoyu
2 tablespoons mirin
2 teaspoons brown rice vine-
　gar
3 small cloves garlic, pressed
　or finely minced
2 teaspoons grated ginger
1 teaspoon dried tarragon
1 block fresh tofu (approxi-
　mately 1 lb.)
¾ cup scallions, cut on the
　diagonal into ½-inch
　lengths

The preparation time of this simple and nutritious dish is very brief, but it must be begun well ahead of mealtime so the marinating tofu will have a chance to absorb flavor.

Combine all ingredients for marinade. Cut tofu crosswise into ½-inch-thick slices, then cut the slices into 1″ by 1½″ pieces. Wrap the tofu pieces in a clean kitchen towel to remove excess water, unwrap and place them in the marinade. Marinate for at least one hour. If marinating any longer, place in the refrigerator.

Remove tofu from the marinade, arrange a single layer in a large skillet, then add the marinade to a depth of ⅓″ (if desired, strain out garlic before adding). Cover, bring to a boil, lower heat, and simmer gently for 5-10 minutes. Sprinkle sliced scallions over the tofu, cover, and cook for 3-5 minutes more. Serve hot.

SERVES 4

# GANMODOKI
## (TOFU-VEGETABLE BURGERS)

This is a variation of a recipe I was taught by a friend in Japan. She added grated jinenjo (*yamaimo*, mountain yam) as a binder, but I was happy to discover that the recipe works well without it. Although they are a traditional Japanese dish, these burgers are well suited to American tastes. *Ganmo* means "mock goose." This recipe was so named because its flavor is reminiscent of wild goose, "a delicacy once forbidden to all but the Japanese nobility " according to *The Book of Tofu*.

Press tofu for 30 minutes as described under Pan-Fried Tofu Cutlets (page 171) . Wrap the pressed tofu in a clean, dry, cotton cloth and wring, squeezing out as much liquid as possible.

Mix the tofu, vegetables, seeds, and salt in a large bowl. Remove from bowl and knead as you would bread for 3-5 minutes (until it is smooth and keeps its shape well when formed into patties or balls) to ensure that the mixture will stick together. Moisten your hands slightly and make small patties. Heat 1½-2 inches of oil to 360° F. Fry the patties until golden-brown and crisp (about 3 minutes on each side) and drain on a wire rack over absorbent paper or directly on the paper.

Sprinkle with shoyu to taste or serve with the dip sauce given for Simmered Tofu (page 174).

MAKES 10 3-INCH BURGERS

*2 pounds fresh tofu*
*2-3 tablespoons grated jinenjo (optional)*
*½ cup finely grated carrot*
*⅓-½ cup finely minced scallion*
*⅓ cup minced parsley (optional)*
*3 tablespoons freshly roasted whole or ground sesame seeds (see page 188)*
*¾ teaspoon sea salt*
*unrefined vegetable oil for deep-frying*
*shoyu or dip sauce*

1 pound fresh tofu

3 tablespoons red (rice) or
barley miso

3 tablespoons tahini or
toasted, ground sesame
seeds

1 tablespoon unrefined light
sesame or Italian olive oil

1½ tablespoons brown rice
vinegar or lemon juice

1 tablespoon ume-su (or omit
and increase vinegar or
lemon juice to 2 table-
spoons)

⅓ cup scallions, minced

¼ cup parsley, minced

2 cloves garlic, pressed or
finely minced

2 tablespoons nutritional yeast
(optional)

¾-1 teaspoon prepared mustard (optional)

## TOFU-MISO SANDWICH SPREAD

Boil tofu in water to cover for 1 minute, turn off, cover, and let rest briefly, then submerge the tofu in cold water for several minutes. Remove tofu, wrap it in cheesecloth, muslin, or a clean kitchen towel, and gently squeeze out excess water. Combine all ingredients in a bowl and thoroughly mash to mix well.

Serve on bread or toast, with lettuce or alfalfa sprouts, or spread on crackers. Refrigerated in a covered container, this nutritious, protein-rich spread will keep for 2-3 days.

**MAKES 3 CUPS**

½ block fresh tofu (approximately 8 oz.)

2 tablespoons unrefined light
sesame or safflower oil

2 tablespoons rice vinegar or
lemon juice

2 cloves garlic, finely minced
or pressed

1 heaping tablespoon minced
onion

½ tablespoon rice syrup
(optional)

pinch of cayenne (optional)

⅓ cup mellow white miso

## CREAMY GARLIC DIP/SPREAD

This is a great dip for chips or vegetables and a delicious, high-protein spread for crackers or rice cakes.

Prepare tofu as in Tofu-Miso Sandwich Spread.

Combine all ingredients and mash well to mix. (To serve as a dip, use a blender for a very smooth consistency.) Let rest, refrigerated, for at least 2 hours before serving to allow flavors to blend and heighten.

**MAKES 1½ CUPS**

# DRIED TOFU (KOYADOFU)

The traditional method for making dried tofu is still being used in the mountains of Japan. Fresh tofu is set out on boards to freeze in the snow overnight. It is then kept out of direct sunlight at below-freezing temperatures for over a week. Next it is hung outdoors in a shady place where it freezes each night and thaws each day until it is perfectly dry and brittle. The tiny air spaces created by the crystallization and subsequent dehydration of tofu's 86 percent water content gives dried tofu its characteristic feather-light, dry, spongy quality. An ingenious precursor to the modern technique of freeze-drying, this process, developed hundreds of years ago, is a natural method of preserving tofu.

Though commonly sold as "Dried Tofu" in this country, "Dried-frozen Tofu" would be a more accurate name. In Japan it is often called *koya-dofu*, after its place of origin, Mt. Koya. Its other Japanese name, *koridofu*, simply means "frozen tofu." A nutritious, convenient, and versatile food that retains many of the wonderful qualities of fresh tofu without the disadvantages of perishability and fragility, dried tofu is a concentrated source of easily digested high-quality vegetable protein (53.4 percent).

Dried tofu readily absorbs flavors and can be used in a variety of ways. Reconstitute it by soaking in warm water for five minutes, then press firmly between your hands. Repeatedly dampen and press until the liquid that comes out is no longer milky. The tofu may then be chopped and added as is to a well-seasoned liquid such as a noodle broth or stew. To use in stir-fried dishes, chef's salads, as cutlets, or deep-fried, first boil in a seasoned broth or marinate, as described in the recipes below.

Good quality traditional dried tofu is now available in many natural foods stores and I suggest that you shop for it there. (I do not recommend the dried tofu sold in Oriental markets because it has almost invariably been soaked in a solution of baking soda before drying so it will expand more during cooking.) Dried tofu comes packaged in cellophane envelopes containing several thin, flat cakes. Though it stores well for several months, it gradually turns yellow-brown with age, so be sure to buy only light beige-colored dried tofu, and store it in a cool, dry place.

*9 cakes dried tofu*

FOR SEASONING TOFU:
*1 cup water*
*1 tablespoon plus 1 teaspoon*
  *shoyu*
*1 tablespoon mirin*
*1 clove garlic, pressed or*
  *finely minced*

*9 whole cabbage or collard*
  *leaves*

FOR SIMMERING
STUFFED CABBAGE:
*4" piece kombu (optional)*
*⅔ cup water*
*2 teaspoons shoyu*
*½ bay leaf*
*pinch rosemary (optional)*

## TOFU IN A BLANKET

Reconstitute dried tofu as described on page 177. Press cakes fairly dry and place them in a saucepan or skillet with the ingredients for seasoning. Simmer, covered, until most of the liquid is absorbed (about 15 minutes). Transfer tofu to a plate.

Meanwhile, parboil cabbage leaves in lightly salted water for about 5 minutes (2 minutes for collards). Remove, cool under running water or in a cold water bath, drain, and set aside. If central ribs of leaves are stiff, cut them out.

Cut each cake of tofu in half and stack two halves in the center of each cabbage leaf. Neatly wrap as you would a package and fasten with toothpicks. Place the ingredients for simmering in a medium-sized skillet, arrange the cabbage packages in it, cover, and simmer for 20-25 minutes. Serve hot.

**SERVES 3**

## TOFU A LA KING

Reconstitute dried tofu as described on page 177. Press fairly dry, then cube each cake into eighths, sprinkle with arrowroot, and toss. Combine marinade ingredients, add tofu, and marinate for at least 30 minutes. Heat the oil in a large skillet, add the mushrooms and a small pinch of salt and sauté over medium heat for 2-3 minutes. Remove tofu from marinade, add to skillet, and sauté briefly. Add greens and sauté for 1-2 minutes more. Add ⅓ cup water or stock to the leftover marinade, swirl, and add to the skillet. Cover, and simmer until the greens are tender (about 10 minutes). Serve hot.

SERVES 3-4

*6 cakes dried tofu*
*2 tablespoons arrowroot*
*  powder*

MARINADE:
*2 tablespoons mirin*
*2 tablespoons shoyu*
*2 tablespoons stock or water*
*1 clove garlic, finely minced*
*¼-½ teaspoon poultry season-*
*  ing or a pinch each thyme,*
*  sage, and celery seed*
*  (optional)*
*2 teaspoons light sesame oil*
*2 cups sliced mushrooms*
*small pinch sea salt*
*4 cups chopped kale (or other*
*  dark, leafy greens)*
*⅓ cup water or stock*

## DRIED TOFU TEMPURA

See About Tempura, page 128.

The batter for this dish is thicker than the usual tempura batter.

Reconstitute dried tofu as described on page 177. Cut each cake into quarters. Combine water, shoyu, and mirin and pour over tofu in a saucepan. Simmer, uncovered, for 10-15 minutes. Remove tofu, allow to cool, and press out about half the liquid from each piece. Dip the pieces in the batter and deep-fry in moderately hot oil (340°F.) until they begin to turn golden (2-3 minutes). Serve hot.

SERVES 4

*4 cakes dried tofu*
*1 cup water*
*1 tablespoon shoyu*
*1 tablespoon mirin*

BATTER:
*2 tablespoons unbleached*
*  white flour*
*2 tablespoons whole wheat*
*  flour*
*¼ cup water*
*small pinch sea salt*

*oil for deep-frying*

The Japanese use a variety of condiments that enhance flavor, add nutrition—especially minerals and vitamins—and promote digestion. Although they are delicious, to avoid masking the natural flavor of food and adding too much salt, condiments should be used sparingly.

For a number of people with various needs, types and levels of activity, and so on, it is impossible for the cook to season foods appropriately for everyone. I find that seasoning grains and some other dishes lightly and providing condiments at the table enables each person to adjust the flavor and saltiness to suit him- or herself. Condiments are especially appealing to people who are used to strong tastes and are making a transition to natural foods.

The following condiments were selected for their flavor, nutritional value, and commercial availability. Most can be found in natural foods stores. It is best, however, to make roasted sesame seeds and gomashio at home since the flavor and aroma are far superior when fresh, and they take but a few minutes. Store condiments in sealed containers in a cool place.


## KUZU

One of Japan's most important and time-tested folk medicines, *kuzu* helps create the alkaline blood condition necessary for restoring and maintaining health. It quickly remedies various intestinal and digestive problems, especially diarrhea, upset stomach, and disorders related to excess acidity. Kuzu is also commonly taken for relief from colds, flu, fever, and hangovers. For a good digestive tonic, see Ume-Shoyu-Kuzu Tea.

A white powder made from the root of one of Japan's more pervasive and vigorous wild plants, kuzu (called "kudzu" in this country) is unsurpassed as a thickening agent in cooking. It provides a smooth texture and has no starchy or interfering taste. Try using kuzu as a thickener in sauces, gravies, soups, and noodle broths for added body. Vegetables and fish dusted with kuzu powder and deep-fried have a light, crisp coating. Since kuzu helps to balance the acidity of sweets, it is ideal in desserts such as kantens, icings, shortcake toppings, puddings, and pie fillings.

When you buy kuzu, the powder will be stuck together in lumps. Always crush the lumps with the back of a spoon before measuring. Use approximately 1 tablespoon per cup for medicinal teas, 1½ tablespoons per cup for sauces and gravies, and 2 tablespoons per cup for jelling liquids. For most preparations, completely dissolve the measured amount of kuzu in a little cold water, then add to the other ingredients near the end of cooking time and gently bring to a simmer, stirring constantly while the kuzu thickens.

Kuzu should not be confused with arrowroot. The latter, from a plant indigenous to the West Indies, is of lower quality and thus less expensive than kuzu. (Arrowroot, however, is of higher quality than the highly processed corn starch.) Kuzu is far superior to arrowroot in jelling strength, taste, texture, and healing qualities. Kuzu should be stored in a sealed jar.

For a thorough account of kuzu's history, processing, culinary and other uses, as well as numerous recipes and medicinal preparations, see *The Book of Kudzu*, by William Shurtleff and Akiko Aoyagi (Avery Publishing, 1986).

## KUZU SAUCE

Unlike most sauces or gravies, this simple recipe contains little oil and no flour, yet has a full, delicate flavor and pleasing texture. Serve it over grains, vegetables, or noodles.

*2 cups water*
*4-inch piece kombu*
*1 teaspoon light sesame oil*
*1 small onion, minced*
*6 mushrooms, sliced*
  *(optional)*
*½ small bay leaf*
*¼ teaspoon sea salt*
*1 tablespoon shoyu*
*½ tablespoon mirin (optional)*
*3 tablespoons kuzu*

Combine water and kombu in a saucepan and bring to a simmer, uncovered, over medium heat. Remove kombu and reserve for another use. In another pan heat the oil, add onion, and sauté for 2-3 minutes. Add mushrooms if using, and sauté briefly. Add the 2 cups stock, bay leaf, and salt, and simmer together for 10 minutes. Add shoyu and mirin, cook for 1 minute more, then remove from heat.

Dissolve kuzu in 2 tablespoons cold water and slowly add to sauce while stirring briskly. Return pan to heat and bring to a simmer, stirring constantly. Simmer for 1-2 minutes.

**MAKES 2½ CUPS**

## CHINESE-STYLE VEGETABLES

*1 large onion*
*12 mushrooms*
*4 cups, lightly-packed, sliced*
*pak choy (or mustard greens*
*or kale)*
*¾ cup peeled, thinly sliced*
*Jerusalem artichoke*
*2 cups snow peas*
*2 teaspoons light or toasted*
*sesame oil*
*pinch sea salt*
*small pinch white pepper*
*(optional)*
*⅔ cup boiling kombu stock or*
*water*
*1 tablespoon shoyu*
*½ tablespoon mirin*
*1½ tablespoons crushed kuzu*

This combination of vegetables, seasonings, and kuzu creates an authentic Oriental appearance and taste. Jerusalem artichoke has a mild flavor. Its bright color and crunchy texture are much like that of water chestnuts, which are more difficult to find fresh.

Cut onion in half lengthwise, peel, then cut in half crosswise and slice thinly. Wash the mushrooms, remove stems, and slice. Separate pak choy leaves and stalks. Cut stalks on the diagonal ½-inch wide. Cut leaves in half lengthwise, then slice ½-inch wide. (Keep leaves and stalks separate since they will be added at different times.) Remove strings from snowpeas if necessary.

Heat the oil over medium heat in a large skillet or wok and sauté the onion for 3-5 minutes. Add the mushrooms along with the salt and pepper and sauté for 2-3 minutes. Add pak choy stems and sauté for 2-3 minutes more. Add artichoke and pak choy leaves, toss, cover, and steam for just 2-3 minutes. Combine the hot stock or water, the shoyu, and the mirin and pour the mixture over the vegetables. Add the snow peas.

Dissolve kuzu in 1½ tablespoons water and add to the vegetables while stirring briskly to avoid lumping. Simmer for 1 minute or just until kuzu thickens. Serve immediately.

**SERVES 5-6**

## CARROTS IN GINGER SAUCE

*1 teaspoon light sesame or*
*toasted sesame oil*
*3 carrots, cut into ⅛ -inch-*
*thick diagonal slices*
*(approximately 2½ cups)*
*small pinch sea salt*
*1 large handful chopped pars-*
*ley or watercress*
*1 teaspoon shoyu*
*1 tablespoon kuzu*
*1½-2 teaspoons juice squeezed*
*from grated fresh ginger*

Heat oil in skillet or saucepan, add carrots, and toss. Sprinkle with a few grains of salt, and sauté for 3-5 minutes. Add one cup water, cover, and simmer over low heat for 5-10 minutes or until just tender. Add greens and shoyu, toss, and simmer for 2 minutes more. Remove from heat.

Dissolve kuzu in 1 tablespoon cold water and slowly add to vegetables while stirring constantly. Return to heat and bring to a simmer while stirring. Cook for 1-2 minutes, add ginger juice, mix, and serve.

**SERVES 3**

# APRICOT PUDDING OR TARTS

Combine apricots, water, and 1 cup of the apple juice in a sauce-pan. Bring to a boil, lower heat, and simmer, covered, for 20 minutes. Pour the liquid remaining in the pot into a measuring cup and add more apple juice to equal 2½ cups total. Purée the cooked fruit with the juice and tahini in a blender, suribachi, or food mill. Return the purée to the pot and add salt and lemon juice.

Crush the kuzu into powder before measuring. Dissolve the 4 tablespoons kuzu in 3 tablespoons cold water, add to the pot, and bring to a simmer over medium heat. Stir constantly as pudding approaches the boiling point. Simmer over low heat for 1-2 minutes. Pour into custard cups or into prebaked and cooled tart shells. If desired, garnish with toasted, slivered almonds or toasted unsweetened coconut flakes. Refrigerate, uncovered. The pudding will set as it cools.

SERVES 5-6

*1 cup (tightly-packed) unsul-fured dried apricots*
*⅔ cup water*
*3 cups apple juice (approxi-mately)*
*1 teaspoon tahini (optional)*
*small pinch sea salt*
*2 teaspoons lemon juice*
*4 tablespoons kuzu*

# FRESH FRUIT TOPPING

This light and cooling fruit dessert can be enjoyed as is or used as a topping for shortcake, vanilla cake, pancakes and waffles, and as a filling for crepes.

Wash the fruit and cut larger fruits into small bite-sized pieces. Delicate, tender fruits such as strawberries and raspberries should not be cooked. Ripe nectarines do not need cooking, but firmer fruits such as blueberries, cherries, and apples should be simmered with the juice.

Combine the juice, syrup, salt, and ¼ cup of the water in a saucepan. Add the fruit, if appropriate, and bring to a simmer uncovered, over medium heat. Meanwhile, crush the lumps of kuzu with the back of a spoon to facilitate measuring. Thoroughly dissolve the kuzu in the remaining ¼ cup water. When the juice mixture begins to simmer, remove the pan from the heat and add the kuzu while stirring briskly. Place the pot over medium-low heat and stir constantly until the mixture returns to a simmer and thickens.

If you are using fruit that does not require cooking, pour the hot liquid over the raw, sliced fruit in a ceramic or glass bowl, mix gently, and place in the refrigerator to cool. If the fruit is already mixed in, simply transfer the contents of the pot to a bowl and cool. The topping will get thicker as it cools. Refrigerated in a covered container, it will keep for several days.

MAKES 5 CUPS

*3 cups sliced or whole fresh fruit such as strawberries, blueberries, raspberries, nectarines, or pitted cher-ries*
*1½ cups apple juice (or juice that combines apple and another fruit, such as apple-strawberry)*
*3-4 tablespoons maple syrup (use 3 with sweet fruits, 4 with tart ones)*
*small pinch sea salt*
*½ cup water*
*4 tablespoons kuzu*

## DARK (TOASTED) SESAME OIL

The delightful, nutty flavor and aroma of toasted sesame oil is a distinctive characteristic of Oriental cooking. Like other oils, toasted sesame oil seals in nutrients and prevents burning when sautéeing, baking, or pan-frying, but its appetizing fragrance and rich taste make this oil most highly prized as a seasoning agent.

Use a small amount of toasted sesame oil in marinades, vinaigrettes, sauces, and dressings, to enhance the flavor of fried noodles, and in sautéed or stir-fried dishes. Add about 10 percent to give background flavor to oil for tempura or deep-frying. In sautéeing, toasted sesame oil may overpower some mild-flavored vegetables if used alone, but it is delicious used in combination with another vegetable oil such as light sesame or corn.

Vegetable oils contain polyunsaturated fats and no cholesterol. The polyunsaturated fats can actually help dissolve artery-clogging cholesterol deposits.

Toasted sesame oil is made from whole sesame seeds that are first carefully toasted then pressed to extract their flavorful oil. No chemicals are used in the processing and, since this oil contains the natural preservatives vitamin E, lecithin, and sesamol, no artificial preservatives are added. Like other natural unrefined oils, toasted sesame oil should be stored in a cool, dark place.

## GINGER FRIED RICE

*1 tablespoon toasted sesame oil*
*4 shiitake mushrooms (soaked for 2 hours then sliced)*
*1 small carrot, cut julienne*
*small pinch sea salt*
*1 tablespoon mirin (optional)*
*4 scallions, sliced into ½-inch lengths*
*1 teaspoon shoyu*
*¾-inch section fresh ginger, peeled and finely minced*
*2 cups cooked brown or white rice*

Delicious and satisfying, yet quick and easy, this dish is a good way to use leftover cooked rice. It goes well accompanied by bean soup and a side dish of steamed greens.

Heat oil in a skillet over medium heat, add mushrooms, then carrots, and toss in the salt. Add mirin and sauté briefly. Add scallions and sauté for 5 minutes (carrots should still be a little crunchy, but not raw tasting). Lower heat, add shoyu and ginger, and toss. Add rice, breaking up clumps with the side of a wooden spoon. Mix thoroughly, cover, and cook for 1-2 minutes more.

SERVES 2

## TOFU SESAMISO SALAD DRESSING

This dressing is excellent on tossed or parboiled salad, or hijiki salad.

Boil tofu in water to cover for 1 minute, then turn off and let rest for a few minutes. Cool tofu in cold water, then wrap in cheesecloth or porous cotton and squeeze out excess water. Combine all ingredients except sesame seeds in a blender or suribachi and mix well. Toast seeds in a dry skillet by stirring constantly over medium heat for 2-3 minutes. Pour dressing into a bowl, mix in seeds, and chill slightly before serving. (A little minced parsley is a flavorful addition.)

MAKES 1⅔ CUPS

*⅓ pound fresh tofu*
*¼ cup unrefined safflower oil*
*1½-2 teaspoons toasted*
*   sesame oil*
*2½ tablespoons brown rice*
*   vinegar*
*¼ cup water*
*3 level tablespoons mellow*
*   white or mellow barley*
*   miso*
*1 clove garlic*
*1 tablespoon rice syrup or ½*
*   tablespoon honey*
*1 tablespoon sesame seeds*

## CARAWAY CABBAGE

Caraway is often cooked with cabbage because the flavors blend so well and because caraway seeds counteract cabbage's gas-forming tendency.

Cut cabbage half into halves, and remove core and slice it very thin. Cut cabbage quarters thin—⅛ -¼-inch thick, starting at the top and working down to the root end. Heat oil in a large skillet, add cabbage, and sauté briefly. Add seeds and salt and continue sautéeing for a few minutes more. Add a *little* water if necessary to prevent scorching, lower heat, cover, and simmer until just tender (about 15 minutes).

SERVES 3

*½ head cabbage*
*2 teaspoons toasted sesame oil*
*1 rounded teaspoon caraway*
*   seeds*
*pinch sea salt*

## GOMA (SESAME SEEDS)

Both black and white sesame seeds are popular ingredients in Japanese cooking. The black seeds are slightly more flavorful and aromatic, but they both are high in protein, calcium, iron, vitamins A, $B_1$, $B_2$, $B_6$, and niacin, and are a source of high quality vegetable oil. Black sesame seeds are often roasted and used whole as a colorful garnish to complement light-colored foods such as rice or delicate white miso sauces. Unhulled white sesame seeds are the usual choice when grinding is called for. Ground seeds are more digestible than the whole seeds. Both black and white are always toasted to bring out their flavor and aroma. Toast only the amount you need since both whole and ground forms are at their best when freshly prepared.

Though toasting sesame seeds is a quick and simple process, it requires attention and care. Overcooking results in a bitter taste. Place unhulled white sesame seeds in a thin-bottomed dry skillet over medium heat and stir constantly for a minute or two or until they are fragrant and begin to pop. Test by squeezing a seed between your thumb and fourth finger. If it crushes easily the seeds are toasted. When done, remove the seeds from the pan immediately or they will continue to cook.

Ground roasted sesame seeds are most commonly used in dressings and sauces and as the delicious condiment, *gomashio*. Grind in a *suribachi* (Japanese grinding bowl; see page 198). Grind the seeds using a steady, gentle pressure and a circular motion until the mixture is fragrant and about 80 percent of the seeds are crushed. Some oil will be released, giving a moist yet flaky texture. If you don't have a suribachi or a mortar and pestle, place seeds between two pieces of wax paper and crush them with a rolling pin.

## GOMASHIO (SESAME SALT)

Sprinkled on rice or other grains, noodles, or vegetables, freshly-ground gomashio adds flavor and concentrated nutrition. The essential amino acids in sesame seeds perfectly complement those in brown rice, so these two foods eaten together provide high-quality complete protein.

Gomashio is prepared the same way as roasted ground sesame, except that sea salt is added and ground with the seeds. Roast the salt separately in a dry pan or skillet for a minute or so, shaking the pan frequently while roasting, then pour the salt into a grinding bowl with the roasted seeds. Though proportions of one part salt to 7-14 parts seeds are often recommended, I prefer to use less salt—1:25 or even 1:50. (There are 16 tablespoons per cup and 3 teaspoons per tablespoon so, for example, 1 teaspoon sea salt to ¼ cup seeds is a ratio of 1:12; ¼ teaspoon sea salt to ¼ cup seeds is a ratio of 1:48.) Children usually love gomashio, and a proportion of about 1:50 is appropriate for them.

It may be tempting to prepare a large quantity, but fresh gomashio is so superior in taste and aroma that it is best to make small amounts frequently.

## GOMA MISO FURIKAKE (SESAME MISO SPRINKLE)

Since its recent introduction to the American natural foods market, this delicious, nutritious condiment has quickly become popular. A rich, crumbly blend of barley miso, whole roasted sesame seeds, and green nori flakes, it goes exceptionally well with brown rice and is also good sprinkled on other grains, vegetables, and noodles.

## GOMA MUSO

Sesame "butter" and barley miso are carefully blended then lightly roasted to produce this flavorful, protein-rich complement to grains and vegetables. Like Goma Miso Furikake, Goma Muso is available packaged in small plastic bags. Both should be stored in covered jars or tightly sealed plastic bags in a cool, dry place.

## TEKKA

Tekka is an iron-rich, moist yet crumbly blend that is delicious sprinkled on grains, noodles, and vegetables. It is made by sautéeing minced burdock root, carrot, and lotus root in unrefined sesame oil, then adding *hacho* (soybean) miso and cooking the mixture over a low heat for 5-7 hours till crumbly and somewhat dry. Minced ginger is added towards the end of cooking. Tekka should be used sparingly since it is concentrated and strong. Convenient and ready to use, tekka is commercially available in plastic pouches and small glass jars in some natural foods stores.

## SHISO MOMIJI (SHISO LEAF CONDIMENT)

Shiso momiji is a delicious and healthful alternative to table salt. It imparts a salty-tart flavor especially appealing sprinkled on grains, salads, and other foods. Made from iron-rich shiso (perilla herb) leaves that are first pickled with umeboshi then sun-dried and powdered, shiso momiji helps the body to maintain an alkaline condition. It is available in well-stocked natural foods stores. Muramoto Shiso Condiment is an organic brand of high quality.

# WASABI (WASABIA JAPONICA)

*Wasabi*, Japanese "horseradish," nicknamed *nami da* (tears) in Japanese, is a strong spice with a definite "bite." Though frequently compared to white horseradish, the two plants are unrelated. Both are strong flavored roots, but wasabi is a little less sharp and more aromatic than horseradish.

Wasabi's biting, yet fresh, stimulating flavor and its abundance of protein-digesting enzymes make it a perfect condiment with raw fish dishes such as sashimi and sushi. Japanese sushi connoisseurs use wasabi to complement the flavor of red-fleshed and oily fish, such as tuna, yellowtail, and salmon, that live close to the surface. These fish are at their peak of flavor in spring and summer. Though wasabi can also be used with white-fleshed bottom fish such as snapper and grouper, grated ginger is often preferred with them. This group is most delicious in winter. A small amount of wasabi is mixed into the shoyu-seasoned dip that accompanies sashimi. In preparing sushi, wasabi is rubbed on bite-sized "fingers" of vinegared rice, then topped with raw fish. Wasabi is also traditionally added to the broth or dipping sauce served with soba noodles.

In Japan, the pale green flesh of the wasabi root is finely grated and used fresh. Unique to the islands of Japan, fresh wasabi roots are rarely available in this country. Powdered wasabi, or a mixture of powdered horseradish and wasabi, is a convenient substitute for the fresh root. It keeps almost indefinitely if stored in a cool, dry place. Packaged in small tins or small plastic-lined foil envelopes, unadulterated powdered wasabi is available in some Oriental markets and in increasing numbers of natural foods stores. However, most commercial "wasabi" is horseradish or a special variety of daikon powder with artificial color added. When mixed with water to make a paste, these are bright green whereas authentic wasabi powder makes a dull greenish-gray paste.

To prepare wasabi, add several drops of lukewarm water to one tablespoon of powder and mix to a paste. Cover the paste and let it sit for about ten minutes to allow the flavor to heighten.

*Tea leaves that have been steamed to preserve their green color are spread out to dry.*

*Sencha, bancha,* and *kukicha,* Japan's most popular teas, are perfect complements to the grain-based vegetarian diet discussed in this book. Mildly stimulating, slightly aromatic, these teas refresh the palate and heighten the aesthetic pleasure of Japanese cuisine.

Originally a medicinal beverage brought to Japan from ancient China by Buddhist monks, for centuries tea (*cha*) was rare and expensive in Japan. The first Japanese cultivation was closely associated with temple life and religious activity. After generations of experimentation and cultivation, tea has become Japan's national beverage. From *Cha-no-yu,* the Zen Buddhist tea ceremony, to *o-cha,* the daily three o'clock tea break, drinking tea is a Japanese institution. Perhaps *Tocha* best illustrates how serious the Japanese are about tea. Tocha was a tea guessing game popular during Japan's feudal period. Beginning in early morning and continuing well into evening, guests would sample as many as fifty varieties of tea, trying to guess their places of origin. The competition was often intense, and elaborate gifts were awarded to the winner. After ten years of drinking this versatile, delicious beverage, I can understand the excitement; properly brewed, Japanese tea is deeply satisfying.

The train ride from Tokyo to Kyoto passes some of Japan's old tea plantations. In spring, the sight of traditionally-dressed workers picking tea leaves on terraced green hillsides is lovely. The earliest leaves of the tea plant are shaded from direct sunlight by slatted bamboo blinds to maintain their tenderness. These small, delicate, aromatic leaves are hand-picked to make *gyokuro,* Japan's highest quality leaf green tea. Ground to a fine green dust, these dried early leaves become *matcha,* the tea used for the tea ceremony. Since caffeine is concentrated in green tea leaves, gyokuro and other green teas contain moderate amounts (but not nearly as much as coffee) of this stimulant. Matcha can be found in many American Japanese community food stores, but gyokuro, which is used in a more fresh state, is hard to come by in this country.

The bright color of all Japanese green tea is produced by a special steaming process that destroys enzymes in the leaf that would naturally turn leaves dark. Though a product of the same bush, typical English, Chinese, and Indian teas are not steamed, so they are dark in color and are referred to as "black" tea.

As tea harvesting continues, the bamboo blinds are removed and *sencha,* Japan's medium-grade green tea is picked. These still-tender leaves are larger and lower on the plant than gyokuro. Sencha, called simply "green tea" in this country, is considered expensive "guest tea" in Japan and is usually only served at the finest restaurants and for special occasions at home.

Even lower on the tea plant, older leaves and small twigs are gathered to make *bancha,* Japan's lowest grade green tea.

Bancha is the tea usually served in Japanese restaurants because it is less expensive than sencha, and it goes well with food. Bancha contains less caffeine than other green teas, so it is appropriate for evening use and for children.

Lightly-toasted, bancha becomes *hojicha*, "roasted tea." Hojicha has a deep, smoky taste quite different from the slightly astringent taste of bancha. Unlike other green teas, which become bitter when cooled, hojicha makes a refreshing cool summer drink.

The final tea cutting is called *kukicha*. Composed of twigs and stems, kukicha is not a green tea. It contains no leaves and therefore is low in caffeine. With a distinctly earthy taste and aroma, kukicha is boiled rather than steeped to extract its flavor. Like hojicha, kukicha is often served cool and is sometimes mixed with apple juice for children. Kukicha is often confused with bancha but the two are quite different. Kukicha, bancha, and hojicha can each be used in combination with shoyu, umeboshi, ginger, and kuzu to make simple medicinal beverages (see page 52).

Excellent quality, even organically-grown varieties of sencha, hojicha, and kukicha are now available in natural and Oriental food stores. However, the Japanese grading system, which values tender, young, green leaves over twigs and stems is reversed by some natural foods advocates. The reason is the caffeine content, and the result is that the price of good quality sencha and kukicha is almost the same in natural foods stores. In Japan green tea is much more expensive.

Perhaps because of an intuitive sense of moderation, in Japan the caffeine issue is not taken seriously by most people. Sencha, which is lower in caffeine than coffee, is slowly sipped in small quantities and always taken with food. Sencha, and to a lesser degree, bancha, are however, mildly stimulating and can be used as stimulants when appropriate.

Two other traditional Japanese teas are barley tea (*mugi cha*) and rice tea (*genmai cha*). Unhulled barley for barley tea is first sprouted to activate its natural sweetness, then roasted to bring out its deep rich flavor. Excellent chilled, barley tea is a favorite of women and children during Japan's hot humid summers.

"Rice tea" is a type of bancha. It is a mixture of bancha leaves and kernels of roasted, popped brown rice. The white color of the popped rice dispersed in green tea leaves gives this tea an interesting appearance. Enjoyed both hot and chilled, rice tea has a mild, nutty flavor. Genmai cha and mugi cha are available in most Japanese foods stores and some natural food stores.

Sencha, bancha, hojicha, barley tea, and rice tea have a long history of daily use in Japan. Other teas such as *kombucha* (kelp tea) and lotus root tea have more special purposes as Oriental medicinal teas. As Americans become more familiar with Japanese culture, more of these special purpose teas will appear in natural foods stores.

Before discussing some principles of tea preparation, two other beverages should be mentioned. George Ohsawa, one of the founders of the macrobiotic movement, spent many years studying classical Oriental herbology. From what he learned about the properties of herbs, Ohsawa blended a strong-tasting herb tea he called "mu tea." There are two varieties, "mu-9" and "mu-16." They can be found only in well-stocked natural foods stores. My family particularly enjoys mu-16 mixed with apple juice and served hot like spiced cider.

Another Ohsawa original is "yannoh," which he suggested as a coffee substitute. It is made from a mixture of roasted and powdered azuki beans, soybeans, and brown rice.

Tea, especially the leaf teas, should be purchased loose in vacuum-packed pouches or tins. (Tea bags and bulk loose tea become stale quickly.) Buy only about a month's supply at a time, and store the tea tightly-closed, preferably in an airtight container, in a cool, dry place.

To develop the art of Japanese tea preparation and presentation, pay attention to water temperature, steeping time, and serving utensils. If the water is hotter than required, the delicate taste of green tea is destroyed. If steeped too long, green tea becomes dark and bitter. Gyokuro and sencha are served in small, delicate tea cups. Bancha, hojicha, kukicha, barley tea, and genmai cha are usually served in somewhat larger handle-less mugs. Japanese tea is never served with sugar or milk. For sweetness, a little rice syrup can be used. Gyokuro and sencha are usually served after meals, whereas the others can be served while eating.

In Japan, when tea is served, whether to family or to guests, it is generally the responsibility of one person, usually the woman of the house or her daughter. The grace and attention with which it is performed is impressive. No matter how many people are being served, or how lively and distracting the conversation, as soon as a cup is empty, the server notices and offers to refill it.

Although preparing and serving matcha, the ceremonial powdered green tea, requires training to master the precise ritual and proper etiquette, following a few simple rules will insure good results in brewing and serving those teas meant for daily use. Kukicha and mugi cha are the easiest. Unlike the varieties of green tea, which are never boiled, these two are simmered to extract their full flavor. Simply add three level tablespoons of either tea to one quart of water, bring to a boil, and simmer gently for 3-5 minutes. Mugi cha should be strained before serving and the barley discarded, but kukicha can be strained as it is being served, and the twigs left in the pot. Kukicha twigs can usually be reused once, though you may need to add a few fresh twigs for a full-bodied flavor. Both are good strained, refrigerated, and served cold in summer. Kukicha can be taken as often as needed to quench thirst. Mugi cha, on the other hand, has a mild laxative effect, so it should not be taken so liberally.

Bancha, genmai cha, and hojicha are closely related and are brewed in the same way. A large teapot is useful if you are serving more than two. Warm the pot by filling it with hot water then pouring it out before adding the tea. Use one level tablespoon of tea for each person. Put the tea in the pot and add about one cup boiling water per serving. Allow it to steep for two to three minutes. If your pot does not have a built-in strainer, strain the tea as you pour it into the cups. Do not allow any tea to remain in the pot or it will become too strong and bitter. If someone wants more, the leaves may be reused once. Fresh leaves should not be added to used ones—discard spent leaves, rinse the pot, and begin afresh.

Though sencha is prepared similarly, there are a few significant differences. First, sencha contains more caffeine and is taken only in small quantities, never to quench thirst. A small Japanese teapot called a *kyusu,* which holds about 1½ cups, is usually used. For three servings, place one rounded tablespoon of sencha in the teapot and add 1½ cups of water that has been brought to a boil then removed from the heat and allowed to cool for a few minutes. Steep for two minutes before serving in small cups. The best method is to pour a little into each cup (strain as you pour if necessary), then add more to each cup, one or two times, until the pot is completely drained. This way the strength of each person's tea will be about the same. The leaves may be reused once if more tea is needed. After that, discard the old leaves before adding fresh ones.

By keeping at least one of each of these three main classes of Japanese tea on hand, you will be sure to have a delicious beverage for every occasion.

The right tool for the job makes cooking easier and more fun. I have selected a few common and useful Japanese cooking utensils which are handy for Oriental, and indeed, all types of cooking. In most cases the Western counterpart can be used. For example, a mortar and pestle will substitute for a *suribachi* and *surikogi*, or a colander for a *zaru*.

The items discussed here are all made from natural materials—wood, bamboo, and ceramic as opposed to plastic or aluminum. They will not chemically interact with food as will aluminum, which easily leaches into foods and can be toxic. Even water boiled in an aluminum pot picks up traces of the metal. Contact with metal or plastic, especially if prolonged, also tends to give food an unpleasant taste. Using natural material utensils creates an aesthetic harmony that most thoughtful cooks find indispensable.

The utensils described below are sold in most Oriental supply stores and many can be found in well-stocked natural foods stores and gourmet kitchen supply outlets.

## OROSHIGANE (CERAMIC GRATER)

The Japanese use two kinds of graters, both of which grate more finely than most American-made graters. The coarser of the two Japanese styles is used mainly for grating daikon radish. Its teeth are higher and set further apart than the fine one used to grate ginger. It is possible to find a Japanese grater with both types of surfaces. Unlike American styles, Japanese graters do not have holes through which the grated material drops. Some have a lip around the edge or a cup at the bottom to catch the juice and gratings. Some are completely flat and should be stood on a plate to grate.

The finest surface on an American-style multipurpose grater gives results comparable to the coarser of the two Japanese types.

## SURIBACHI (JAPANESE CERAMIC GRINDING BOWL) AND SURIKOGI (WOODEN PESTLE)

The Japanese-style mortar and pestle is a "non-violent" alternative to the electric blender and can be used for many of the same purposes. The suribachi is more appropriate than a blender for certain grinding jobs such as gomashio. The unique aspect of the suribachi is its pattern of narrow grooves that makes grinding quick and easy. Suribachis come in various sizes. I have found the medium size, about ten inches in diameter, appropriate for any purpose from grinding seeds and nuts to puréing or blending ingredients for sauces and dressings.

The proper method of grinding is to place the palm of one hand loosely on top of the pestle while guiding the pestle in a circular motion with your other hand, which is held halfway up the stick. Gentle pressure is usually all that is necessary to accomplish the task. In most cases, simply placing the suribachi on a towel or other non-slippery surface while grinding will work fine. However, if you are puréing thick substances you may find it necessary to hold the suribachi firmly with your knees or thighs as you grind.

The suribachi is easy to clean with a stiff brush. If not cleaning immediately after use, fill the bowl with water to prevent the ground material from drying in the grooves.

## MUSHIKI (BAMBOO STEAMER)

Steaming is a popular method of cooking because it preserves food's natural flavor, nutrition, and moisture. Bamboo steamers are usually found as sets of two or three round, flat tiers with wooden sides and loosely woven bamboo bottoms that allow steam to circulate freely. The tiers, filled with separate foods, are stacked and covered with a wood and bamboo lid. The steamer is placed over a wok or other appropriate vessel containing rapidly boiling water. For best results, put the filled tiers in only after the pot is full of steam. Cooking vegetables quickly over high or medium-high heat maintains their vibrant color and texture and prevents uneven cooking.

Most vegetables and seafoods can be steamed. However, tough vegetables such as burdock, or those with a strong bitter taste are best cooked by another method such as sautéeing or boiling. When mixing different ingredients in the steamer, cut foods that take longer to cook, in smaller pieces or add a tier of quick-cooking ingredients after others are partially steamed, so that everything is done at the same time. To test whether the foods are cooked, pierce with a skewer or taste. If done the food will offer little resistance to skewer or teeth, but be careful not to overcook to a mushy consistency. Steamed foods should be served immediately. They are often accompanied by a delicate sauce, and any seasoning to be used is almost always added after cooking.

## ZARU (BAMBOO BASKET)

Like colanders, zaru are used mainly for draining, rinsing, and tossing foods such as noodles, vegetables, and salads. Bamboo baskets are preferred over metal or plastic colanders because they are made from a natural material. Since they should not be stored in a cupboard (because the lack of ventilation can cause mildew); they can add a decorative touch if hung on a wall of your kitchen.

Wash zaru under tepid running water. It is best to avoid lengthy soaking or soapy water, which can cause warping.

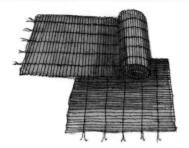

## MAKI-SU (BAMBOO SUSHI MAT)

Thin strips of bamboo are tied together with heavy cotton string for these strong, flexible mats. They are most commonly used to roll cooked foods, such as rice or noodles wrapped in nori seaweed, into a firm cylinder (see Nori-maki, page 148). Steamed or boiled greens can be tightly rolled to squeeze out excess moisture, then cut in one-inch rounds for an interesting presentation.

Bamboo mats are also used to cover bowls before serving, since they retain heat yet allow steam to escape. Used to cover leftovers, the mats allow for ventilation while preventing food from drying out excessively.

After washing, allow the mats to dry thoroughly before putting them away, to avoid the growth of mildew.

## TAWASHI (VEGETABLE BRUSH)

This natural coconut fiber vegetable brush is ideal for scrubbing root vegetables. Tawashi are stiff enough to do the job effectively, yet flexible enough not to injure the skin of unpeeled vegetables.

## CHOPSTICKS (HASHI) FOR COOKING

If you are accustomed to handling chopsticks, you will find the long, slender bamboo or wooden type used for cooking, to be handy. They come in different lengths and are often joined at the top with string. Cooking chopsticks of any length can be used for stirring, sautéeing, tossing; and picking up foods and arranging them on the serving plate. The longest ones will enable you to stir foods in deep pots, and in deep-frying they give more distance from hot oil that might splatter.

## CHOPSTICKS (HASHI) FOR EATING

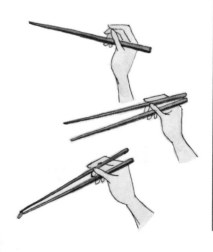

There are many types and sizes of eating chopsticks made from various materials—wood, bamboo, lacquer, and plastic. Some are long and round with blunt tips while others are square and taper down to a point. The shape is a matter of personal preference. The attractive, shiny lacquer chopsticks are best avoided since they are slick and difficult to manage. Unfinished bamboo or wooden chopsticks are preferred, and unless you are already a pro you will probably find shorter ones easier to handle.

If you are not accustomed to using chopsticks it won't take long to learn. Simply rest the bottom stick on the first joint of your fourth finger and in the saddle between your thumb and index finger. This stick remains stationary and is held in place by the middle finger and thumb. The top stick is held between the thumb and index finger. If your hand is kept relaxed and the sticks held loosely, you will soon have no trouble manipulating them and picking up food. One common mistake beginners make is to hold the sticks too close to the tips, which makes them more difficult to control.

## WOODEN SPOONS

Wooden stirring spoons and ladles are basic. They were humanity's first cooking utensils and there have been no better substitutes since the dawn of cooking. Besides aesthetic and earthy considerations, such as wood's personalized mellowing with age and its harmonious interaction with food, wooden utensils do not cut and tear food in preparation and serving, like metal and plastic do, with their sharp edges. Also, the sound of wood on metal is much more pleasant than metal on metal.

You might want to keep near your main work area a ceramic container, such as a wide-mouthed pitcher, filled with an array of wooden spoons, ladles, and spatulas of various sizes.

## DONABE (EARTHENWARE CASSEROLES)

Donabe are thick-walled covered earthenware casseroles, that come in sizes ranging from single-serving, to one that holds enough for six to eight people. Unlike stoneware and other ovenproof materials, donabe can be used over a direct flame as well as in the oven. Mainly used for cooking one-pot winter dishes simmered in a broth, donabe cook evenly and retain heat well.

Small donabe are perfect for serving boiling hot noodles in broth, with or without vegetables or fish. A variety of lightly cooked vegetables can be arranged on top of parboiled noodles and broth and heated together for a beautiful and warming entrée (see Soba Sukiyaki, page 68).

Larger donabe make attractive cooking and serving utensils. In Japan these are used for the style of food preparation called *nabemono* ("things in a pot"). Like Europe's fondue, this type of cooking, done at the table on a portable gas or electric burner, creates a lively social atmosphere. The ingredients, which include a variety of fresh vegetables, fish, and tofu, are all cut in advance and artfully arranged on a large platter. Diners add these foods, small amounts at a time, to simmering kombu stock in the large donabe, allow them to cook lightly, then remove and dip them in individual bowls containing some of the cooking broth seasoned to taste with shoyu and, if desired, ginger, scallion, and lemon. Parboiled noodles or baked mochi are often added last to top off this delightful meal.

Though they appear indestructible (and properly treated they will last indefinitely), donabe must be tempered before being used for the first time. This is done by filling the donabe with water and placing it over low heat for an hour. Both when tempering and subsequently using donabe, always be sure the unglazed outside of the body is *thoroughly* dry before heating. Heating one when wet may cause it to crack. Also, always heat and cool donabe gradually. Sudden extreme changes of temperature such as placing over high heat or submerging in cold water is likely to cause cracks.

Donabe might be more difficult to find than the other utensils described here. Not many natural foods stores carry them, so your best bet is probably a well-stocked Oriental market.

## PRESSURE COOKER

The traditional Japanese cast iron cooking pot worked on the same principle as our modern pressure cooker. Rice or other grains were put into the pot with water and salt, and the pot was fitted with a thick wooden cover that allowed little steam to escape during cooking, thus building interior pressure. The intense steam produced within the pot would thoroughly cook the rice to delicious tenderness in a short time.

Today's pressure cookers are lightweight, dependable, long-lasting, simple to use, and safe. A pressure cooker cooks food quickly and uses less water and fuel than pot-boiling. A cook concerned with nutrition will find the pressure cooker economical in this respect, too. The absence of air prevents oxidation of vitamins, and because so little water is needed, soluble nutrients are not so easily dissolved. Cooking with pressure also enhances the flavor of foods rather than losing it in vapor.

There are many excellent pressure cookers on the market, both American-made and imported, in a variety of shapes and sizes. Shop around, ask friends, and choose one most appropriate to your needs. Most pressure cookers are constructed of stainless steel or aluminum. Stainless is by far the better choice—it is easy to clean and does not leave the unpleasant taste and discoloration in foods that aluminum can.

Pressure cooking is advantageous for grains, beans, and a wide variety of other foods. However, there are some foods, such as split peas, oatmeal, and so on, that should not be cooked in the pressure pot because they can lose their integrity and clog the steam vent. These will be listed in the manufacturer's brochure that accompanies the cooker. The brochure will also explain operating and maintenance procedures, which you should follow carefully each time you use your cooker.

It takes very little practice to become skilled in using a pressure cooker, and the advantages in your daily cooking will soon become apparent.

# COMPOSING MEALS

The art of composing a meal is probably nowhere more highly refined than in Japan. Whether it is a grand meal of as many as ten or twelve delicate and beautiful courses served by women in kimonos who seem to float in and out at precisely the right time, or a more simple, family-style dinner, certain basic principles are followed.

Only foods that are fresh and in season are selected. Besides flavor, appearance, and healthfulness, the constant variation of available ingredients helps provide the interest and stimulation so important to a grain-centered vegetarian diet. Every effort is made to provide a harmonious balance of colors, flavors, textures, and nutrition in a wide range of ingredients. An ingredient is not used in more than one dish in a meal. For example, if tofu is used in the soup, it would not be added to a stir-fry in the same meal.

Interest is also heightened by varying cooking techniques. A typical Japanese meal begins with soup and ends with rice, pickles, tea, and often fruit. The middle course consists of a grilled dish, a steamed dish, and a simmered dish. American cooks tend to use techniques such as baking and pressure cooking more often than the Japanese, and also incorporate more raw foods into their meals. Steaming, simmering, stir-frying, and raw foods are used more in summer, while baking, broiling, deep-frying, and pressure cooking are more often used in winter cooking.

In most traditional cultures, some type of grain provides the focus of each meal. An African friend once told me that if his mother came to this country and was served an elaborate meal of the finest foods, but there was no cornmeal, it would be as if she had not eaten. Generally, vegetables and beans or some other type of protein-rich food rounds out the meal. The sample menus that follow all include some form of grain and vegetables. Most of them include beans, bean products such as tofu or miso, or other high protein foods such as

seitan, fu, or fish. The lunch suggestions are simpler, lighter, and quicker to prepare than the dinners.

Visualize the meal before you begin. Imagine how the foods will taste and how they will look together. Is there enough variety and color? Take a minute for this simple exercise and you will serve beautiful, well-balanced meals.

## WARM WEATHER LUNCHES

*Mellow Miso Soup*
*Macaroni Salad*
*Corn on the Cob with*
   *Umeboshi Paste*
*Black Beans*

*Tofu-Watercress Soup*
*Noodle Rolls*
*Green Beans in Sesame Miso*

*Summer Soba*
*Tossed Salad with Miso-Tofu or*
   *Tofu Sesamiso Salad Dressing*

*Clear Soup with Fu*
*Udon Salad*
*Braised Carrots and Snowpeas*

*Kyoto Style Miso Soup*
*Nori-Maki*
*Parboiled Greens Salad*

*Fish Chowder*
*Assorted raw or lightly steamed*
   *vegetables (carrot, broccoli,*
   *cauliflower, green beans)*
   *with Creamy Dill Dip*
*Corn-Buckwheat Bread*

*Sake-Seasoned Clear Soup*
*Roasted, Boiled Rice with*
   *Gomashio or Mushroom Gravy*

Hijiki Salad
Tangy Greens

## WARM WEATHER DINNERS

Mushroom Soup
Nori-Maki
Teriyaki Tofu
Parboiled Greens Salad

Wakame White Miso Soup
Rice with Shrimp
Steamed Green Beans sprinkled
 with Gomashio
Tossed Salad with Mellow Miso
 Salad Dressing
Carob Amazake Brownies

Clear Soup with Fu
Johnny's Stir-fried Shrimp
 and Vegetables
White Rice
Sliced Cucumber Rounds
 with Umeboshi
Apple-berry Cooler

Tofu-Watercress Soup
Parsley Rice
Marinated Vegetable-Bean salad
Daikon Rounds with Miso Sauce

Egg-Drop Soup
Ginger Fried Rice
Chilled Tofu
Steamed Broccoli with Ume Su
Blueberry Cake with
 Walnut Topping

Udon in Broth
Tofu Burgers
Vinegared Greens
Vanilla Cake with Fresh
 Fruit Topping

FESTIVE DINNER:
Kyoto Style Miso Soup

Broiled Marinated Haddock
Somen Salad
Carrots in Ginger Sauce
Neopolitan Parfait

## COOL WEATHER LUNCHES

Onion Soup
Delicatessen Seitan Sandwich
Parboiled Salad with
 Japanese Dressing

Split Pea Soup with Hato Mugi
Fried Soba
Simmered Hokkaido Pumpkin

Navy Bean Soup
Corn-Buckwheat Muffins
Pressed Chinese Cabbage Salad

Miso Soup with Shiitake
Pan-fried Mochi
Carrots in Ginger Sauce

Seitan Stew
Unyeasted Amazake Bread with
 Miso-Tahini Spread/Sauce

Tempura Udon
Chinese Cabbage Rounds

Mushroom-Barley Stew
Pan-fried Tofu Cutlets
Ume Kuzu Broccoli

## COOL WEATHER DINNERS

Seitan Pasta E Fagioli
Whole Wheat
 Buckwheat Muffins
Baked Hokkaido Pumpkin
Parboiled Greens Salad

Nabemono or Soba Sukiyaki
Sweet Mochi

*Azuki Soup*
*Millet-Pumpkin Loaf with*
  *Kuzu Sauce*
*Hijiki with Shiitake,*
  *Carrot & Dried Tofu*
*Caraway Cabbage*


*Miso Soup with Shiitake*
*Sesame Rice*
*Carrot-Burdock Tempura*
*Steamed Broccoli Seasoned with Ume Su*
*Vanilla Amazake Pudding*

*Deep-Fried Mochi in Broth*
*Chinese Style Vegetables*
*Black Beans*
*Almond Cookies*

*Udon with Shrimp Flowers*
*Kinpira*
*Steamed Broccoli with White Sauce*
*Banana Creme Pie*

*FESTIVE DINNER:*
*Sake-Seasoned Clear Soup*
*Seitan Bourgignonne*
*Cranberry Sauce*
*Pumpkin Flowers*
*Parboiled Greens Salad*
*Amazake Creme Puffs*

## JAPANESE PRONUNCIATION GUIDE

Japanese pronunciation is surprisingly easy. It isn't necessary to hear a word to know where to place the accent, since all syllables are given equal weight. Except for the letter "e," which has two distinct sounds, the vowels have only one pronunciation. Although vowels can be either long or short, we will not go into that here since our purpose is simply feeling comfortable in using the Japanese words, not in mastering the fine points of the language.

With only a few exceptions, the consonants are pronounced the same as in English. The only exception worth noting is the letter "r." Whereas we retract our tongue to pronounce the letter "r," the Japanese "r" is said with the tongue forward and touching the roof of the mouth, as it is when we pronounce the letter "l." So, to pronounce the Japanese "r," place your tongue as you would to make and "l" sound, then try to make an "r" sound. It should come out somewhere between the two, which is what you're looking for.

The vowel sounds are as follows:

a—*like the "a" in "father," though generally a little shorter. In the list below, it is written "a."*

e—*this can be either like the "e" in send or like the "e" in "obey." In the list below, the former is written "e," the latter "ay."*

i—*like the "i" in "machine," though usually shorter. Below it is written "ee."*

o—*like the "o" in "comb." Below it is written "o."*

u—*very similar to the double "o" sound as in "toot," but usually shorter. In the following list it is written "oo."*

| | |
|---|---|
| amazake | *a ma za kay* |
| arame | *a ra may* |
| azuki | *a zoo kee* |
| bancha | *ban cha* |
| bonito | *bo nee to* |
| daikon | *da ee kon* |
| donabe | *do na bay* |
| fu | *foo* |
| furikake | *foo ree ka kay* |
| ganmodoki | *gan mo do kee* |
| genmai cha | *gen ma ee cha* |
| gobo | *go bo* |
| goma | *go ma* |
| goma muso | *go ma  moo so* |
| gomashio | *go ma shee o* |
| hashi | *ha shee* |
| hato mugi | *ha to  moo gee* |
| hijiki | *hee jee kee* |
| hojicha | *ho jee cha* |
| Hokkaido | *Hok ka ee do* |
| ita | *ee ta* |
| jinenjo | *jee nen jo* |
| kabocha | *ka bo cha* |
| kanten | *kan ten* |
| kinpira | *keen pee ra* |
| koji | *ko jee* |
| kombu | *kom boo* |
| kombu maki | *kom boo  ma kee* |
| kukicha | *koo kee cha* |
| kuruma | *koo roo ma* |
| kuzu | *koo zoo* |
| maki-su | *ma kee-soo* |
| mirin | *mee reen* |
| miso | *mee so* |
| mizu ame | *mee zoo a may* |
| mochi | *mo chee* |
| mugi cha | *moo gee cha* |
| mushiki | *moo shee kee* |
| natto | *nat to* |
| niboshi | *nee bo shee* |
| nori | *no ree* |
| nuka | *noo ka* |

| | |
|---|---|
| oroshigane | *o ro shee ga nay* |
| renkon | *ren kon* |
| sake | *sa kay* |
| seitan | *say ee tan* |
| sencha | *sen cha* |
| shiitake | *shee ta kay* |
| shiso momiji | *shee so mo mee jee* |
| shonai | *sho na ee* |
| shoyu | *sho yoo* |
| soba | *so ba* |
| somen | *so men* |
| suribachi | *soo ree ba chee* |
| surikoji | *soo ree ko jee* |
| sushi | *soo shee* |
| takuan | *ta koo an* |
| tamari | *ta ma ree* |

| | |
|---|---|
| tawashi | *ta wa shee* |
| tekka | *tek ka* |
| tempura | *tem poo ra* |
| tofu | *to foo* |
| tororo | *to ro ro* |
| udon | *oo don* |
| ume | *oo may* |
| umeboshi | *oo may bo shee* |
| ume su | *oo may soo* |
| wakame | *wa ka may* |
| wasabi | *wa sa bee* |
| yamaimo | *ya ma ee mo* |
| yudofu | *yoo do foo* |
| zaru | *za roo* |
| zeni fu | *ze nee foo* |
| zenryu fu | *zen ree oo foo* |

# SUPPLIERS

The companies listed below supply high
quality Japanese foods through their import and
distribution systems. These companies are
direct importers from Japan, yet there are other
companies who distribute these foods
throughout the U.S. You can contact any of
them for additional information on the availability of their product line.

Erewhon, Inc.
5 Waltham Street
Wilmington,MA 01887
(617) 657-8120

Eden Foods
701 Tecumseh Rd.
Clinton,MI 49236
(517) 456-7424

Granum
2901 NE Blakely St.
Seattle, WA 98105
(206) 525-0051

Great Eastern Sun
92 MacIntosh Rd.
Asheville, NC 28806
(704) 258-1821

Edward & Sons
Box 3150
Union, NJ 07083
(201) 964-8176

Mt. Ark
120 S. East Street
Fayetteville,AR 72701
(800) 643-8909

Oak Feed Store
3030 Grand Ave.
Coconut Grove, FL 33133
(305) 448-7595

Ohsawa America
P.O. Box 12717
Northgate Station
San Rafael, CA 94913
(800) 647-2929

San-J International
384 Liberty
San Francisco,CA 94114
(415) 821-4040

Tree of Life, Inc.
PO Box 410, 315 Industrial St.
St. Augustine, FL 32084
(904) 824-8181

Westbrae Natural Foods
4240 Hollis Street
Emeryville,CA 94608
(415) 658-7521

Aihara, Cornellia. *The Chico-san Cookbook*. Oroville, CA: George Ohsawa Macrobiotic Foundation, 1976.

Aihara, Cornellia. *The Do of Cooking*. Oroville, CA: G.O.M.F., 1972.

Aihara, Cornellia. *Macrobiotic Kitchen*. New York: Japan Publications, 1983.

Arasaki, Seibin and Teruko. *Vegetables From The Sea*. Tokyo: Japan Publications, 1983.

Belleme, John. "The Miso-Master's Apprentice." *East West Journal*, April, 1981.

Colbin, Annemarie. *The Book of Whole Meals*. New York: Ballantine Books, 1983.

Esko, Edward and Wendy. *Macrobiotic Cooking for Everyone*. New York: Japan Publications, 1980.

Hall, Alan. *The Wildfood Trailguide*. New York: Holt, Rinehart and Winston, 1976.

Hanson, Larch. *Edible Sea Vegetables of the New England Coast*. Box 15, Steuben, Maine 04680.

Hirasuna, Delphie and Diane J. *Flavors of Japan*. San Francisco: 101 Productions, 1981.

Hutchens, Alma R. *Indian Herbology of North America*. Ontario, Canada: Merco, 1973.

Jacobs, Barbara and Leonard. *Cooking with Seitan*. New York: Japan Publications, 1986.

Jacobson, Michael. *The Changing American Diet*. Washington, DC: Center for Science in the Public Interest, 1978.

Jarvis, D.C., M.D. *Folk Medicine*. Greenwich, CT: Fawcett Publications, 1958.

Kohno, Sadako. *Home Style Japanese Cooking in Pictures*. Tokyo: Shufunotomo Co., Ltd., 1977.

Konishi, Kiyoko. *Japanese Cooking for Health and Fitness*. Tokyo: Gakken Co., Ltd., 1983.

Kuriwa, Togo. *Rice Vinegar: An Oriental Home Remedy*. Tokyo: Kenko Igakusha Co., Ltd., 1977.

Kushi, Aveline with Alex Jack. *The Complete Macrobiotic Cookbook: Cooking for Health, Harmony and Peace*. New York: Warner, 1985.

Kushi, Michio. *The Book of Macrobiotics*. New York: Japan Publications, 1977.

Kushi, Michio and Alex Jack. *The Cancer Prevention Diet*. New York: St. Martin's Press, 1983.

Kushi, Michio. *Natural Healing Through Macrobiotics*. New York: Japan Publications, 1978.

Matsumoto II, Kosai. *The Mysterious Japanese Plum*. Santa Barbara, CA: Woodbridge Press, 1978.

Mayo, Patricia. *The Sugarless Baking Book*. Brookline, MA: Autumn Press, 1979.

Mendelsohn, Robert S., M.D. *Confessions of a Medical Heretic*. Chicago: Contemporary Books, 1979.

Muramoto, Noboru. *Healing Ourselves*. New York: Avon Books, 1973.

Nutrition Search, Inc. *Nutrition Almanac*. New York: McGraw-Hill Book Co., 1979.

Ohsawa, George. *You Are All Sanpaku*. Ed. by William Dufty. New York: University Books, 1965.

Ohsawa, George. *Zen Macrobiotics*. Los Angeles: Ohsawa Foundation, 1965.

Ohsawa, Lima. *The Art of Just Cooking*. Hayama, Japan: Autumn Press, 1974.

Price, Weston A., D.D.S. *Nutrition and Physical Degeneration*. Santa Moncia, CA: Price-Pottenger Nutrition Foundation, 1945.

Rombauer, Irma S. and Marion Rombauer Becker. *Joy of Cooking*. New York: The New American Library, Inc., 1964.

Sacks, Castelli, Donner, and Kass. "Plasma Lipids and Lipoproteins in Vegetarians and Controls." *The New England Journal of Medicine*, May 29, 1975.

Sacks, Rosner, and Kass. "Blood Pressure in Vegetarians." *American Journal of Epidemiology*, Vol. 100, No. 5.

Sattilaro, Anthony, M.D. with Tom Monte. *Recalled by Life: The Story of My Recovery from Cancer*. Boston: Houghton-Mifflin, 1982.

Shurtleff, William and Akiko Aoyagi. *The Book of Kudzu*. Wayne, NJ: Avery Publishing Group, 1985.

Shurtleff, William and Akiko Aoyagi. *The Book of Miso*. New York: Ballantine Books, 1976.

Shurtleff, William and Akiko Aoyagi. *The Book of Tempeh*. New York: Harper and Row, 1979.

Shurtleff, William and Akiko Aoyagi. *The Book of Tofu*. New York; Ballantine Books, 1975.

Smith, Allan K., Ph.D., and Sidney J. Circle, Ph.D. *Soybeans: Chemistry and Technology*. Westport, CT: AVI Publishing Co., 1980.

Tanaka, Seno. *The Tea Ceremony*. New York· Kodansha International, 1973.

Tara, William. *Macrobiotics and Human Behavior*. New York: Japan Publications, 1984.

Tsugi, Shizuo. *Japanese Cooking: A Simple Art*. New York: Kodansha International, 1980.

Yamaguchi, Mas. *World Vegetables*. Westport, CT: AVI Publishing Co., 1983.

Yamaoka, Masako. *A First Book of Japanese Cooking*. New York: Kodansha International, 1984.

Yoneda, Soei. *Good Food from a Japanese Temple*. New York: Kodansha International, 1982.